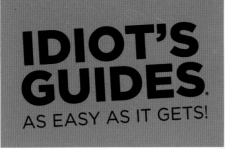

IDIOT'S GUIDES.
AS EASY AS IT GETS!

D0886374

Knitting Sweaters

by Megan Goodacre

ALPHA

A member of Penguin Random House LLC

For my boys (all three of you). You don't knit, but you make me laugh, you feed me, and you keep me sane.

ALPHA BOOKS

Published by Penguin Random House LLC

Penguin Random House LLC, 375 Hudson Street, New York, New York 10014, USA • Penguin Random House LLC (Canada), 90 Eglinton Avenue East, Suite 700, Toronto, Ontario M4P 2Y3, Canada (a division of Pearson Penguin Canada Inc.) • Penguin Books Ltd., 80 Strand, London WC2R 0RL, England • Penguin Ireland, 25 St. Stephen's Green, Dublin 2, Ireland (a division of Penguin Books Ltd.) · Penguin Random House (Australia), 250 Camberwell Road, Camberwell, Victoria 3124, Australia (a division of Pearson Australia Group Pty. Ltd.) • Penguin Books India Pvt. Ltd., 11 Community Centre, Panchsheel Park, New Delhi—110 017, India • Penguin Random House (NZ), 67 Apollo Drive, Rosedale, North Shore, Auckland 1311, New Zealand (a division of Pearson New Zealand Ltd.) · Penguin Books (South Africa) (Pty.) Ltd., 24 Sturdee Avenue, Rosebank, Johannesburg 2196, South Africa · Penguin Books Ltd., Registered Offices: 80 Strand, London WC2R 0RL, England

International Standard Book Number: 978-1-61564-832-0
Library of Congress Catalog Card Number: 2015933120

17   16   15   8   7   6   5   4   3   2   1

Interpretation of the printing code: The rightmost number of the first series of numbers is the year of the book's printing; the rightmost number of the second series of numbers is the number of the book's printing. For example, a printing code of 15-1 shows that the first printing occurred in 2015.

Printed in China

Note: This publication contains the opinions and ideas of its author. It is intended to provide helpful and informative material on the subject matter covered. It is sold with the understanding that the author and publisher are not engaged in rendering professional services in the book. If the reader requires personal assistance or advice, a competent professional should be consulted. The author and publisher specifically disclaim any responsibility for any liability, loss, or risk, personal or otherwise, which is incurred as a consequence, directly or indirectly, of the use and application of any of the contents of this book.

Most Alpha books are available at special quantity discounts for bulk purchases for sales promotions, premiums, fundraising, or educational use. Special books, or book excerpts, can also be created to fit specific needs. For details, write: Special Markets, Alpha Books, 375 Hudson Street, New York, NY 10014.

Trademarks: All terms mentioned in this book that are known to be or are suspected of being trademarks or service marks have been appropriately capitalized. Alpha Books and Penguin Group (USA) Inc. cannot attest to the accuracy of this information. Use of a term in this book should not be regarded as affecting the validity of any trademark or service mark.

Photo credit, page 10 (measuring tape): Steve Gorton © Dorling Kindersley.

Publisher: Mike Sanders

Associate Publisher: Billy Fields

Development Editorial Supervisor: Christy Wagner

Cover Designer: Laura Merriman

Book Designers: Rebecca Batchelor and Laura Merriman

Production Editor: Jana M. Stefanciosa

Indexer: Celia McCoy

Layout: Ayanna Lacey

Proofreader: Cate Schwenk

Contents

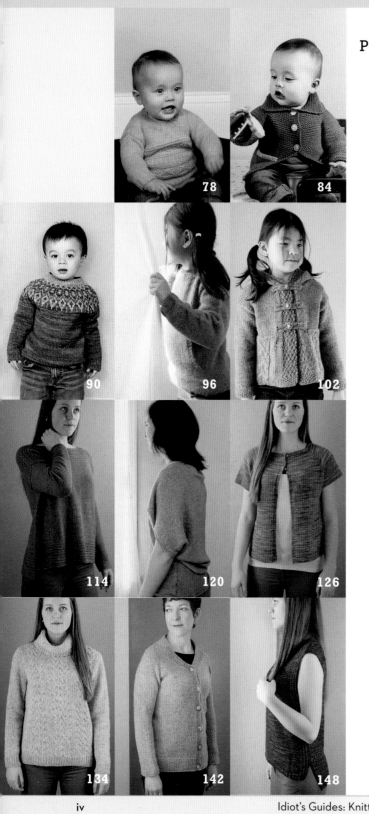

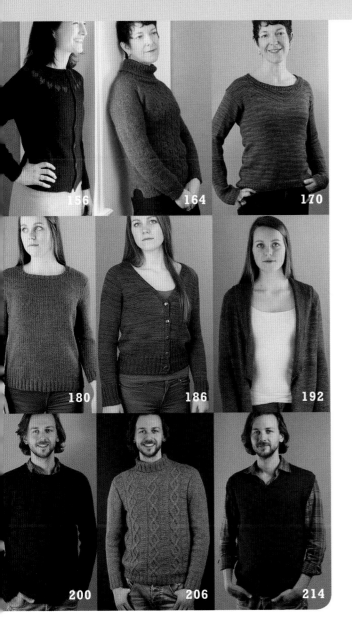

Introduction

The sweater. For many knitters, it's the ultimate goal. It can also be an imposing one. I've spoken to so many knitters who earnestly inform me, even as a hat or pair of socks is flying off their needles, "I could never knit a *sweater*." To that I say, "Oh yes you *can*."

Knitting a sweater is wonderfully fulfilling, from beginning to end. Planning the sweater, choosing the perfect yarn, sculpting the fabric, blocking each piece to perfection, and weaving in that last end—each step in the process adds up to a profound sense of accomplishment. And imagine the thrill that comes when someone says, "I love your sweater!" and with a rush of pride you can say, "Oh this? Thanks! I made it myself."

Whether you're a newer knitter who has successfully tackled some other projects and now want to make your very first sweater or an experienced sweater knitter looking to pick up some new techniques, this book is for you. In the following pages, I explain how to choose the right yarn, share suggestions on selecting the right size and shape sweater to flatter your body, teach you how to tailor a pattern to fit just right, offer pointers on finishing your sweaters perfectly, and much more. You also learn advanced techniques like working short rows and setting in a sleeve, and you'll conquer your fear of sewing pieces together. All the lessons are accompanied by clear, step-by-step photos that show you just what you need to know.

Feel free to jump in anywhere and start looking for inspiration. Before casting on, do look at Part 1, especially the "Flatter and Fit" and "Knitting Like a Pro" chapters, which are chock full of helpful tips and tricks.

As you browse the patterns in this book, I hope you'll feel among friends, with keywords like *simple, comfortable, classic,* and *elegant.* The patterns have just enough knitterly detail to make beautiful garments without demanding extreme technical skills—perfect for knitters who already know the basics and want to create something more. Even after many years of knitting and many sweaters, I still enjoy the simple patterns the most. These are the sweaters that, when I first put them on, feel immediately like home.

Acknowledgments

This book took shape over many long days and nights, but of course it wasn't a solo act. I'm grateful to my family, who continue to be unphased by the knitting paraphernalia spilling from our home's every orifice. When you say to your friends in complete seriousness, "You can't sit there. That's where the knitting is," thank you for that. Charles, thank you for doing all the cooking; you amazed us with your perfect challah braids on the first try.

A huge thank you to the folks at Alpha Books for letting me write another book! In particular Christy Wagner, my editor, and Laura Merriman, the designer who made this book look as good as it does.

Thank you to the knitters who brought the sweaters to life and knit as fast as I could put words on the page: Deborah, Donna, Jacey, Jan, J'lene, and Pam. And of course, my mom, who would have knit all 20 if I had asked, and who taught me to knit in the first place.

Thank you to my models for their poise and patience: Alex, Amy, Blake, Evan, Iris, J'lene, and Rebecca.

And of course, one of the great pleasures of putting this book together was getting to work with such beautiful yarns. I'm very grateful to the yarn suppliers for their generous contributions: Americo Original, Berroco, Blue Sky Alpacas, Brooklyn Tweed, Cascade Yarns, The Fibre Company, Knit Picks, Lorna's Laces, Madelinetosh, Malabrigo, The Plucky Knitter, Quince & Co., Skacel, Swans Island Company, and SweetGeorgia Yarns.

And finally, thanks to all my knitting peeps out there, online, on Ravelry, in my classes, and in the yarn stores, for your kind words and encouragement. Happy knitting!

learning to knit sweaters

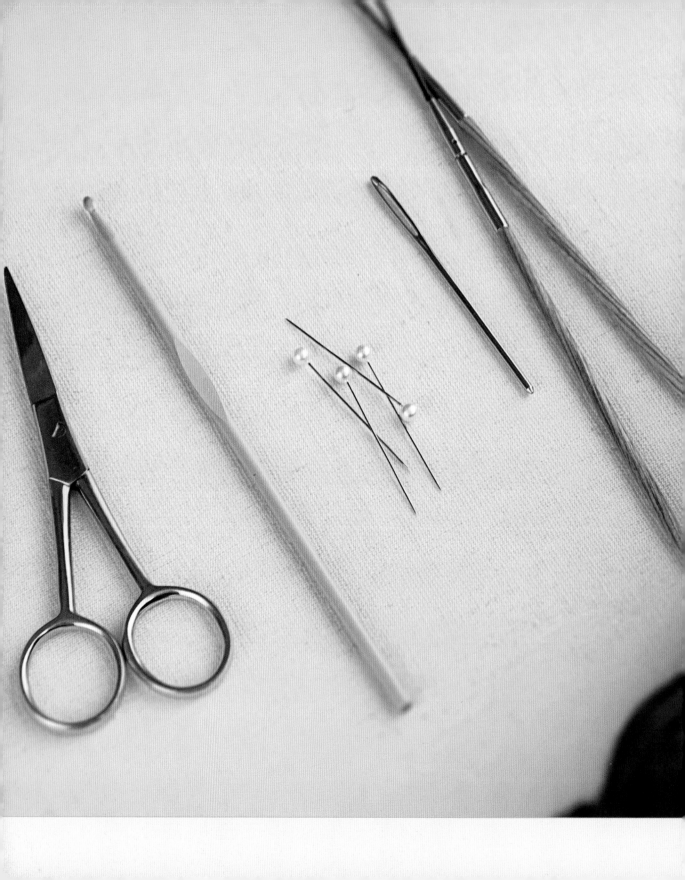

before you begin

IN THIS CHAPTER

The skills you need to knit a sweater

Stocking your sweater toolkit

Selecting your yarn

skills

If you can cast on and off, knit, purl, decrease, increase, and sew a simple seam, you already have all the skills you need to knit almost half the sweaters in this book!

Add picking up stitches, making a cable, and working in color, and you're well on your way to stitching some very sophisticated knits. And believe it or not, if you can measure and do a few simple sums, you can be your own designer and create your own unique knitted pieces!

The following table outlines the skills you need to knit the sweaters in this book.

Required Knitting Skills

basic skills	intermediate skills	finishing skills
Cast on	Reading from a chart	Picking up and knitting stitches
Bind (cast) off	Shaping with increases and decreases	Mattress stitch
Knit and purl	Knitting with two colors	Sewing buttons
Knitting in the round	Making knitted cables	Blocking
	Making basic knitted lace	Kitchener stitch
		3-needle bind (cast) off

Skill Ratings

Each pattern in this book is given a skill rating of 1 to 5, with 1 being the easiest and 5 being the most advanced. Here's what the ratings mean:

1 These patterns are suitable for the beginner. They require only a few basic skills like knit/purl, mattress stitch, and basic finishing.

2 Patterns rated 2 are suitable for the new knitter. They combine basic skills with one or two finishing techniques.

3 These patterns are suitable for a new knitter who has some experience. Patterns rated 3 add a technique to the skills needed for a 1 or 2 rating, such as working with color, reading from a chart, or adding buttons.

4 Patterns rated 4 are suitable for the new intermediate knitter or the knitter who is comfortable using several techniques in one pattern and is ready to learn more advanced skills, such as short rows or following multiple steps at once.

5 The most challenging, 5 patterns are suitable for the intermediate knitter. This highest skill rating means the patterns combine several techniques in one project and include at least one advanced technique.

Use these ratings as a general guide; even the projects labeled 5 are well within the grasp a new intermediate knitter. A higher rating might mean there's one advanced technique beyond what you might already know. For example, the Fine-Knit Pullover is a very simple sweater, but it's rated 4 because it has set-in sleeves worked in the round.

The transition from smaller projects like knitted hats to full-size sweaters can be exciting and ambitious. If you're not sure where to start, check out the "Easy First Sweaters" chapter. It contains three simple but surprisingly elegant options—the Silver Shrug is made entirely from a single rectangle. But really, in this book, you could start almost anywhere. Even when a pattern calls for an advanced technique—like short rows—I describe each step in detail.

your sweater
toolkit

In theory, all you need to knit a sweater are two needles and some yarn. However, knitting is much more enjoyable when you have a few slightly more sophisticated tools.

Knitting Needles

As a somewhat experienced knitter already, you likely have at least one set of needles in your toolkit, and maybe more. By far, your needles are the most important tools you need to knit a sweater, but you don't need to invest in each and every size your local yarn store stocks—as tempting as that might be!

When you're starting a sweater, choose quality needles in the sizes the pattern or the yarn you're using recommend. You'll appreciate having good tools and further build your needle inventory at the same time. Keep in mind that you might have to experiment with needle size to match the gauge (tension) called for in a pattern, and you often knit flat and in the round in the same project.

What needles do you need? When knitting a sweater, you usually need the following needles:

- One set for the main body of the sweater in the size needed to achieve gauge (tension)
- Another set in a smaller size for the cuffs, edges, and button bands
- A third set in the smaller size for working in a small round for necklines or armholes

Which size to use? Although you don't need to have every existing size needle in your toolkit, it is convenient to have the most commonly used sizes. (*Size* here refers to the diameter of the needle, not the length.) This enables you to test your knitting gauge (tension) thoroughly before starting a project.

For sweater knitting, you'll probably use needle sizes in this range—and the majority of the patterns in this book are worked on these commonly used sizes:

U.S. 4 (3.5mm/UK 10)

U.S. 5 (3.75mm/UK 9)

U.S. 6 (4mm/UK 8)

U.S. 7 (4.5mm/UK 7)

U.S. 8 (5mm/UK 6)

If you often work in fine-weight yarn, consider getting a set of U.S. 2 or 3 (3.25mm/UK 11) needles as well. And if you like knitting with bulky yarn, add U.S. 9 and 10 (5.5 and 6mm/UK 5 and 4) needles.

Straight or circular? I started knitting with straight and double-pointed needles (dpns), but I now knit exclusively on interchangeable circular needles. A good collection of circulars can do everything straights and dpns can do—and more. Interchangeable needles, on which the needle tips can be removed from the cables, are even more versatile.

Circular needles are quite versatile. You can knit 4 or 400 stitches on a circular needle, flat or in the round, and the soft, flexible cable is essential for working the button bands or collar of many cardigans. Circulars also have ergonomic benefits, as the weight of the knitting sits in your lap rather than on the ends of straight needles, putting less strain on your hands and wrists. And when you're ready to set your work aside, circular needles coil up neatly to fit in your knitting bag.

With interchangeables, you don't need to buy separate needles to change needle length—ideal for seamless knits where the rows vary in length throughout the project. And to set stitches aside, you simply remove the needle tips and leave the stitches on the cable.

When choosing circular needles, keep the following points in mind:

- The length of a circular needle is measured from tip to tip.

- When knitting flat on one circular needle, any length will work, but don't get one so short that the stitches are very crowded.

- When knitting in the round on one circular needle, it should be *shorter* than the total length of the stitches.

- When knitting in a small round (for example, a sleeve) on two circular needles, the needles can be any length, but a mid-length needle that's comfortable to work with is best.

- When knitting in a small round on one looped circular needle, a long flexible cable works best.

Other Tools

Here are some other items your sweater-knitting toolkit should contain:

- Stitch markers (the inexpensive ring style are fine)

- Blunt yarn needle with a big eye for seams and weaving in

- Sharp sewing needle for sewing on buttons with small holes

- Safety pins

- Sturdy straight pins for blocking

- Crochet hook (try a U.S. G/6 [4mm/UK 8])

- Cable needle

- Stitch holders

- Small, sharp scissors

- Measuring tape

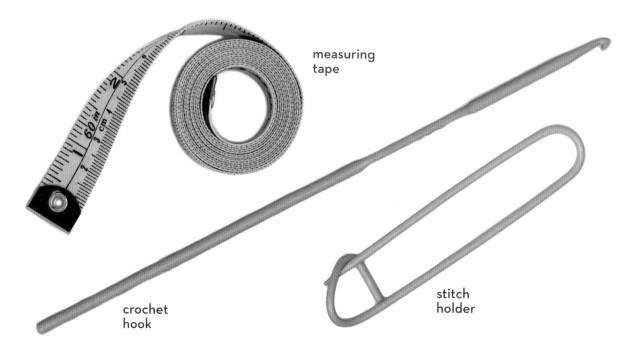

measuring tape

crochet hook

stitch holder

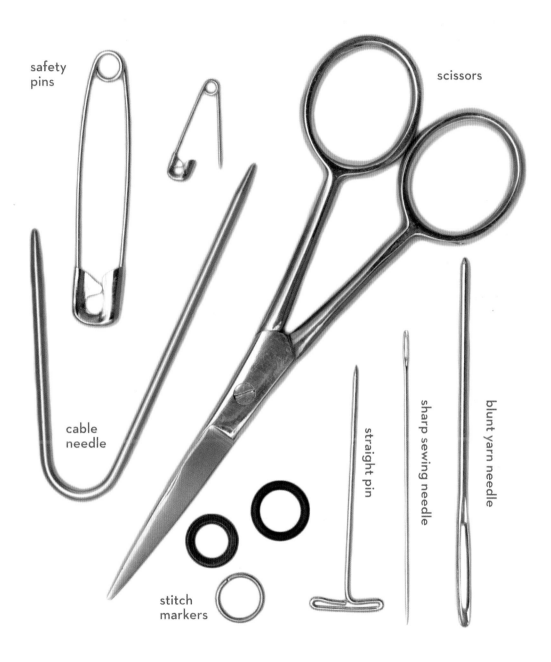

safety
pins

scissors

cable
needle

stitch
markers

straight pin

sharp sewing needle

blunt yarn needle

choosing your
yarn

When you're beginning to consider knitting a sweater, you probably think of two factors first—what style of sweater you'd like or the pattern you'll use, and your yarn. We look at patterns in more detail in the next chapter, so for now, let's think about yarn. After all, you want to choose something you'll enjoy knitting and wearing.

Yarn Weight

Most of the sweater patterns in this book are designed for sport to worsted (fine to medium) weight yarns. For your first sweater, DK or worsted (light and medium) yarns are great choices. They yield a light, wearable garment and are easy to work with.

If you prefer a finer knit, a fingering or sport (superfine and fine) yarn makes a beautiful sweater. Of course, finer yarn means more stitches, so the sweater will take longer to finish.

It might seem that heavier, chunky, or bulky yarns would be a good choice, and yes, a heavier yarn requires fewer stitches and can be faster to knit. However, it can be more challenging to get a comfortable fit and nice finish with a very heavy yarn.

Yarn Fiber

One of the secrets to an expertly knit sweater is the right fiber. An ideal yarn for a first sweater is fairly lightweight with a little bounce and elasticity. Wool is a great choice, making it easy to keep an even gauge (tension) and sew great-looking seams. Smooth fibers that have a lot of sheen and drape (like silk and cotton) do make beautiful knits but can make it challenging to achieve the perfect finish and the right fit.

Find pure wool a little itchy and silk too heavy to knit with? Look to the fiber blends! For example, a slippery silk can be stabilized when it's blended with a soft merino wool.

- -

Hand-painted or hand-dyed yarns look incredible in the skein, and the more multi-colored they are, the more appealing they can be. But be careful when choosing one for a sweater. Highly variegated yarn isn't always suitable, and the yarn could form unexpected pools or bands of color. If you'd like to work with hand-dyed yarns, look for something with very little color variation or something kettle dyed.

- -

How Much Yarn Do You Need?

Yarn requirements vary depending on the details a sweater pattern calls for and the size you're knitting, as well as your gauge (tension). Even the type of knitting needles you use can affect how much yarn you need.

Start with the pattern's yarn requirements as a guide, and be sure to have a contingency plan if you run out of yarn. For example, if you're buying yarn that's been discontinued, it's a good idea to buy 1 or 2 balls extra.

Based on a long-sleeved, hip-length sweater, plain or slightly textured, the following table offers a rough guide on how much yarn you'll need. Of course, it's always best to use the pattern's requirements.

Approximate Yarn Requirements

Finished Chest Circumference	Fingering or Sport (Superfine or Fine) Yarn in 50g Balls	DK or Worsted (Light or Medium) Yarn in 50g Balls
Women's bust 30 (34, 38, 42, 46, 50, 54, 58, 62) inches (76 [86.5, 96.5, 106.5, 117, 127, 137, 147.5, 157.5] cm)	8 (9, 10, 11, 12 or 13, 13 or 14, 14 or 15, 16, 17)	8 (8 or 9, 9 or 10, 10 or 11, 12, 12 or 13, 14, 15, 16)
Men's chest 36 (40, 44, 48, 52) inches (91.5 [101.5, 112, 122, 132] cm)	10 (11 or 12, 13, 14, 15 or 16)	10 (11, 12, 13, 14 or 15)
Baby or child ages 3 months (12 months, 2 years, 4 years, 8 years, 12 years): 18 (20, 23, 25, 28½, 32) inches (45.5 [51, 58.5, 63.5, 72.5, 81.5] cm)	2 (3, 3 or 4, 4, 5 or 6, 7)	2 (3, 3, 4, 5, 6 or 7)

sweater
talk

IN THIS CHAPTER

Deciphering sweater patterns

Sweater construction secrets

Tips for knitting seamless sweaters

reading sweater
patterns

Sweater patterns contain numerous pieces of information, all compactly organized into a few pages. When you first read through a pattern, it might feel like you're looking at a foreign language. But don't worry. You'll learn the lingo of sweater patterns quickly and easily.

Anatomy of a Sweater Pattern

A pattern's opening section is full of useful material. Here you find crucial information such as gauge (tension), yarn requirements, recommended needle size, construction information, how the garment fits, skills required, and how to work special techniques. Read this section carefully before casting on a single stitch.

The bulk of the pattern contains the actual steps you'll take to knit the sweater. Scan through these instructions to familiarize yourself with the steps, particularly the parts that require a little multitasking (the neck, armhole, and shoulder shaping, for example). Highlight the numbers for the size you're knitting as well as any areas that possibly require special attention.

Finally, take the time to examine the pattern's schematic. This drawing contains vital information on the size of the garment plus clues on the construction. Check that the finished sweater will fit the way you like; if not, decide on the modifications you'd like to make before starting, and make notes on the pattern.

bulk of pattern

opening section

schematic

Cracking the Code

Abbreviations, special punctuation, and short phrases are used to keep patterns brief and easy to scan. You're probably familiar with abbreviations like "rep from *," but some key phrases need special attention in a sweater pattern. The following table gives you keys to cracking the sweater-pattern code.

what to watch for	example	what it means
ending with a	Knit until back measures 12 inches (30cm) from cast-on edge, ending with a WS row.	The final row worked should be the side specified. In this example, the final row should be a WS (wrong side) row.
as set; as established; in pattern	Begin neck shaping, maintaining the stitch pattern as established.	As the neck is shaped, continue to work the fabric in the same stitch texture you've been knitting.
keep(ing) pattern correct	Keeping pattern correct, shape front neck.	The front neck shaping interrupts the established stitch pattern, creating partial multiples at the edges. In those partial multiples, maintain the stitch pattern as established.
at the same time	Dec 1 st at the underarm every RS row for 8 rows, while at the same time, begin shaping the neck on Row 4 as follows ...	Knitting often requires multitasking. In this case, continue to shape at the underarm after you begin shaping the neck.
work even	Work even for 12 more rows.	This usually comes after a shaped portion. It tells you to work without shaping in the stitch pattern as established.
switch to larger/ smaller needles	Work 12 rows rib and then switch to larger needles.	Change to the needles specified in the pattern. Usually the larger size is needed to achieve gauge (tension), while the smaller size is used for edges, so it's crucial to switch.
place marker (pm)	K12, pm, k2.	Knit 12 stitches, place a movable marker such as a ring marker on the right needle, and knit 2. The correct placement of markers is crucial, as it affects subsequent steps. On rows where the markers aren't referenced, simply slip them.
bind (cast) off at ...	On the next 4 rows, bind (cast) off 4 sts at the armhole edge.	Binding (casting) off is worked at the beginning of a section or row (not the end because the yarn would be at the wrong end of the work). In this case, on each of the 4 rows, bind (cast) off 4 and work to end, binding (casting) off a total of 16 stitches.
every nth row	Work a sleeve inc every 18th row 5 more times.	If the first increase was done on Row 1, then work increases on Rows 19, 37, 55, 73, and 91.
every nth RS row	Inc every other RS 5 more times.	It's important to watch out for the "RS" in this instruction. In this case, increase every second right side row, or every 4th row.
n sts inc'd/dec'd	Work a sleeve inc 5 more times. 10 sts inc'd, 100 sts.	The stitch change and the new stitch count follow a shaping instruction where there was a bind (cast) off, a decrease, or an increase. It's useful information, and it's a good idea to count your stitches to confirm you have the correct number.

sweater
construction

Sweater construction refers to how a knitted sweater is put together, and quite a variety of construction methods are available.

One traditional way, called *pieced,* or *knit flat,* is to knit the front (or fronts if it's a cardigan), back, and sleeves; sew them together; and pick up and work the neckline. Another traditional method, called a *yoked* or *seamless construction,* is to knit the body and the sleeves in the round to the underarms, join them into one piece, and work the yoke in the round to the neck. And there are variations on both pieced and seamless constructions. A seamless sweater, for example, can be worked from the top down, starting at the neck. Many hybrid construction methods exist as well. Some sweaters are worked seamlessly in the round to the underarms and then worked flat to the neck with seams at the shoulders and sleeves.

Because each construction method has its own pros and cons, I've included several varieties in this book so you can try different combinations and decide which ones you enjoy most.

Pieced Sweater Constructions

The shape of the pieces in a pieced sweater is largely decided by the type of sleeve (and of course whether it is a pullover or cardigan). The sleeve is a key element, and its shape affects the armhole, shoulder, and underarm.

A **set-in sleeve** is the most tailored sleeve, with a curved sleeve cap that fits around the top of the arm where it meets the body. The top of the sleeve cap usually hits the shoulder at the widest point or a little higher. Set-in sleeves tend to be relatively fitted and work well in a sweater that isn't overly roomy.

A **drop shoulder** is the simplest sleeve shape, with the armhole following the vertical line of the body. The seam where the sleeve is joined to the body falls over the shoulder to the upper bicep. The top of the sleeve is a straight line, making it easy to join to the body. Drop shoulder sweaters are generally boxy and comfortable.

The **modified drop shoulder,** a variation on the drop shoulder, has an armhole set in slightly from the side of the body, and the sleeve cap mimics the shape of the armhole. The modified drop is a little less boxy than a drop shoulder, and it's almost as easy to work.

set-in sleeve

drop shoulder

modified drop shoulder

raglan sleeve

dolman sleeve

sleeveless

The *sleeve cap* is the part of the sleeve above the underarm. A drop shoulder sleeve has no cap. The *shoulder drop* or *slope* is the vertical distance from the highest point of the shoulder at the side of the neck to the point where the sleeve joins. *Armhole depth* is the vertical distance from the underarm to the shoulder.

A **raglan sleeve,** instead of curving like a set-in sleeve, is shaped at a diagonal from the underarm to the neck—there's no shoulder seam in a raglan sweater. Raglan sleeves aren't overly tailored and are quite comfortable. Because of the prominent diagonal lines, they tend to accentuate the shoulders and chest.

Dolman sleeves are worked with the body, with the sleeve coming out in a curve before the underarm. Dolman sleeves are roomy at the underarm and bust, making them very comfortable. They work best with a sweater that fits snugly at the hip.

And of course, don't forget **sleeveless** construction. The shoulder seam in a sleeveless vest usually ends at the widest point of the shoulder, but it can vary for different styles.

Seamless Sweater Constructions

Many knitters don't enjoy sewing the seams of pieced sweaters, and seamless sweaters are a great solution to that problem. In knitting, unlike in sewing, you build the fabric as you go, and you're able to sculpt it however you wish.

Seamless sweaters can be worked from the bottom up, much like a typical pieced sweater, but in the round. The advantage to this is that the construction is fairly logical as you're knitting the sweater in the direction you'll eventually wear it. Another advantage is that most of the knitting happens below the underarms, so once you join the sleeves to the body, the sweater comes together quickly.

Note that when a pattern uses *left* or *right,* it means "as worn." For example, the left front of a cardigan is the left side to the person wearing it.

Seamless sweaters also can be worked from the top down. This makes for a slightly counterintuitive way to work, but it's a neat trick: you start with a small cast on, and you can try on your sweater as you go, which is nice because you can tweak the chest circumference and length very easily.

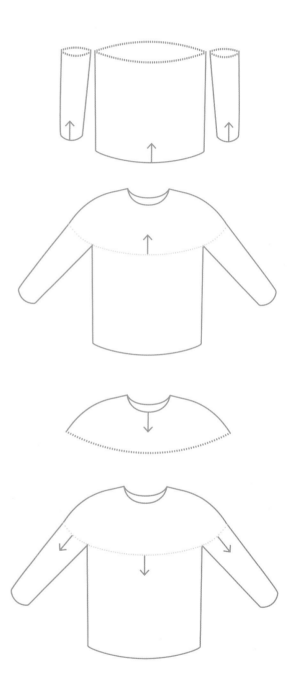

In either a bottom-up or top-down seamless sweater, the yoke (the part of the sweater from the underarm to the neck) is shaped with either evenly spaced decreases, forming a circular yoke, or at the diagonal raglan lines, making a raglan yoke. A seamless raglan yoke appears very similar to a pieced raglan construction, but without the seams, of course. A circular yoke is frequently used with patterned colorwork, as in the Mini Icelandic Sweater and the Sweetheart Cardigan patterns later in this book.

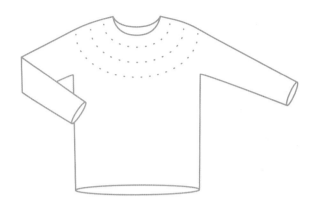

When working a bottom-up seamless sweater, you make the sleeves and body in the round and then join them at the underarms. The first few rounds after joining the sleeves to the body can be very tight near the underarms, but that will ease up after a few rounds. To ease the strain, try using two sets of circular needles, just as you would when using two sets of circulars for knitting in a small round.

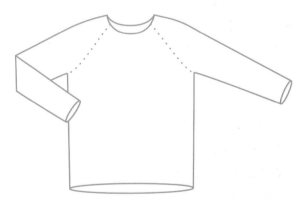

Necklines

A sweater's neckline, like the sleeve style, is an important defining characteristic of the garment. Thanks to the variety of necklines, you can customize a pattern to use your preferred neckline.

A **cowl neck collar** is a tall, wide tube that folds over and is wider at the outer edge. It fits more looser than a turtle neck.

A **turtle neck collar** is a long tube that folds over.

A **mock collar** is a short tube neck. It's usually straight or slightly wider at the top.

A **funnel collar** is a short tube neck that's slightly narrower at the top than at the base.

A **straight collar** is similar to a boat neck and is very easy to shape. It also can be off the shoulder.

A **boat (or bateau) collar** is wide and slightly oval shaped and can be off the shoulder. It's easy to work.

A **V-neck collar** is a traditional diagonally shaped neck. It can be shallow or deep and is a good choice for cardigans.

A **scoop collar** has a deep round shape and is very feminine.

A **crew collar** is a versatile round shape. It works with a variety of collars.

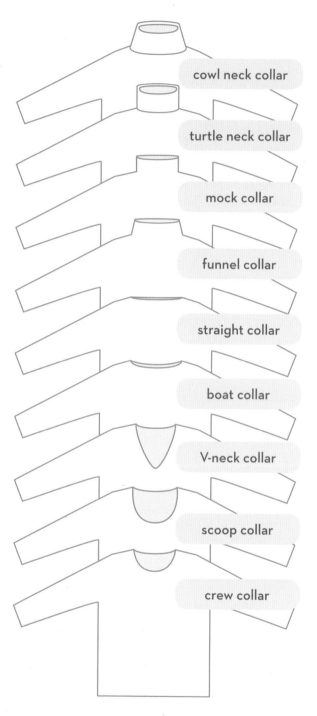

cowl neck collar

turtle neck collar

mock collar

funnel collar

straight collar

boat collar

V-neck collar

scoop collar

crew collar

Silhouettes

The shape formed by the sides of a sweater is referred to as its *silhouette*. Although you don't need to venture outside the straight-bodied sweater, many women find a gently shaped hourglass silhouette is most flattering. (In Chapter 3, I show you how to customize the silhouette in your sweaters.)

A **straight silhouette** is the same width at the chest, waist, and hip and has no shaping in the body to the underarm.

Hourglass shaping is narrower at the waist and sometimes wider at the hip than the bust.

A **tapered silhouette** is narrower at the waist and gradually widens to the chest.

Sweaters with an **A-line silhouette** are noticeably wider at the hip than the chest and have little or no shaping at the waist.

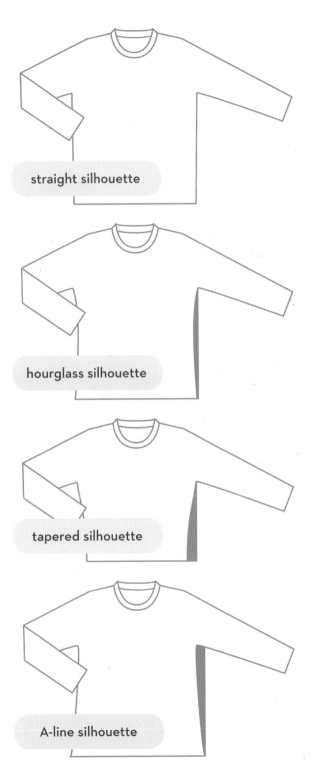

straight silhouette

hourglass silhouette

tapered silhouette

A-line silhouette

The hourglass, tapered, and A-line silhouettes are all shaped in the body.

flatter and fit

IN THIS CHAPTER

Taking your measurements

The best ways to flatter your figure

Customizing your sweaters
for the perfect fit

taking
measures

Careful measuring is essential when making any kind of clothing, but it's especially important when you're creating a garment and building the fabric at the same time, as when you knit a sweater. Also, alterations are difficult to make in a knitted sweater, unlike a sewn skirt or shirt.

So before you begin your sweater, it's a good idea to record your measurements, or the measurements of whoever you're knitting for.

Measuring Yourself

A guy might know that a particular waist size always fits when he's shopping for pants, and a woman might know her bra size, but you need much more detailed—and accurate—measurements when knitting a sweater to fit your body. So you'll need to take some measurements.

Use a flexible measuring tape to measure various areas of your body, and fill in your numbers in the Body Measurement Worksheet. As you measure, stand relaxed and breathe naturally, and hold the tape close but not tight.

Measuring yourself can be awkward. If you don't have a helper, use a string instead of a measuring tape, marking the length with your finger and thumb and then measuring the string with a yard (meter) stick. It can be helpful to tie a string around your waist as a guide.

Measuring kids? Most small children don't love standing still while you measure, so try to get at least their chest, shoulder to hip length, and arm length before setting them free to play.

In knitting terminology, *cross back* is the distance from shoulder to shoulder, measuring between the outer edges of the shoulder bones. It's an important measurement to record, especially for women, because it gives you a better indicator of width than the bust measurement.

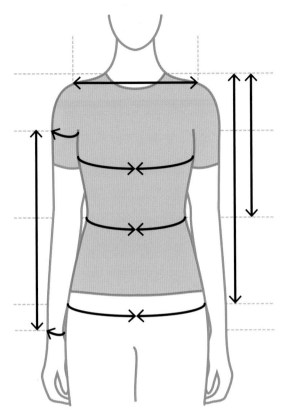

Body Measurement Worksheet

area	measurement
Hip	_____
Waist	_____
Chest/bust	_____
Shoulder to shoulder (cross back)	_____
Highest point of shoulder to waist	_____
Highest point of shoulder to hip	_____
Upper arm	_____
Wrist	_____
Arm from wrist to underarm	_____

Determining Ease

Ease is the difference between the garment's measurements and your body measurements. *Positive ease* means the garment is larger, and *negative ease* means the garment is smaller and stretches to fit. Because knit sweaters can stretch, they can have either negative or positive ease.

The amount of ease found in machine-made sweaters tends to change as fashions change.

Large amounts of positive ease are trendy one season, while fitted Lycra blends are de rigueur the next. Personal preference, on the other hand, tends to be more stable and doesn't change as often. Take the time to calculate your preferred ease, based on the Body and Garment Measurement Worksheets. This will help you when deciding which size of sweater to knit.

Measuring Other Sweaters

I find that one of the most useful pieces of information for deciding on a sweater size to knit is to measure something I already wear and like the fit of. To start, try to measure one with long, set-in sleeves. As you become more familiar with sweater construction, it's useful to measure other constructions, such as raglan sleeves.

Lay the garment flat, measure its dimensions, and make a note of them. This helps you know which parts you like close fitting and which parts you like loose.

Also, make a note of any aspects of the existing garment you'd change if you could. For example, you might have a sweater that you love the feel of but wish the sleeves were a little longer.

For the hip, waist, chest/bust, sleeve cuff, and sleeve upper arm in the Garment Measurement Worksheet, you multiply the flat measurement by 2 to get the circumference measurement.

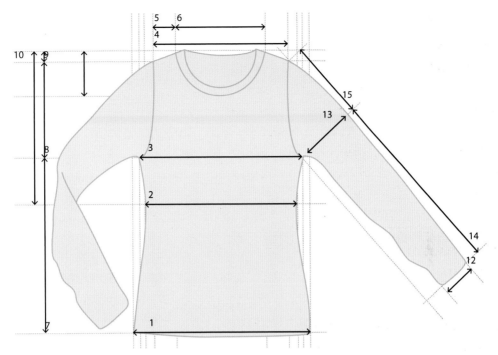

Garment Measurement Worksheet

area	measurement	area	measurement
1 Hip	_____ (x2)	**9** Shoulder drop	_____
2 Waist	_____ (x2)	**10** Highest point of shoulder to waist	_____
3 Chest/bust	_____ (x2)	**11** Front neck drop	_____
4 Shoulder to shoulder (cross back)	_____	**12** Sleeve cuff	_____ (x2)
5 Shoulder to neck (seam to seam)	_____	**13** Sleeve upper arm	_____ (x2)
6 Neck (seam to seam)	_____	**14** Cuff to underarm	_____
7 Bottom edge to underarm	_____	**15** Cap height	_____
8 Underarm to shoulder	_____		

flattering your
figure

Do you know someone who always looks fabulous even though they don't have a (so-called) perfect figure? It's not because they necessarily follow the trends, avoid horizontal stripes, or heed any other fashion "rules." It's because they know what clothes fit their body best, and they feel confident in what they're wearing.

Learn from the clothes you already have that fit and flatter you, and trust your instincts. If a garment feels great when you wear it, you'll feel great. Focus on finding a fabric that feels good and a fit that's right for you.

Knitting for Different Body Types

When we talk about body types, let's face it—we're usually talking about women. But you'll need to think about some specifics when knitting for babies, kids, and men.

Babies

The great thing about knitting for babies is that they don't care about flattering clothes or silhouettes. Here are some considerations:

- Babies have proportionally large heads and don't always enjoy getting dressed. Be sure sweaters have a wide enough neck opening so they can go on comfortably over baby's head and face.

- Babies' arms are fairly short, and their cuffs tend to get wet. You can make the sleeves a little shorter for a baby than you would for a child or adult, or at least be sure the sleeves can be rolled back.

- Babies range from tiny to stocky. One brand-new baby might be swimming in a garment labeled "newborn," while another fits nicely into something labeled "12 months." When in doubt, knit a larger size; they'll grow into it.

Kids

Children's clothing, like babies', is sized by age. But as any parent knows, these labels don't always match reality. When you can, knit to measurement, rather than age. Here are some other things to keep in mind:

- Kids all seem to grow at uneven rates. They'll go through phases where nothing is quite in proportion, be short and stocky one year, and then shoot up to long and lanky the next.

- Unlike babies, children can be very particular about the fit and style of their clothes but often don't know how to explain what they like. Try measuring one of their favorite sweaters to get an idea of their preferred fit.

- Older kids reach a point where they adamantly don't want to wear "little kid" clothes. And they might have the chest size of an XS adult but not the height or arm length. You can use an XS adult pattern, shorten the body and sleeves, and make the neck narrower if necessary.

Men

Although men certainly come in a variety of shapes and sizes, just like women do, they don't seem to get the same amount of choice when it comes to clothing sizes. Here are some points to ponder when knitting for men:

- Men are usually wider at the shoulder and taper in slightly to the hip.

- Many men complain about sleeves never being long enough. Take the time to measure from his underarm to his wrist.

- Allow enough ease at the chest, underarms, wrists, and neck for a comfortable fit. If you can, measure their favorite garment to compare.

- -

Remember that most sweaters are made for layering. It's perfectly fine—and sometimes necessary—for them to be a little roomy. A tailored shirt in woven cotton might be flattering, but that doesn't mean the sweater worn over that shirt needs to be equally snug. Most sweaters look nice when they're a little relaxed.

- -

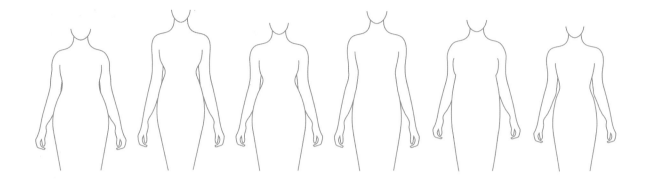

Women

With their curves out at the hip, rear, bust, and shoulder, and curves in at the waist, wrist, and neck, women's body types can be complicated. Issues women face usually have to do with proportion:

- Shoulders can be narrow or broad in proportion to the hips.

- Hips can be narrow or full in proportion to the bust.

- Busts can be small or large.

- Waists can be small or wide.

- Upper arms can be lean or full.

Because the issue is usually about proportion, rather than which particular category a body fits into (pear, hourglass, triangle, rectangle, etc.), think about knitting to flatter a body type in these general terms:

Balance: If a section of the body is proportionally narrow, broaden it. Narrow shoulders? Visually broaden them with a boat neck or raglan yoke and a few stripes at the shoulders. If a section of the body is proportionally large, soften and narrow it. Big bust and broad shoulders? Go for soft drape that skims the bust and a deep, round neckline that shortens the bust.

Counterbalance: To help balance proportion, pay attention to the complementary body part. For example, counterbalance narrow hips by softening the shoulder. Counterbalance broad shoulders by emphasizing the hips.

Break up lines: Our eyes seek out lines, especially horizontal and vertical straight lines. So throw in some gentle curves such as side shaping, a dropped hem, a scooped neck, undulating cables, or a draped front. Or break up the lines with details like pockets or vertical texture.

Skim: Don't try to cover up the feature you don't like. That just leads to big, baggy, shapeless garments. And covering up can actually have the opposite effect. Big hips took larger when covered by long cardigans. A busty upper body looks much bulkier in a baggy, boxy top. You're usually better off trying to skim your figure with a well-fitting sweater.

Finding Your Best Fit

The biggest favor you can do yourself to get a flattering knitted sweater is to concentrate on fit. Use the worksheets earlier in this chapter; pay close attention to a pattern's schematics; and be aware of the necessary ease at the hips, bust, and upper arms.

When choosing a size for yourself, look at the schematic and find one that best suits your shoulder to shoulder (cross back) and your upper arm measurements. If you need to compensate for a proportionally large bust, you can make adjustments, like adding some shaping to the body. (I show you how to do that in the next section.)

If you're busty, avoid high necklines or big collars that increase the distance between your underarm and neck and make your bust look heavy and bulky instead of curvy. Don't want to reveal too much décolletage? You can always layer a deep sweater neckline over a thin tank or camisole. Also, steer clear of a sweater with a shapeless upper body, which will make your bust and shoulders look shapeless in turn. Go for set-in sleeves and a fitted bust.

If you have wide hips or are a bit bottom-heavy, sidestep long sweaters that hit at or below your hips. This draws attention to your hips and makes you look hippier than you are. Instead, opt for a sweater that fits with little or no ease above the hips. If you feel like you want a little extra length, try a dropped hem with side vents; this breaks up the hem line in a flattering way.

If you have a round figure, stay away from short sleeves that end just below your bust or high waist shaping. Both can make your stomach more prominent. Instead, consider a straight or A-line silhouette and three-quarter sleeves.

tailoring
your knits

The patterns in this book, like most knitting patterns, are based on "average" measurements ranging from petite to plus sizes. But if you've ever gone jean shopping and come home with no jeans after hours in the fitting room, you know "average" isn't always the right fit.

The topic of tailoring or modifying knitted sweaters is worth an entire book unto itself, but unless you're going to knit for a lot of different people who have a lot of different sizes, you probably don't need to know how to tailor to *every* shape, just your own.

The sweater designs in this book are intentionally uncomplicated; you won't find any intricate tailoring or advanced shaping techniques in them. But you *will* find shapes you can easily adjust to fit your body.

Easy and More Difficult Modifications

Some adjustments are more difficult than others. A hand-knit sweater is like a puzzle with several interconnected sections. Some sections are more interconnected than others, so you want to avoid changing them if you can.

Here are some of the easier and the more difficult changes you can make when modifying a pattern to flatter your figure:

Easy changes:

- Body length
- Shaping at the hip, waist, and bust
- Sleeve length
- Neck shape

Changes to avoid:

- Sleeve cap and upper arm (affects the shape of the armhole, which affects the length of the body and cross back width)
- Yoke (affects the shoulder, back and front widths, neck circumference, and height from shoulder to underarm)
- Cross back and shoulder (affects the armhole and neck width)

If you need to modify a pattern, which size do you choose as your starting point? To determine this, examine the pattern's schematic; choose the size that offers the best match in cross back, shoulder, and upper arm measurements; and modify from there.

- -

When you start tailoring your knits, you might have to make as many as a dozen calculations to change a long sleeve to a three-quarter sleeve, or to add a little shaping at the waist. But don't worry; all the calculations are simple. If math really isn't your cup of tea, or if you need to calculate a complex curve, skip the math and plot the shapes on graph paper instead.

- -

Calculating Shaping

In knitting, most shaping involves decreasing or increasing stitches over a length of a section to create a slope: the tapered shape of a sleeve or a V neck or the rows of decreasing for the

waist. Even the curve of a round neck can be broken down into a series of gradually changing slopes.

The Shaping Formula

The *shaping rate* tells you how often to increase or decrease. Here's how it's calculated:

> Shaping rate = total rows available for shaping ÷ shaping rows needed

You'll need to do a few more calculations to fill in this equation.

If you're working back and forth, use this formula to determine the rows available for shaping:

> Total *right side* rows available for shaping = (length × row gauge [tension]) ÷ 2

If you're working in the round, here's how to determine the rounds available:

> Total *rounds* available for shaping = length × row gauge (tension)

To calculate how many shaping rows you need, use this equation:

> Shaping rows needed = (width of shaping × stitch gauge [tension]) ÷ stitches changed each shaping row

Let's plug in some numbers to see how the equations work. Say you want to increase the width of a sleeve by 2 inches (5cm) over 13¾ inches (35cm) of length. Your gauge (tension) is 20 stitches and 28 rows over 4 inches (10cm), or 5 stitches and 7 rows over 1 inch (2.5cm). Here's what to do next:

1. Calculate how many rows are available for shaping:

   Total right side rows available for shaping = (length × row gauge [tension]) ÷ 2

   = (13¾ inches × 7 rows per inch) ÷ 2

   = 48 right side rows (rounded down from 48.125)

2. Calculate how many shaping rows are needed to increase the desired width:

   Shaping rows needed = (width of shaping × stitch gauge) ÷ stitches changed each shaping row

   = (2 inches × 5 stitches per inch) ÷ 2 stitches per increase row

   = 5 shaping rows needed

   Note that a sleeve is increased at the left and right edges, with 2 stitches added each increase row.

3. Now calculate how often to increase:

   Shaping rate = total right side rows available for shaping ÷ shaping rows needed

   = 48 right side rows ÷ 5 shaping rows

   = 9.6 (shape every 9th RS row with a remainder of 3 RS rows)

4. If necessary, deal with a remainder.

If you're lucky, the final calculation will give you a whole number with no remainder. (For example, if you had to increase 10 stitches over 100 rows, you'd increase 1 stitch every 10th row. But knitting math is rarely so convenient!)

If a remainder is very low or very high, you can round the shaping rate up or down. For example, 46 ÷ 5 = 9 with a remainder of 1, so drop the 1. 44 ÷ 5 = 8 with a remainder of 4, which is almost the value of the divisor (5), so round up the result to 9 and drop the remainder.

It's easy to deal with the remainder of 3 RS rows by distributing them over the shaping rate:

   Alternate shaping rate = shaping rate + 1

   = 9th RS row + 1

   = 10th RS row (sometimes you'll increase every 9th, and sometimes every 10th, RS row)

   Number of times to use the alternate shaping rate = remainder = 3 times

   Number of times to use the basic shaping rate = shaping rows needed – remainder

   = 5 – 3 = 2 times

Either distribute the alternate shaping rate at one end of the slope …

   Shape every 9th RS row 2 times and then every 10th RS row 3 times

… or distribute the shaping more gradually for an evenly sloped shape. This requires a little more fiddling with numbers:

   Shape on the 10th, the 9th, the 10th, the 9th, and then the 10th RS rows.

That's quite a bit of math and working with formulas, but if you take it step by step, you'll find it's not that difficult.

Changing Length

Luckily, one of the most effective tailoring moves you can make is also the easiest! Making your sweater the optimal length is easy.

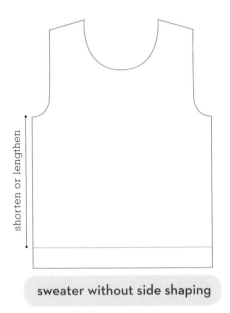

shorten or lengthen

sweater without side shaping

For a sweater *without* side shaping:
Calculate the goal length from the underarm to the bottom edge, and knit the body to the underarm to that length. You don't need to change the height of the ribbing or edge pattern. But don't forget to modify both the front *and* the back.

For a sweater *with* side shaping: If you change the length of a shaped sweater, you also have to change the distribution of the increases or decreases.

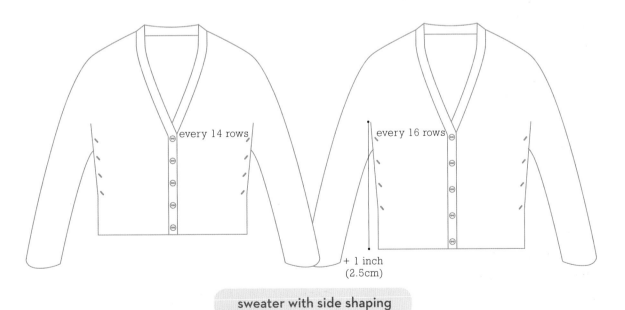

every 14 rows

every 16 rows

+ 1 inch
(2.5cm)

sweater with side shaping

Say you want to modify the Cropped Cardigan. The second to smallest size measures 12½ inches (32cm) from the bottom edge to the underarm. You want to *add* 1 inch (2.5cm) to this or, in the gauge (tension) of the pattern, 7.25 rows, which we'll round down to 7. The shaping section of the body decreases 1 stitch at each side every 14 rows 4 times over 56 rows from the underarm to the waist. (The Cropped Cardigan is worked from the top down.)

To tailor your sweater length use the shaping formula:

> Right side rows available for shaping = (56 rows + added length) ÷ 2
>
> = (56 + 7) ÷ 2
>
> = 32 right side rows (rounded up from 31.5)
>
> Shaping rows needed = 4 (this number is from the pattern and doesn't need modifying)
>
> Shaping rate = 32 right side rows ÷ 4 shaping rows
>
> = 8

So here's your tailored shaping rate:

> Decrease every 8th right side row 4 times over 64 rows.

- -

When modifying length in a sweater that has shaping below and above the waist, it's easiest to adjust the length below the waist.

- -

Adjusting Sleeve Length

Another easy bit of tailoring is the sleeve length. Again, as with modifying a shaped sweater length, you need to calculate the distribution of the sleeve shaping. Most sleeves are tapered between the cuff and the underarm.

Small _increase_ in length: If you want to increase the sleeve length less than 1 inch (2.5cm), you can simply add rows before and after the tapered portion of the sleeve and work the tapered section as written.

Small _decrease_ in length: When shortening by 1 inch (2.5cm) or less, work some of the sleeve shaping rows closer together. Calculate the length difference in rows. If your gauge (tension) is 8 rows to 1 inch (2.5cm) and you want to shorten by ½ inch (1.25cm), work 4 rows fewer. If, for example, the pattern increases every 5th RS row, work the final 2 increases every 4th RS row.

Tailor a sleeve: If you're making significant modifications—from a long sleeve to a three-quarter sleeve, for example—you have several calculations to make because you'll have to modify the cuff width as well as the sleeve length. Remember, you want to avoid changing the upper arm width, so that number remains as written in the pattern.

So to turn a long sleeve into an elbow-length sleeve 12 inches (30cm) long, keep the upper arm width and cuff height the same, but calculate a new cuff width and new shaping rate. Your gauge (tension) is 4 stitches and 6 rows per 1 inch (2.5cm).

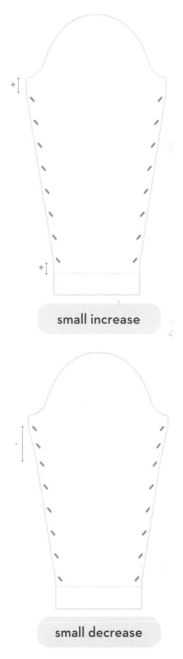

small increase

small decrease

Here's how to tailor your sleeve use the shaping formula:

> Total right side rows available for shaping = (length × row gauge) ÷ 2

Two parts of the sleeve are not shaped: the cuff, 2 inches (5cm) high, and about ½ inch (1.25cm) at the underarm.

> Length = 12 – 2 – ½
>
> = 9½ inches (24cm)
>
> Total right side rows available for shaping = (9 inches × 6 rows per inch) ÷ 2
>
> = 28 right side rows (rounded down from 28.5)
>
> Shaping rows needed = (width of shaping × stitch gauge [tension]) ÷ stitches changed each shaping row

The last two parts of this formula are easy: the stitch gauge (tension) is 4, and the stitches changed each shaping row is 2.

You decide the cuff should be 10½ inches (26.5cm) and the upper arm is 14 inches (35.5cm).

> Width of shaping = upper arm – cuff
>
> = 14 – 10½ inches
>
> = 3½ inches

Shaping rows needed = (width of shaping × stitch gauge) ÷ stitches changed on every shaping row

> = (3½ inches × 4 sts per inch) ÷ 2 sts changed per shaping row
>
> = 7 shaping rows needed

Your tailored shaping rate = total rows available for shaping ÷ shaping rows needed

> = 28 right side rows ÷ 7 shaping rows
>
> = Increase every 4th right side row

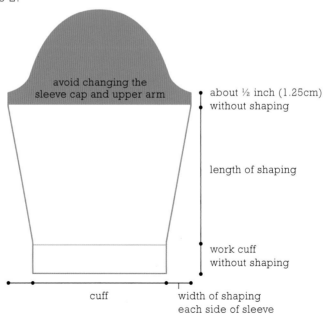

avoid changing the sleeve cap and upper arm

about ½ inch (1.25cm) without shaping

length of shaping

work cuff without shaping

cuff

width of shaping each side of sleeve

Modifying the Neck

Shaping a neck is usually worked in several steps to form a smooth curve or V. The best way to tailor a neckline is to draw the desired shape on graph paper.

For example, say someone with a busty figure finds a deep neckline a little too revealing and wants to raise it. Working with the existing width of the neck, a new neckline can be designed quite easily.

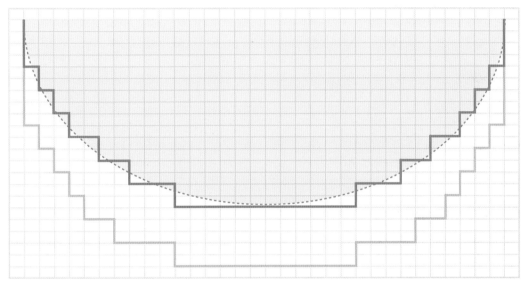

- Neck as written
- New neck curve
- New neck shaping

Start by plotting the existing neckline as written in the pattern, draw the goal neckline shape, and then plot out the neckline shaping using your goal as a guide. Keep in mind that changes to the neck width affect the shoulder width.

If you can, draw your neckline on knitter's graph paper, which is proportionally closer to knitting than square graph paper.

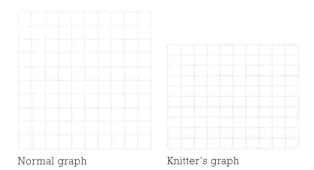

Normal graph   Knitter's graph

Adjusting Shaping

Alter the silhouette of a sweater to suit the hips, waist, or bust, and you're truly tailoring to fit. And the good news is, the calculations are relatively simple, and they all use the shaping formula.

The patterns in this book that have shaping in the body are shaped at the sides. This is for simplicity; to shape a piece of knitting next to a seam is relatively easy and, I think, intuitive. It's also fairly discreet, with the increases or decreases tucked away at the sides of the body.

You also could place the decreases or increases in each quadrant of the body with darts. This is a more sophisticated way to shape your knits, but it's a good deal more complicated. It needs to be executed neatly because the shaping is prominent. Also, it can be difficult to incorporate if a stitch texture such as cables is used in the body. If you'd like to try this style of shaping, instead of placing the decreases or increases near the sides, place them about ¼ to ⅓ of the width in from the sides.

shaping at sides

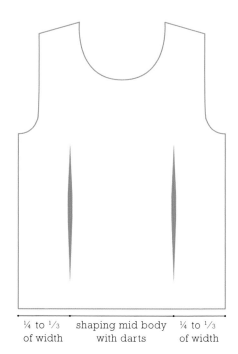

¼ to ⅓ of width   shaping mid body with darts   ¼ to ⅓ of width

When shaping the sides of a sweater, use the shaping formula as we you did when changing the body length or sleeve. Then, calculate the length of the sections to shape, as follows:

> Shaping length from hip to waist = total length – center back neck to waist length – height of edge – ½ to 1 inch (1.25 to 2.5cm) at waist]

> Shaping length from waist to underarm = length from the bottom edge to the underarm – shaping length from hip to waist – [1 or 2 inches (2.5 to 5cm) at waist] – ½ inch (1.25cm) at underarm]

Here's what you need to know when shaping the sides:

- The placement of the waistline (see "Taking Measures" for how to measure)

- The desired width of the hip, waist, and bust (avoid dramatic changes between hip, waist and bust; don't make the difference between the bust and waist more than 4 inches [10cm]; and stay closer to 2 inches [5cm])

- Work about 1 or 2 inches without shaping at, or a little higher than, the waistline

- Just as with the sleeve, work a few rows, about ½ inch (1.25cm) without shaping below the underarm

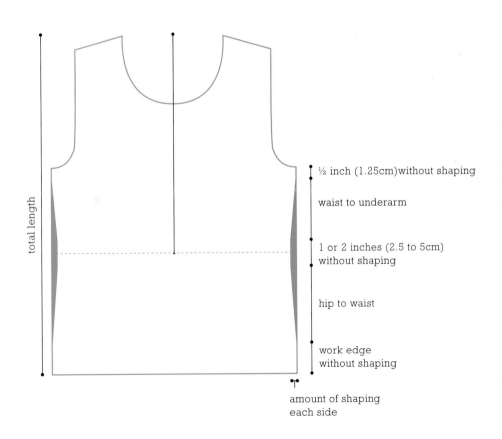

total length

½ inch (1.25cm) without shaping

waist to underarm

1 or 2 inches (2.5 to 5cm) without shaping

hip to waist

work edge without shaping

amount of shaping each side

knitting like a pro

the importance of
swatching

The usual advice for avoiding knitting mistakes applies to sweater knitting as well: count your stitches often, check for dropped stitches, read the pattern completely through before starting, have enough yarn in the same dye lot, and measure carefully.

I'd like to share some tips I've learned specifically from knitting sweaters. The first up is swatching. You probably know you need to knit a swatch before you begin a larger project, but with sweaters, it's especially important. A swatch is a test-run with your yarn and needles, before you invest time and energy (and more yarn) in a larger project.

By swatching, you can discover potential problems. With a swatch, you can try out a new stitch pattern or yarn and better visualize what your finished sweater might look like. Also, you can check gauge (tension). It's all too easy to cast on impulsively without making a swatch, confident you can match the pattern's stitch size through sheer force of will. But even the tiniest variation in the size of a stitch can have a significant impact when thousands of stitches

are combined to make a sweater. *Take the time to make a gauge (tension) swatch,* and adjust your needle size up or down until your knitting matches the pattern.

To measure gauge (tension), knit a square at least 5 inches (12.5cm) in stockinette (stocking) stitch, block it, and measure the number of stitches and rows in 4 inches (10cm).

If your pattern has texture or colorwork, make a swatch in that texture or color pattern. Many knitting patterns specify which stitch to use for your swatch. For example, cable patterns tend to be narrower than plain knitting.

When looking at gauge (tension) in the round versus worked flat, many knitters find that their stitches tend to be tighter when they're knitting in a small round. This isn't necessarily an issue when you're making a pair of socks, but it can become a problem in a sweater, where the sleeves are worked in the round and the body is worked back and forth.

There are a few potential reasons for this. For example, many knitters purl more loosely than they knit. Stockinette (stocking) stitch in the round has no purling, meaning tighter stitches. Also, knitting in a small round confines the yarn and needles, adding a little bit of tension to the stitches. Finally, the rounds in a small tube are slightly curved away from the knitter, meaning the yarn has a slightly shorter distance to travel from stitch to stitch.

So how can you test gauge (tension) when working in the round? The truly accurate way is to knit in the round and measure. However, this is time-consuming and uses a lot of yarn.

Instead, try using circular or double-pointed needles, and knit only the *right side rows*. To do this, don't turn your work at the end of a row. Instead, bring the yarn loosely across the

gauge (tension) differences

back of the beginning of the next row, and slide the stitches to the right side of the needle.

This is one method, but you also can simply use a larger needle. As you get to know your own knitting habits, you'll know how much larger of a needle you need, but I use one (U.S.) size larger.

the right
cast on

All sweaters—and all knitting, really—start with a cast on.

Many cast-on methods are available. When I teach a group of knitters, I almost always discover a new variation someone learned from their grandmother. You'll develop your own preferred technique as you become a more advanced knitter.

Unless otherwise stated in the pattern instructions, for the sweaters in this book, I recommend using a long tail or cable cast on for any knitted edge that needs to be fairly sturdy with a little bit of stretch—which is most edges in a sweater. The long tail creates a row of stitches that look like a row of purls from the back, so I usually like to begin with an extra wrong side row.

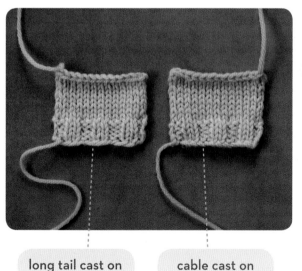

long tail cast on   cable cast on

The highlighted row shows a wrong side row worked immediately after a long tail cast on.

the right (bind)
cast off

You have many ways to cast *on* a sweater, but you usually use one method of binding (or casting) *off*.

Unless otherwise noted in the pattern, bind (cast) off as usual—knit 2, pass a stitch over, knit 1, pass over, etc. On a textured edge, like a ribbed neckline, binding (casting) off *in pattern* is a nice touch. This simply means working the stitches in the stitch pattern as established (K2/P2, for example), instead of knitting them.

Do be mindful of your tension when binding (casting) off neck edges and button bands. Keep your tension a little relaxed without being too tight or too loose.

edgings

Most sweaters have some kind of edge treatment, usually a firm, non-curling stitch like ribbing or garter stitch. The edge is often worked with a smaller needle than the one used for the body of the sweater.

Take some time to get to know a few of the edge stitches. This helps you avoid mistakes—the edge can be the most complex component of a simple sweater—and also empowers you to make substitutions to suit your own taste.

K1/P1 ribbing: This edging is very stretchy and slightly open.

Twisted K1/P1 ribbing: This isn't as stretchy as K1/P1, and it's more tightly knit.

Broken K1/P1 ribbing: Not as stretchy as K1/P1, this edging is more textured.

K2/P2 ribbing: This ribbing is very stretchy and not as open as K1/P1.

Garter stitch: This classic makes a firm edge that doesn't pull in as much as ribbing.

Seed (moss) stitch: This produces a pretty, firm, alternative to a garter stitch edge.

We learn to knit flat, working back and forth in rows. But what if you want to knit in a tube, or *in the round?* Knitting in the round is useful for socks and hats of course, but many sweater patterns also require it for necklines, sleeves, and armhole edges.

When working in the small round, you have a few options:

- A set of double-pointed needles (dpns)
- Two circular needles (works for any size of round for knitting of any complexity—this is my preferred method)
- One long circular needle, also called a *magic loop* (works for knitting of any complexity but requires a very long cable)
- One very short circular needle (only works for rounds longer than the total length of the needle, which might work for a neckline, but not for a sleeve)

If you usually work in the round with dpns, consider learning one of the other methods, especially if you get into sweater patterns with seamless components. For example, working a sleeve with a complex stitch pattern can be awkward with dpns. Try two circulars or a Magic Loop instead.

working in the
round

For more information on the "magic loop," check out the booklet *The Magic Loop* by Bev Galeskas with Sarah Hauschka.

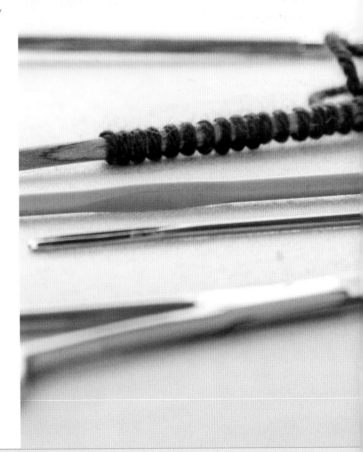

shaping

The first shaping a knitter learns is probably a knit 2 together. But in this book, you get to try out several sophisticated techniques for shaping your knits.

Fully Fashioned

Fully fashioned shaping refers to a piece of knitting that's shaped with visible decreases or increases, rather than hiding the shaping at the edge. Fully fashioned shaping can give your knits a professional look, and it also lends visual interest. It can be flattering as well, breaking up a large, featureless section of knitting.

The tailored shoulder of the Layering Vest is a nice example of fully fashioned shaping. The double decreases shape the shoulder and also create a textured diagonal detail in what would otherwise be a relatively plain garment.

Most decreases and increases slant either to the left or the right. This slant is important to successful fully fashioned shaping. A right-leaning decrease on a sleeve cap, for example, might be paired with a left-leaning decrease on the underarm. A neck might be shaped with right-leaning decreases on one side and left-leaning on the other.

The following table shows which decreases work well together.

right-leaning		left-leaning
Knit 2 together (k2tog)	works with	Slip, slip, knit 2 together through back loop (ssk)
Knit 3 together (k3tog)	works with	Slip 1, knit 2 together, pass slipped stitch over (sl1-k2tog-psso)
Make 1 by picking up the strand between the needles and working into the front of it (m1R)	works with	Make 1 by picking up the strand between the needles and working into the back of it (m1L)

Short Rows

A short row is simply a row that's short. Specifically, you work part of a row but turn before reaching the end. Short rows are used to shape sections of knitting by working extra height.

Here's an example of short rows in action in the collar of the Walking Jacket. The short rows get gradually shorter, creating a gently rounded collar that's several rows deeper at the back of the neck than it is at the base of the front neck.

Short rows take a little experience to master, but when you need them for a sweater in this book, I show you how to use them in a way that doesn't require advanced knitting skills!

Sloped Bind (Cast) Off

When shaping a curve or diagonal edge—such as a shoulder, neckline, or underarm—you bind (cast) off at the *beginning* of a row. This means you can only bind (cast) off *every other* row, resulting in a series of steps. These steps can create unwanted bulk in seams.

The solution? A *sloped* bind (cast) off:

When picking up and knitting from a sloped bind (cast) off, be sure to pick up from the stitch *below* the bound (cast) off chain, not from the chain itself.

1

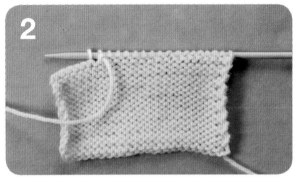

2

On the first row of shaping, bind (cast) off at the beginning of row as usual, and work to the end.

On the return row, *slip the final stitch* purlwise instead of working it.

3

4

On the next row, slip the first 2 stitches purlwise.

Pass the farthest stitch over the first. This is your first bound (cast) off stitch. Proceed binding (casting) off as usual.

Repeat the steps 2 through 4, slipping the final stitch on return rows and slipping the first 2 stitches to bind (cast) off. A sloped bind (cast) off is worked the same on right and wrong sides.

joining
new yarn

In a sweater that uses several balls of yarn, you'll have to join new yarn multiple times. Joining new yarn isn't difficult, but here are some tips for doing it right:

- Avoid joining yarn at the neck edge of a cardigan. That's one of the most visible areas of the sweater.

- Try to join new yarn in a discreet spot, like the side of the body.

- If you're joining new yarn in a seamless sweater yoke, where there are no seams in which to hide the ends, try to join at the back of a shoulder where it will be the least noticeable.

- When joining new yarns in a sweater, leave a long tail. Long tails give you more to work with when weaving in, and they also can be used in the finishing for seams.

Variegated or hand-dyed yarns differ slightly from one skein to the next. And when they're knit next to each other, even the slightest difference in color can be dramatically visible—something you don't want in the middle of a sweater!

While you have several yards or meters left on the current skein, join the new one. Work 2 rows in the new skein and then 2 rows in the current one. Continue alternating for several rows and then switch to the new skein. This blends any potential color differences.

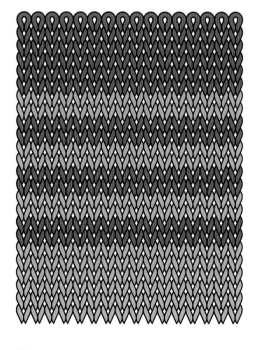

 current skein   new skein

Sometimes you need to set aside stitches.

This is easy to do using a stitch holder:

Using a stitch holder, simply slip the stitches from the needle to the holder and fasten the holder to retain the stitches.

When you need to use the held stitches, transfer them to a knitting needle first, before working them.

You also can use a piece of scrap yarn. Here's how:

Use a blunt yarn needle to thread a piece of scrap yarn in a contrasting color through the stitches and slip them off the knitting needle. Tie the ends of the scrap yarn.

When transferring from scrap yarn, leave the tied scrap yarn in place until all the stitches have been placed on the needle. Untie it, remove it, and knit as usual.

holding
stitches

blocking

Blocking is an essential step in finishing your sweater. Although it might seem daunting to tame those curling pieces of knitting, the process is easy, straightforward, and deeply satisfying.

In textiles, *block* means making something smooth and giving it shape. In knitting, it means using moisture or steam to set stitches into their final position and fit knitted pieces to their final measurements. A thorough blocking will make your knitting look fantastic.

What You Need

Here's what you need to block your work:

- Sturdy pins (without plastic heads if you're using steam)
- Clean towels
- A large, flat surface to pin into (blocking mats, made from dense foam rubber, are specifically designed for this)
- The garment schematics
- Ruler or measuring tape
- If you're using steam: a clothes steamer or an iron
- If you're spritzing: a spray bottle with water
- If you're soaking: wool soak or mild detergent
- A clean container (the kitchen sink will do if your family doesn't mind)

When to Block

Sewing, picking up bands, and weaving in ends are much easier after you've blocked your knitted fabric. Also, the blocking process is a great time to check one last time for dropped stitches or any errors. It's much easier to fix a piece before sewing than it is after! Some patterns instruct you to weave in your ends before blocking, but I prefer to block first; the seams can be a handy place to hide the ends.

It's also a good idea to spot-block after adding neck bands, button bands, pockets, or armhole edges. You might also spot-block areas where you weave in ends to help them blend in. To do this, simply lay the garment flat and spot-block the areas with a little spritz of water.

You have a few options when it comes to blocking methods.

Soaking

This is my preferred method. Unless you're never going to wash that sweater, you'll have to get it wet eventually. Although steam blocking is faster, a thorough wet block really smooths out your knitting.

To soak, fill a large, clean container with tepid water and a very small amount of detergent. Add your knitting, and soak it until the fiber is completely wet. This should take 10 minutes to an hour, depending on the fiber and size of your project.

Run clean, cool water into the container until the soaking water runs clear, carefully gather together your knitting, and lift it out of the water, holding it in one clump. Squeeze—*never wring*—out the excess water.

Place the wet knitting on a large, clean towel. Roll the towel, and press it thoroughly to remove as much water as you can from the knitting.

Lay the damp knitting on a dry towel on your blocking surface. Using your pattern's schematics and your ruler, arrange each piece of knitting and straighten the edges. Pin at frequent intervals along all the edges, and allow to dry.

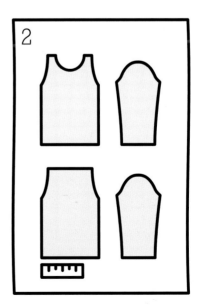

This is also how you can wash your hand-knit sweaters. You won't need to pin as thoroughly on subsequent soaking because the sweater will hold much of its shape from the first blocking.

- - - - - - - - - - - - - - - - - - - -

Before applying steam or water to your knitting, check the care instructions on the yarn ball band. Some fibers require special care such as dry cleaning.

- - - - - - - - - - - - - - - - - - - -

Spritz or Steam

With this method, you pin the dry pieces on a dry towel on your blocking surface, using the schematic as a guide. Then spritz thoroughly or apply steam—but *don't touch the iron to the fabric directly.* Allow to dry.

In the Dryer

Some fibers benefit from a very short, very *careful* spin in the dryer when they're almost dry after lying on a towel. I sometimes zip moist superwash wool or cotton knits in a mesh laundry bag and place in the dryer on low heat for 5 to 10 minutes, checking them frequently.

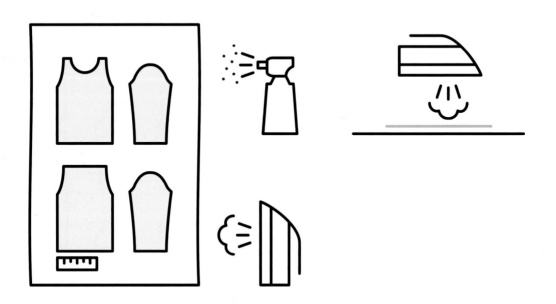

joining

Sweater patterns often end with the instruction to join, seam, or sew pieces together. How to join is usually left up to the knitter. Which method you use depends on what you're joining, but mattress stitch is the most frequently used. Mattress stitch is a user-friendly joining technique that makes an attractive and sturdy seam.

Before you sew, anchor the pieces together loosely with safety pins.

Start with a length of yarn three times the length of the seam. If you can, use the same yarn for the seams as you used for the sweater. If the yarn is too fragile or lumpy, use a fine yarn in a matching color.

Joining Side Seams

The sides of a sweater or sleeve, where you usually join row to row, can be sewed nicely with mattress stitch. Be sure you work in a well-lit area so you can see the running threads (the horizontal strands between the columns of stitches). Pass the needle under 1 or 2 running threads between the two columns of stitches at the edge of one piece, and repeat on the other piece.

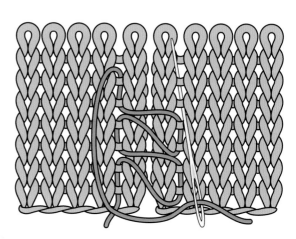

Joining Garter Stitch

To join the edges of garter stitch, you can make a flatter seam than the one made by mattress stitch. Instead of passing the needle under the running threads, pass it through the bumps made by the garter stitch ridges. Use a finer needle if necessary and pass through the bottom half of the bump on one piece and the top half of the bump on the other.

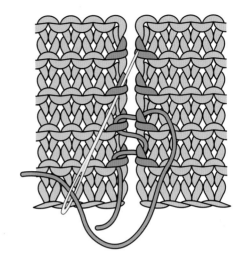

Joining Shoulders

Again, mattress stitch is an appropriate method for joining two bound (cast) off edges. Pass the needle cleanly through the center of 1 stitch and back up through its neighbor, and repeat on the other edge.

If the shoulder stitches are not bound (cast) off, you can join them using a 3-needle bind (cast) off.

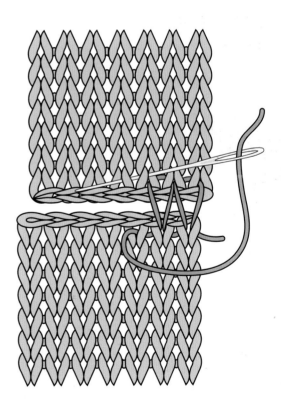

Joining Sleeves

With shoulders and sides, you usually join row to row or stitch to stitch, making the job of lining up seams quite simple. When you join a sleeve to a body, however, you join stitches to a different number of rows. This means more pinning is required before you start sewing.

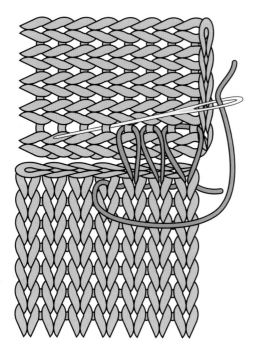

The basic idea of mattress stitch still applies when joining a sleeve: pass the needle through the stitches at the top of the sleeve and under the running threads on the body. Note that, because there will be more rows than stitches, you need to vary how many running threads you pass the needle under. Pass the needle under 1, 2, or 3 running threads as needed to keep the pieces lined up from end to end.

Joining Set-In Sleeves

A set-in sleeve is the most tailored join you'll need to make because the sleeve cap is a different shape from the armhole and needs to be carefully eased in. You can fit in the sleeve before or after sewing the side seams. Before is a little easier to work.

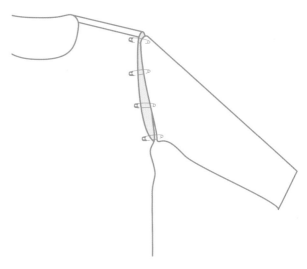

Fit the sleeve in the armhole, lining up the center of the sleeve cap with the shoulder, and pin at the underarm and center. Add more pins at intervals, adjusting the pins as you go to make a smooth fit. Starting at the top of the sleeve, sew to the underarm using mattress stitch, as described earlier.

Joining Live Stitches

Sometimes you need to join two sets of "live," or not yet bound (cast) off, stitches. Joining live stitches is not quite sewing and not quite knitting.

Three-Needle Bind (Cast) Off

By binding (casting) off two sets of stitches at the same time, you can form a smooth, lightweight seam. I use it for some shoulders and the top of hoods.

Arrange the two sets of stitches you want to join on two needles, with the right sides of the pieces facing and needle tips pointing to the right. With a third needle, bind (cast) off normally—except when you knit, put the needle through the first stitches on both the front *and* the back needle and then knit, pulling the yarn through both stitches.

From the wrong side, the seam looks like a normal bind (cast) off.

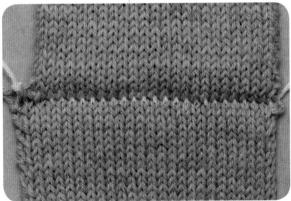

From the right side, the yarn you used for binding (casting) off is barely visible.

Kitchener Stitch (Grafting)

Using Kitchener stitch is another way to join two sets of live stitches. It makes an invisible, smooth join that's nice for seamless sweaters, shawls, and socks. In the patterns in this book, it's used to join the underarm stitches in seamless sweaters, but you can substitute the simpler 3-needle bind (cast) off if you like. Kitchener stitch isn't difficult, but be sure to follow each step carefully.

Arrange the two sets of stitches you want to join on two needles, with wrong sides of your work facing each other and the needle tips pointing to the right. Thread a blunt needle with yarn three times the width of the seam.

First things first: *For the first stitch, thread the yarn through the first stitch on the front needle as if to purl, and leave the stitch on the needle. Then thread the yarn through the first stitch on the back needle as if to knit, and leave stitch on the needle.*

Thread the yarn through the first stitch on the front needle as if to knit, and slip the stitch off the needle.

Thread the yarn through the next stitch on front needle as if to purl, and leave the stitch on.

Thread the yarn through the first stitch on the back needle as if to purl, and slip the stitch off.

Thread the yarn through the next stitch on the back needle as if to knit, and leave the stitch on the needle.

Repeat steps 1 to 4, pausing to adjust the tension of the seam every 8 stitches or so, until you reach the end.

Your finished seam will look just like a row of stockinette (stocking) stitch from the right side.

picking up and
knitting

Traditional sweater construction requires finishing around the edges. Raw edges need to be tidied and strengthened, necklines need detailing, and curling stockinette (stocking) stitch needs something to anchor it flat. Picking up and knitting—adding new knitting to an existing piece—does the job nicely.

In theory, picking up and knitting is easy. But when you're faced with a curling edge, with its bumps and loose strands, it can be daunting: *where* to pick up?

When picking up from stitches, put the needle through the center of the stitch below the bound (cast) off edge. When picking up from rows, put the needle *between* the first two stitches. This will make a tidier pick-up than putting the needle into the edge stitch. And when picking up from rows, don't pick up a stitch for each row; use a ratio of 3 to 4 or 2 to 3 stitches per row.

Also, pick up cleanly without splitting the yarn. If it's difficult to get the needle through the knitting, use a finer needle for the pick-up row.

Finally, as you go, pay attention to the multiple of stitches picked up. Most edges are worked in pattern, such as ribbing.

Be mindful of the ratio of stitches to rows in your gauge (tension). Most of the patterns in this book use the *general* ratio of picking up 3 stitches for every 4 rows. But because row gauge (tension) tends to vary from knitter to knitter and from yarn to yarn, if your row gauge (tension) is on the high side—i.e., your stitches are short—you might find a ratio of 2 stitches every 3 rows is a better fit. And remember, the best way to calculate how many stitches to pick up is to measure the edge and calculate based on your stitch gauge (tension).

You'll pick up and knit in several spots during sweater construction.

Front Bands

The button and buttonhole bands on a cardigan are a prominent detail, and it's important that they lie flat. Take time to measure the edges and calculate ahead of time how many stitches you need to pick up. Even though the number might be provided by the pattern, every sweater varies in length a little, which affects how many stitches need to be in the front bands.

Armholes

It's better for armhole edging to pull in than flare out on a sleeveless sweater. If in doubt, pick up fewer stitches.

Necklines

The neck of a sweater can be its defining characteristic. A neckline requires a careful pick up because you have to negotiate curves and seams. But don't worry; follow the logic of the neckline and avoid picking up from any loose stitches, and you'll get a lovely result.

- 1 stitch for each obund (cast) off stitch
- 3:4 ration of stitches:rows
- ignore ratio for 1 stitch to end up with odd number of stitches

This photo shows the neckline of the Baby Gansey with colored dots indicating where to pick up. It's tempting to pick up *between* the stitches, or to pick up a stitch on *every* row, to bridge the gaps. But it's more important to follow the existing logic of the stitches than it is to have a gapless pickup row. And to end up with an odd number of stitches for K1/P1 rib, you pick up 1 extra stitch near the seam.

Here's how it works:

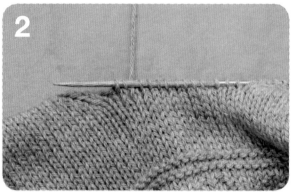

With the right side facing, working from right to left, pick up 1 stitch for each stitch on the back neck and then 3 stitches for every 4 rows of the front neck. You can pick up at a seam if the gap between stitches is too large.

Pick up 1 stitch for each stitch of the center front, making sure to put the needle through each stitch below the bound (cast) off edge. Small gaps will disappear when the neck is worked.

Continue to the end, picking up and knitting as established. Here's the final pick up, ready to work.

And here's the finished neck, after a little spritz blocking. Notice how the gaps have disappeared and the stitches of the center front neck flow directly out of the stitches of the front.

Before adding the front bands to a cardigan, try on your sweater to decide on the ideal button placement. Use the pattern as a guide, but feel free to customize the number and location of the buttons.

Buttons

When choosing buttons, be mindful of their weight. Large novelty buttons that work on heavy woven fabric might pull too much on a knitted sweater.

Before sewing on your buttons, be sure they fit through the buttonholes and the sewing needle fits through the holes in the button.

Buttonholes

Use safety pins or scrap yarn to mark the top and bottom buttonhole positions. Then mark the remaining buttonholes at even intervals.

The easiest buttonhole, an eyelet, is done with a yarn over and a decrease. And for simplicity, most of the patterns in this book use the eyelet method.

However, an eyelet is relatively small and, therefore, limits you to a smallish button. If you want to use a larger button, substitute the 1-row buttonhole technique used in the Sweetheart Cardigan.

buttons and
buttonholes

weaving in
ends

Some sweaters have dozens of ends to weave in, and it feels good to tidy them up and finalize your sweater.

Thread the end onto a blunt yarn needle, and weave it under and over stitches. You don't need to weave them in over a long distance; a few stitches is enough. Snip the yarn end close to the fabric when you're done, being careful not to cut the knitting.

Seams

If the end is near a seam (after sewing the pieces together), weave it in and out of the selvedge stitch.

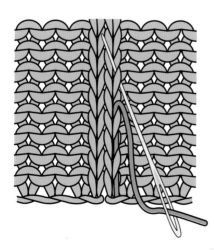

Duplicate Stitch

Sometimes an end is in the middle of the work and there's no place to hide it. In this case, use a duplicate stitch to weave the end under the bumps on the back of the work, tracing the shape of the stitches.

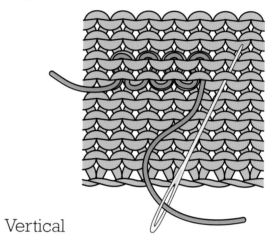

Vertical

Another way to hide an end is to weave it vertically under every other bump. Then, skipping the first bump, bring the needle back through the same bumps. This nicely hides an end in the back of ribbing, where duplicate stitch would be overly visible.

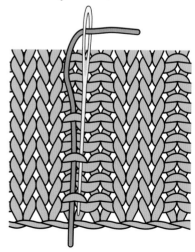

Knitting an entire sweater involves many steps: choosing a pattern, picking yarn, matching gauge (tension), knitting all the pieces, and finishing. I'm confident you can get through them all successfully with a little patience and help from this book.

One pitfall many knitters experience—I certainly do!—is the unfinished sweater. It's a classic scenario: the partially knitted sweater, collecting dust in the knitting basket, with all but one sleeve completed. Why is knitting closure so challenging? The reasons can vary, but here's a tip I've learned: *choose a combination of yarn and pattern you really love.* Take the time to pick a pattern you can visualize yourself wearing, and choose a yarn that suits you and feels nice, and you increase your chances of sweater-finishing success.

Also, look at how much yarn a pattern calls for. A 1,200-yard (1,100m) sweater could be finished in a few weeks. However, knitting a fine-knit sweater might stretch on for multiple months. If the thought of working on a sweater for that long is daunting, start with something that requires less yarn.

Sleeves are a hurdle for many knitters. They're not difficult, but the momentum that carries you through the first sleeve might fizzle by the time you get to the second. A solution is to knit both

sleeves at the same time on one needle. It's easier to keep track of shaping, and it lets you keep an eye on how much yarn you have left. If sleeves are *really* a hurdle for you, try knitting them first, before the body.

When you find a mistake, don't immediately rip it out. First, take a deep breath and assess the damage. Can you repair the problem without undoing anything? You can fix a dropped stitch, for example, in plain knitting with a crochet hook. If you have a larger mistake that requires unraveling, don't procrastinate.

Finally, position yourself among like-minded folks. Knit-alongs, or KALs, are a great way to maintain momentum. You can share pointers with each other as you encourage the others to succeed.

the
sweater
patterns

sweaters for little ones

IN THIS CHAPTER

baby
gansey

● ● ● ○ ○

Knit a wee piece of tradition with this sweet little pullover. The fishermen's *guernsey*, or *gansey*, has a rich history that goes back centuries. Densely knit in warm wool, ganseys are known for their understated textures and distinct construction. This miniature interpretation is an easy introduction to the tradition. You'll enjoy the simple knit-purl textures and the straightforward drop shoulder construction. And the small button closure makes it easier to fit over a baby's head.

Skills Needed

Knit/purl, mattress stitch, picking up and knitting

Finished Measurements

To fit 3 months (6 months, 12 months, 18 months, 2 years)

Choose a size 1 to 3 inches (2.5 to 7.5cm) larger than the actual chest measurement

Chest: 18 (19, 20, 20½, 23) inches (45.5 [48.5, 51, 52, 58.5] cm)

Length: 10¼ (11, 11½, 12, 12½) inches (26 [28, 29, 30.5, 32] cm)

Yarn

1 (2, 2, 2, 2) skeins worsted (medium-weight) yarn, 100 grams/218 yards (199m) each. I used Americo Original Mezcla de Lujo, 70 percent merino wool, 30 percent cashmere, in Heathered Grey.

Gauge (Tension)

19 stitches and 25 rows = 4 inches (10cm) in stockinette (stocking) stitch

Needles

1 set circular or straight needles and 1 set in your preferred method of working in small round: U.S. 8 (5mm/UK 6) or size needed to obtain gauge (tension)

1 set circular needles: U.S. 7 (4.5mm/UK 7) or 1 size smaller than gauge (tension) needle

Other Supplies

2 safety pins, 1 small (about ⁷⁄₁₆-inch [11mm]) button

Construction Notes

This sweater is worked flat in four pieces and then sewn together at the shoulders, sides, and underarms. The neck edge is picked up and knit with a button closure at the center back neck.

2½ (2¾, 2¾, 2¾, 3¼) inches (6.5 [7, 7, 7, 8.5] cm) 4 (4¼, 4¾, 5, 5¼) inches (10 [11, 12, 12.5, 13.5] cm)

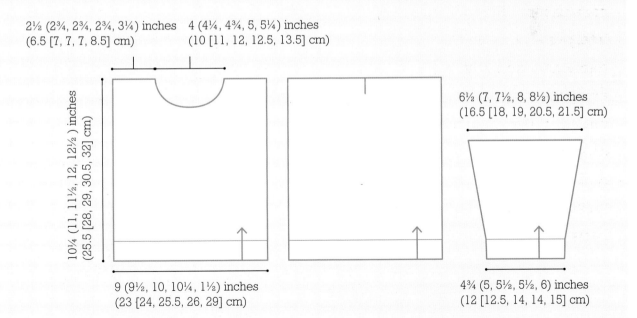

10¼ (11, 11½, 12, 12½) inches (25.5 [28, 29, 30.5, 32] cm)

6½ (7, 7½, 8, 8½) inches (16.5 [18, 19, 20.5, 21.5] cm)

9 (9½, 10, 10¼, 1½) inches (23 [24, 25.5, 26, 29] cm)

4¾ (5, 5½, 5½, 6) inches (12 [12.5, 14, 14, 15] cm)

Tips for Modifying

- Use the pattern as a blank canvas for your own textural or color motifs.

- To make a jacket, work the front in two halves, skip the back neck closure, and pick up and work the button bands.

- Add some knit-purl texture to the sleeves instead of working them in plain knitting.

- Play with the chart to design your own textures.

Chart

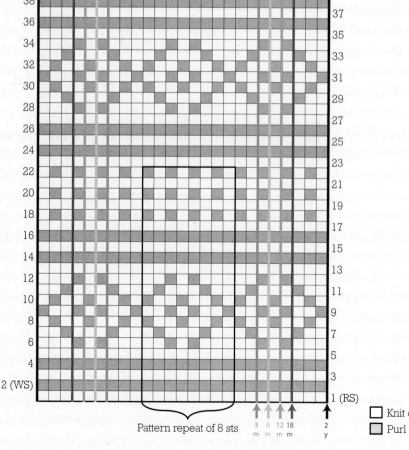

Pattern repeat of 8 sts

3 6 12 18
m m m m

2
y

☐ Knit on RS, purl on WS
▨ Purl on RS, knit on WS

Stitch Patterns and Techniques

K1/P1 rib (worked over a multiple of 2 sts):

All rows: *K1, p1; rep from * to end.

Stockinette (stocking) stitch (worked over any number of sts):

All RS rows: Knit all sts.

All WS rows: Purl all sts.

Shaping Notes

Sleeve inc (RS): K2, m1L, knit to 3 before end, m1R, k2. 2 inc'd.

Baby Gansey

Back

With smaller needles, cast on 44 (46, 48, 50, 56) sts.

Work 8 rows K1/P1 rib.

Switch to larger needles.

Next row (RS) (inc): K2, m1L, knit to end. 45 (47, 49, 51, 57) sts.

Work 1 (3, 5, 7, 9) more row stockinette (stocking) stitch.

Work from chart for 38 rows, *being sure to start and end as indicated for your size.*

Work in stockinette (stocking) stitch until piece measures 8½ (9½, 10, 10½, 11) inches (21.5 [24, 25.5, 26.5, 28] cm) from cast-on edge, ending with a WS row.

Back Neck

Divide back neck (RS): K21 (22, 23, 24, 27), k2tog. Join new ball, and k22 (23, 24, 25, 28) to end.

Next row (WS): Purl to 2 sts before end of 1st group of sts, k2. K2 at beg of 2nd group of sts, purl to end.

Next row (RS): Knit all sts.

Cont as set until back measures 10 (11, 11½, 12, 12½) inches (25.5 [28, 29, 30.5, 32] cm) from cast-on edge.

Bind (cast) off back shoulders and neck.

Front

Work same as back until piece measures 7¾ (8½, 9, 9¼, 9¾) inches (19 [21.5, 23, 23.5, 25] cm) from cast-on edge, ending with a WS row.

Shape Neck

Next row (RS): Work 19 (20, 20, 21, 24), join 2nd ball of yarn, bind (cast) off center 7 (7, 9, 9, 9), work to end.

Next 2 rows: Bind (cast) off 2 (2, 2, 3, 3) at neck edge.

Next 4 (5, 5, 5, 5) RS rows: Knit to 4 before end of 1st group of sts, ssk, k2. K2, k2tog at beg of 2nd group of sts. 13 (13, 13, 13, 16) sts each shoulder.

Cont without shaping until front is same length as back.

Bind (cast) off front shoulders.

Sleeves

With smaller needles, cast on 22 (24, 26, 26, 28) sts.

Work 8 rows K1/P1 rib.

Switch to larger needles.

With a sleeve inc (see "Shaping Notes") every 2nd (2nd, 3rd, 2nd, 2nd) RS row 6 (6, 6, 7, 8) times, work in stockinette (stocking) stitch until sleeve measures 6 (6½, 7½, 8, 8½]) inches

(15 [16.5, 19, 20.5, 21.5] cm) from cast-on edge. 34 (36, 38, 40, 44) sts.

Bind (cast) off.

Finishing

Block all pieces to schematic measurements.

Join front to back at shoulders.

With a safety pin, mark center of top edge of each sleeve (fold sleeve lengthwise to find center).

Line up safety pin with shoulder seam. Sew sleeves to body.

Fold sweater at shoulder seams to line up sides and sleeves. Sew sides and sleeves together.

Neck

With smaller circular needles and RS of neck edge facing you, starting and ending at center back, pick up and knit 45 (51, 55, 59, 59) sts. If you modify the number of sts picked up, be sure you have an odd number of sts.

Row 1 (WS): Starting and ending with p1, work in K1/P1 rib.

Next row (RS): Work in rib as set by Row 1 to 4 sts before end, k2tog, yo, work 2 to end.

Work 1 more row in K1/P1 rib.

Bind (cast) off.

Sew button to neck, matching buttonhole position.

Weave in ends.

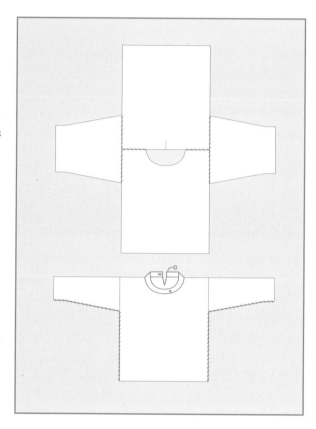

baby
jacket

●●●○○

You'll love the squishy warmth of garter stitch for baby sweaters. This cozy little jacket is knit in one piece from the top down, without seams. It's simple to knit, but it has just the right details: long sleeves, buttoned front, comfy raglan yoke, a warm collar, and contrasting pocket linings. The only sewing you need to do is to stitch the optional pockets in place.

Skills Needed

Knit/purl, picking up and knitting, working in the round, basic sewing

Finished Measurements

To fit 3 months (6 months, 12 months, 18 months, 2 years)

Choose a size 1 to 3 inches (2.5 to 7.5cm) larger than the actual chest measurement

Chest: 17 (18 ½, 20, 21½, 23) inches (43 [47, 51, 54.5, 58.5] cm)

Length: 10¼ (11, 11½, 12, 12½) inches (26 [28, 29, 30.5, 32] cm)

Yarn

2 (2, 3, 3, 3) skeins Main Color (MC), plus 1 (optional) skein Contrast Color (CC), sport (fine-weight) yarn, 100 grams/225 yards (206m) each. I used Louet Gems Sport, 100 percent superwash merino, in Pewter (MC) and Sea Foam Green (CC).

Gauge (Tension)

22 stitches and 48 rows = 4 inches (10cm) in garter stitch

22 stitches and 36 rows = 4 inches (10cm) in stockinette (stocking) stitch

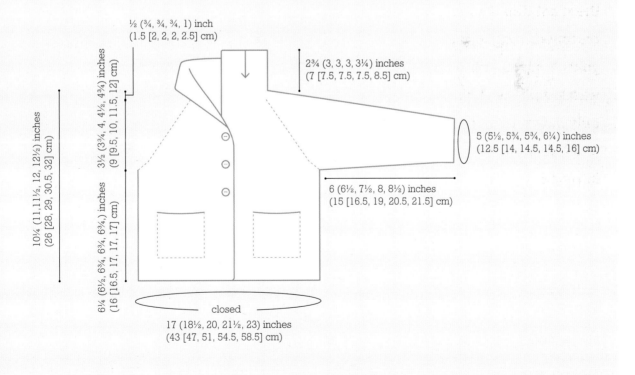

Needles

1 set circular plus 1 set in your preferred method for working in the round: U.S. 5 (3.75mm/UK 9) or size needed to obtain gauge (tension)

Other Supplies

4 stitch markers, 3 small (about 7/16- to 1/2-inch [11 or 12mm]) buttons, scrap yarn, 1 dpn 1 or 2 sizes smaller than gauge (tension) needle

Construction Notes

This sweater is worked from the top down in one piece, beginning with the collar. The raglan yoke is shaped from the neck down, and the sleeves and body are worked separately from the underarms. The pockets are marked while working the body and then picked up and knit in the finishing.

Tips for Modifying

- Simplify the pattern, and skip the pockets.

- Make it a little girlier with short sleeves and a simple lace stitch on the bottom edge.

- Splash a few stripes across the body for a sporty team jacket.

Stitch Patterns and Techniques

K1/P1 rib (worked flat over odd number of sts):

All RS rows: K1, *p1, k1; rep from * to end.

All WS rows: P1, *k1, p1; rep from * to end.

K1/P1 rib (worked in the round over a multiple of 2 sts):

All rnds: *K1, p1; rep from * to end.

Garter stitch (worked flat over any number sts):

All rows: Knit all sts.

Garter stitch (worked in the round over any number sts):

Rnd 1: Knit all sts.

Rnd 2: Purl all sts.

Rep Rnds 1 and 2 for pattern.

Stockinette (stocking) stitch (worked flat over any number of sts):

All RS rows: Knit all sts.

All WS rows: Purl all sts.

Baby Jacket

Collar

With MC, cast on 55 (63, 65, 67, 77).

Work 4 rows K1/P1 rib.

Work 30 (32, 32, 32, 36) rows garter stitch. Then shape yoke.

Shape Yoke

Marker setup (RS): K12 (13, 13, 13, 15) (front), pm, k6 (8, 8, 8, 10) (sleeve), pm, k19 (21, 23, 25, 27) (back), pm, k6 (8, 8, 8, 10) (sleeve), pm, k12 (13, 13, 13, 15) to end (front).

Knit 1 WS row.

Row 1 (RS) (inc, buttonhole): *Knit to 2 sts before marker, kfb, k1, sm, kfb, rep from * 3 more times, knit to 5 sts before end, k2tog, yo, k3. 8 sts inc'd. 13 (14, 14, 14, 16) sts each front, 8 (10, 10, 10, 12) each sleeve, 21 (23, 25, 27, 29) back, 63 (71, 73, 75, 85) total.

Knit 3 rows.

Row 5 (RS) (inc): *Knit to 2 sts before marker, kfb, k1, sm, kfb, rep from * 3 more times, knit to end. 8 sts inc'd. 14 (15, 15, 15, 17) sts each front, 10 (12, 12, 12, 14) each sleeve, 23 (25, 27, 29, 31) back, 71 (79, 81, 83, 93) total.

Working a buttonhole on Rows 19 (21, 23, 25, 27) and 39 (43, 47, 51, 55), cont in garter stitch and inc *every other* RS row 8 (9, 10, 11, 12) more times. 22 (24, 25, 26, 29) sts each front, 26 (30, 32, 34, 38) each sleeve, 39 (43, 47, 51, 55) back, 135 (151, 161, 171, 189) total.

Work 1 row without shaping. Then divide body and sleeves.

Divide Body and Sleeves

Next row (RS): *Knit to marker, transfer sleeve sts to spare circular needle or scrap yarn, removing markers on either side of sleeve. Cast on 4, pm, cast on 4; rep from * once, knit to end. 26 (28, 29, 30, 33) sts each front, 47 (51, 55, 59, 63) back, 99 (107, 113, 119, 129) total.

Cont in garter stitch until body measures 2¾ (2¾, 3, 2¾, 2½) inches (7 [7, 7.5, 7, 6.5] cm) from underarm, ending with a WS row. Then mark pockets.

Mark Pockets

Next row (RS): K7, and with long piece of scrap yarn, k16 (17, 18, 19, 21) to mark pocket opening, slip pocket sts back to left needle, and with MC k3 (4, 4, 4, 5) to marker, sm, knit to 2nd side marker, sm, k3 (4, 4, 4, 5), with 2nd piece of scrap yarn k16 (17, 18, 19, 21) for top of 2nd pocket, slip pocket sts back to left needle, with MC knit to end. (If you're not adding pockets, skip this row.)

Knit until body measures 5¾ (6, 6¼, 6¼, 6¼) inches (14.5 [15, 16, 16, 16] cm) from underarm.

Work 4 rows K1/P1 rib.

Bind (cast) off. Then work sleeves.

Sleeves

Transfer sleeve sts to needles for working in the round.

With MC, carefully pick up and knit 4 from body underarm, pm, pick up and knit 4 more. Knit across sleeve to marker. 34 (38, 40, 42, 46) sts.

Beg with a purl rnd, work 5 rnds garter stitch.

Next row (dec): K1, k2tog, knit until 3 sts remain, ssk k1. 2 sts dec'd. 32 (36, 38, 40, 44) sts.

Working a dec every 29th (21st, 25th, 19th, 17th) rnd (always on a knit rnd) 2 (3, 3, 4, 5) more times, cont in garter stitch until sleeve measures 6 (6½, 7½, 8, 8½) inches (15 [16.5, 19, 20.5, 21.5] cm) from underarm. 28 (30, 32, 32, 34) sts.

Work 4 rows K1/P1 rib.

Bind (cast) off.

Finishing

Pocket Linings

With a dpn, pick up the sts above the pocket marker. Be sure you get all the sts anchored by the scrap yarn.

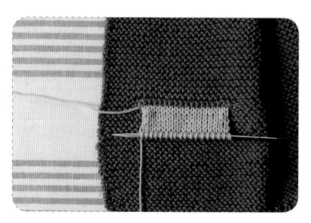

Join CC, and work 18 (20, 20, 22, 26) rows stockinette (stocking) stitch. Bind (cast) off.

With a dpn, pick up the sts below the pocket marker. Be sure you get all the sts anchored by the scrap yarn. You'll end up with 1 more st than the width of the pocket marker. This is because you're picking up the bottom of the sts instead of the tops, and you're picking up 1 extra ½ st on either side. Carefully remove scrap yarn.

Join CC at right end of dpn, and knit 1 row, then 3 rows K1/P1 rib. Bind (cast) off.

Sew pocket edge to RS and pocket linings to WS of fronts.

Block jacket to schematic measurements.

Sew buttons to left front edge, matching button-hole position.

mini icelandic
sweater

● ● ● ● ○ ○

A *lopapeysa* is a traditional sweater from Iceland known for its fleecy wool, kaleidoscopic color patterns, and circular yoke. This miniature take on the Icelandic sweater is a great introduction to working in color. Use a hand-dyed superwash wool like the one shown here, and you'll make a beautiful heirloom— that's washable, too!

Skills Needed

Knit/purl, stranded color work, grafting

Finished Measurements

To fit 3 months (6 months, 12 months, 18 months, 2 years, 3 years, 4 years, 6 years, 8 years)

Chest: 17½ (19, 20½, 21¼, 22, 23½, 25¼, 27½, 29¾) inches (44.5 [48.5, 52, 54, 56, 59.5, 64, 70, 75.5] cm)

Length: 12¼ (13, 13½, 13½, 14¼, 15, 15¼, 16¼, 18¼) inches (31 [33, 34.5, 34.5, 36, 38, 38.5, 41.5, 46.5] cm)

Yarn

1 (1, 1, 1, 1, 2, 2, 2, 2) skein Main Color (MC) and 1 skein Contrast Color (CC) worsted (medium-weight) yarn, 115 grams/270 yards (247m) each. I used Plucky Knitter Plucky Sweater, 90 percent superwash merino wool, 10 percent nylon, in Starling (MC) and Old Lace (CC).

Gauge (Tension)

21 stitches and 25 rows = 4 inches (10cm) in stockinette (stocking) stitch

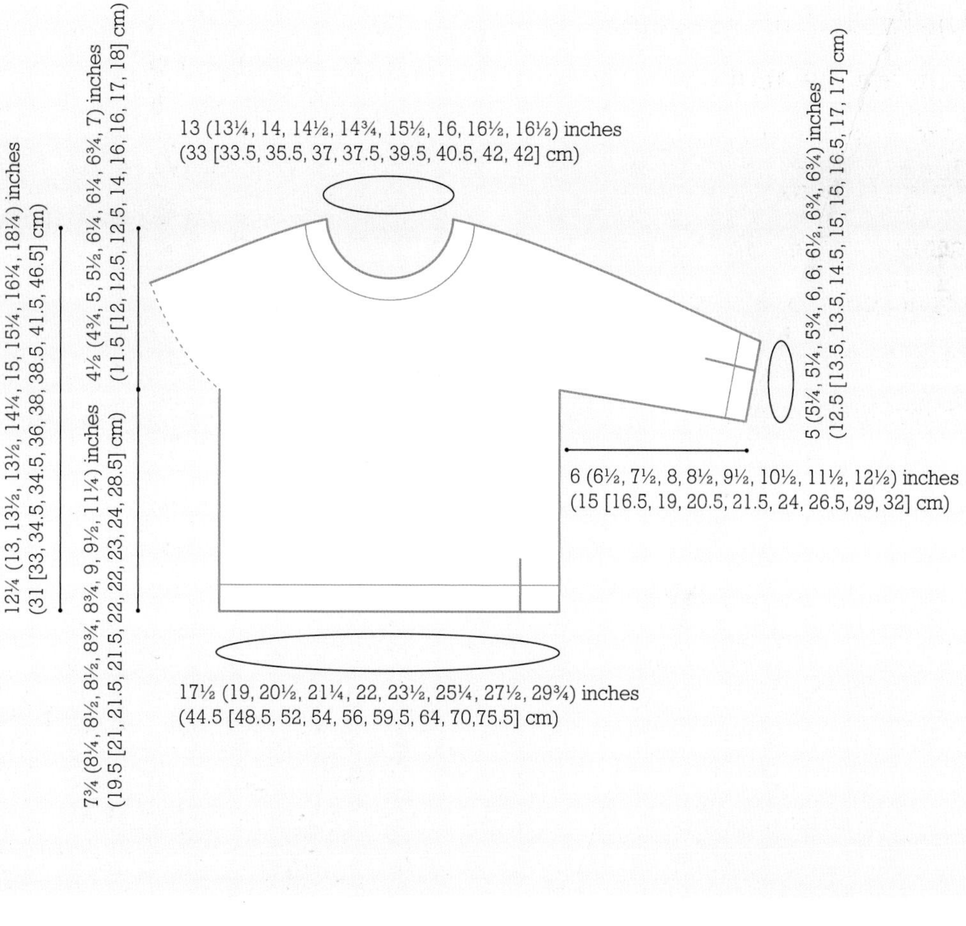
12¼ (13, 13½, 13½, 14¼, 15, 15¼, 16¼, 18¼) inches
(31 [33, 34.5, 34.5, 36, 38, 38.5, 41.5, 46.5] cm)
7¾ (8¼, 8½, 8½, 8¾, 8¾, 9, 9½, 11¼) inches
(19.5 [21, 21.5, 21.5, 22, 22, 23, 24, 28.5] cm)
4½ (4¾, 5, 5½, 6¼, 6¼, 6¾, 6¾, 7) inches
(11.5 [12, 12.5, 12.5, 14, 16, 16, 17, 18] cm)
13 (13¼, 14, 14½, 14¾, 15½, 16, 16½, 16½) inches
(33 [33.5, 35.5, 37, 37.5, 39.5, 40.5, 42, 42] cm)
5 (5¼, 5¼, 5¾, 6, 6, 6½, 6¾, 6¾) inches
(12.5 [13.5, 13.5, 14.5, 15, 15, 16.5, 17, 17] cm)
6 (6½, 7½, 8, 8½, 9½, 10½, 11½, 12½) inches
(15 [16.5, 19, 20.5, 21.5, 24, 26.5, 29, 32] cm)
17½ (19, 20½, 21¼, 22, 23½, 25¼, 27½, 29¾) inches
(44.5 [48.5, 52, 54, 56, 59.5, 64, 70,75.5] cm)

Needles

1 set circular for the body, plus 1 set in your pre-ferred method of working in a small round:

U.S. 6 (4mm/UK 8) or size needed to obtain gauge (tension)

U.S. 4 (3.5mm/UK 10) or 2 sizes smaller than gauge (tension) needle

Other Supplies

Blunt yarn needle, 1 small (about 7/16- to 1/2-inch [11 or 12mm]) button, scrap yarn for holding stitches

Construction Notes

The body and sleeves are worked in the round to the underarms and then joined. The yoke is worked in the round and decreased gradually to the neck opening. The underarm stitches are grafted using Kitchener stitch.

Tips for Modifying

- Make a quick, seamless sweater in a single color.

- Change the edge stitches for a different look.

- Play with the chart to make your own color patterns.

Stitch Patterns and Techniques

K1/P1 rib (worked in the round over a multiple of 2 sts):

All rnds: *K1, p1; rep from * to end.

Stockinette (stocking) stitch (worked over any number of sts):

All rnds: Knit all sts.

Chart

☐ Knit in MC
☐ Knit in CC
☑ K2tog in MC
☑ Ssk in MC
■ (no stitch)

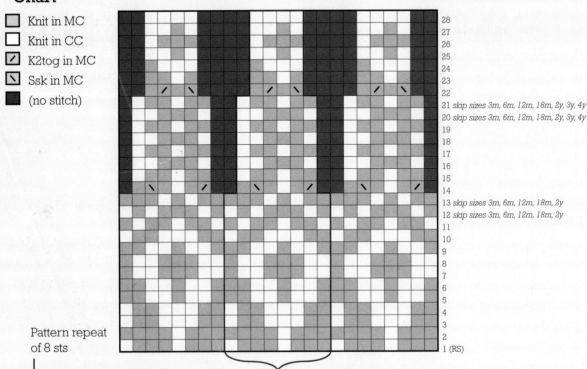

28
27
26
25
24
23
22
21 *skip sizes 3m, 6m, 12m, 18m, 2y, 3y, 4y*
20 *skip sizes 3m, 6m, 12m, 18m, 2y, 3y, 4y*
19
18
17
16
15
14
13 *skip sizes 3m, 6m, 12m, 18m, 2y*
12 *skip sizes 3m, 6m, 12m, 18m, 2y*
11
10
9
8
7
6
5
4
3
2
1 (RS)

Pattern repeat of 8 sts

Mini Icelandic Sweater

See "Sweater Construction" for additional tips.

Sleeves

With MC and smaller needles for working in a small round, cast on 26 (28, 28, 30, 32, 32, 34, 36, 36) sts.

Join for working in the round, being careful not to twist sts.

Work 8 rnds K1/P1 rib.

Switch to larger needles.

Rnd 1 (sleeve inc): K2, m1L, knit to 2 sts before end, m1R, k2. 2 sts inc'd. 28 (30, 30, 32, 34, 34, 36, 38, 38) sts.

Working a sleeve inc every 6th (8th, 0, 7th, 0, 9th, 0, 13th, 12th) rnd 3 (2, 0, 4, 0, 2, 0, 2, 2) times and then every 5th (7th, 6th, 6th, 7th, 8th, 11th, 12th, 11th) rnd 2 (2, 6, 2, 6, 4, 5, 3, 4) times, work in stockinette (stocking) stitch until sleeve measures 6 (6½, 7½, 8, 8½, 9½, 10½, 11½, 12½) inches (15 [16.5, 19, 20.5, 21.5, 24, 26.5, 29, 32] cm) from cast-on edge. 38 (38, 42, 44, 46, 46, 46, 48, 50) sts.

Underarms: Set aside 1st and last 3 (3, 4, 4, 4, 4, 4, 5, 5) sts of rnd [total of 6 (6, 8, 8, 8, 8, 8, 10, 10) sts] on scrap yarn or holder. 32 (32, 34, 36, 38, 38, 38, 38, 40) sts each sleeve. Set aside sleeves on spare circular needle or scrap yarn. Then work body.

Body

With MC and smaller needles, cast on 92 (100, 108, 112, 116, 124, 132, 144, 156) sts.

Join for working in the round, being careful not to twist sts.

Work 8 rnds K1/P1 rib.

Switch to larger needles.

Stopping 3 (3, 4, 4, 4, 4, 4, 5, 5) sts short of end on final rnd, cont knitting until body measures 7¾ (8¼, 8½, 8½, 8¾, 8¾, 9, 9½, 11¼) inches (19.5 [21, 21.5, 21.5, 22, 22, 23, 24, 28.5] cm) from cast-on edge. Then join sleeves to body.

Join Sleeves to Body

Beg 3 (3, 4, 4, 4, 4, 4, 5, 5) sts short of end of rnd, set aside next 6 (6, 8, 8, 8, 8, 8, 10, 10) sts on scrap yarn or holder for underarm.

PM for new beg of rnd, work across sleeve, joining it to body.

K40 (44, 46, 48, 50, 54, 58, 62, 68) across body (front). Set aside next 6 (6, 8, 8, 8, 8, 8, 10, 10) sts of body for 2nd underarm.

Work across 2nd sleeve, joining it to body.

Work across body (back) to end of rnd. 144 (152, 160, 168, 176, 184, 192, 200, 216) sts, plus 4 sets of 6 (6, 8, 8, 8, 8, 8, 10, 10) sts set aside for underarms. Beginning of rnd is at the left back underarm. Proceed with yoke.

Yoke

Knit 0 (1, 1, 2, 5, 7, 7, 8, 10) rnds.

Work chart, switching to needles for working in a small round when necessary. 72 (76, 80, 84, 88, 92, 96, 100, 108) sts.

Next rnd (dec): *K2tog, k16 (10, 11, 8, 6, 7, 6, 5, 3), * rep from * 3 (5, 5, 7, 9, 9, 11, 13, 19) times, k0 (4, 2, 4, 8, 2, 0, 2, 8). 68 (70, 74, 76, 78, 82, 84, 86, 88) sts.

Knit 1 rnd.

Switch to smaller needles.

K1/P1 rib for 7 rnds.

Bind (cast) off in pattern.

Finishing

Block sweater to schematic measurements.

Underarms

(Work 1 underarm at a time.) Arrange sleeve underarm sts on 1 needle and body underarm sts on another. Working from the RS and using Kitchener stitch, graft the 2 sets of sts together.

Weave in ends.

kids' cocoon
pullover

■ ■ ■ ■ ○

This is the perfect layering sweater for girls or boys. In a soft baby alpaca like this, it's delicate and fuzzy. Or try it in a rugged tweed for a totally different look. Bottom-up seamless construction makes it as easy to knit as it is to wear. And you'll love the way the pouch pocket is worked at the same time as the sweater.

Skills Needed

Knit/purl, picking up and knitting, working in the round, grafting

Finished Measurements

To fit 2 (3, 4, 6, 8, 10, 12) years

Meant to be worn with 2 to 4 inches (5 to 10cm) of ease

Chest: 25 (27, 27, 29, 31, 32, 34) inches (63.5 [68.5, 68.5, 73.5, 78.5, 81.5, 86.5] cm)

Length: 14 (14, 15, 16, 18, 19½, 20½) inches (35.5 [35.5, 38, 40.5, 45.5, 49.5, 52] cm)

Yarn

3 (3, 3, 3, 4, 4, 5) balls worsted (medium-weight) yarn, 50 grams/137 yards (125m) each. I used Knit Picks Reverie, 80 percent baby alpaca, 20 percent acrylic, in Hawk. (Reverie is a particularly fluffy yarn, and a little goes a long way. If you substitute a different yarn, allow 2 extra balls.)

Gauge (Tension)

16 stitches and 24 rows = 4 inches (10cm) in stockinette (stocking) stitch

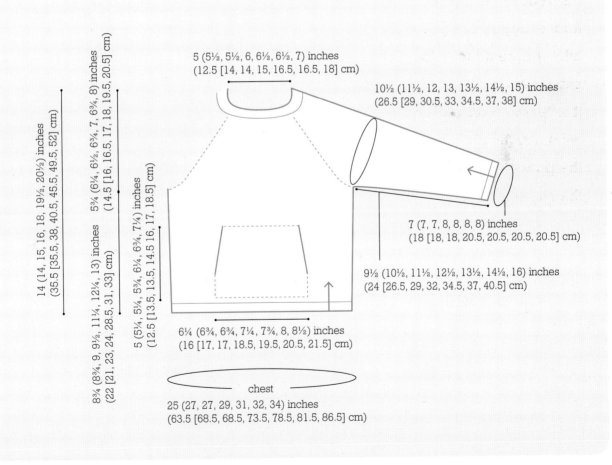

5 (5½, 5½, 6, 6½, 6½, 7) inches
(12.5 [14, 14, 15, 16.5, 16.5, 18] cm)

10½ (11½, 12, 13, 13½, 14½, 15) inches
(26.5 [29, 30.5, 33, 34.5, 37, 38] cm)

7 (7, 7, 8, 8, 8, 8) inches
(18 [18, 18, 20.5, 20.5, 20.5, 20.5] cm)

9½ (10½, 11½, 12½, 13½, 14½, 16) inches
(24 [26.5, 29, 32, 34.5, 37, 40.5] cm)

14 (14, 15, 16, 18, 19½, 20½) inches
(35.5 [35.5, 38, 40.5, 45.5, 49.5, 52] cm)

5¾ (6¼, 6½, 6¾, 7, 6¾, 8) inches
(14.5 [16, 16.5, 17, 18, 19.5, 20.5] cm)

8¾ (8¾, 9, 9½, 11¼, 12¼, 13) inches
(22 [21, 23, 24, 28.5, 31, 33] cm)

5 (5¼, 5¼, 5¾, 6¼, 6¾, 7¼) inches
(12.5 [13.5, 13.5, 14.5, 16, 17, 18.5] cm)

6¼ (6¾, 6¾, 7¼, 7¾, 8, 8½) inches
(16 [17, 17, 18.5, 19.5, 20.5, 21.5] cm)

chest
25 (27, 27, 29, 31, 32, 34) inches
(63.5 [68.5, 68.5, 73.5, 78.5, 81.5, 86.5] cm)

Needles

1 set circular and 1 set for your preferred method for working in a small round:

U.S. 8 (5mm/UK 6) or size needed to obtain gauge (tension)

U.S. 7 (4.5mm/UK 7) or 1 size smaller than gauge (tension) needle

1 spare circular in gauge (tension) size

Other Supplies

4 stitch markers, blunt yarn needle, stitch holders or scrap yarn

Construction Notes

The body and sleeves are worked in the round to the underarms and then joined. The yoke is worked in the round from the underarms to the neck. The front pouch pocket is knitted at the same time as the body. Finishing is minimal: the pocket lining is sewn to the body, and the underarm stitches are grafted together.

Tips for Modifying

- Skip the pocket for a quick knit.
- Easily change the length of the body or sleeves.
- Try adding stripes or colorwork.

Stitch Patterns and Techniques

Stockinette (stocking) stitch (worked in the round over any number of sts):

All rnds: Knit all sts.

K2/P2 rib (worked in the round over a multiple of 4 sts):

All rnds: *K2, p2; rep from * to end.

Kids' Cocoon Pullover

Pocket Lining

With larger needle, cast on 26 (28, 28, 30, 32, 32, 34) sts and work 10 (12, 12, 12, 14, 14, 16) rows stockinette (stocking) stitch.

Do not bind (cast) off. Cut yarn, leaving a tail about 1 yard (1m) long. Set aside on spare needle. Then work sleeves.

Sleeves

With smaller needles for working in a small round, cast on 28 (28, 28, 32, 32, 32, 32) sts.

Join for working in the round, being careful not to twist sts.

Work 6 rnds K2/P2 rib.

Switch to larger needles.

Rnd 1 (sleeve inc): K2, m1L, knit to 2 sts before end, m1R, k2. 2 sts inc'd. 30 (30, 30, 34, 34, 34, 34) sts.

Working a sleeve inc every 6th rnd 1 (6, 7, 4, 5, 10, 9) time and every 8th rnd 5 (2, 2, 5, 5, 2, 4) times, work in stockinette (stocking) stitch until sleeve measures 9½ (10½, 11½, 12½, 13½, 14½, 16) inches (24 [26.5, 29, 32, 34.5, 37, 40.5] cm) from cast-on edge. 42 (46, 48, 52, 54, 58, 60) sts.

Underarms: Set aside 1st and last 3 (3, 3, 4, 4, 4, 4) sts of rnd (total of 4 sts) on scrap yarn or holder. 36 (40, 42, 44, 46, 50, 52) sts each sleeve. Set aside sleeves on spare circular needle or scrap yarn. Then work body.

Body

With smaller needles, cast on 100 (108, 108, 116, 124, 128, 136) sts.

Join for working in the round, being careful not to twist sts.

Work 6 rnds K2/P2 rib.

Switch to larger needles.

Work 16 (18, 18, 18, 20, 20, 22) rnds stockinette (stocking) stitch. Then shape pocket front.

Shape Pocket Front

K12 (13, 13, 14, 15, 16, 17) sts.

The pocket front is worked separately, back and forth, on spare needles.

Pocket front Row 1 (RS): Join new ball, and with spare gauge (tension) needle, k26 (28, 28, 30, 32, 32, 34). Turn work.

Pocket front Row 2 (WS): K3, p20 (22, 22, 24, 26, 26, 28), k3. Turn work.

Cont as set by these 2 rows for 2 (2, 2, 4, 4, 4, 4) more rows.

Next row (RS) (dec): K3, k2tog, knit to 5 sts before end, ssk, k3. 2 sts dec'd. 24 (26, 26, 28, 30, 30, 32) sts.

Work a dec row every 6th (6th, 6th, 6th, 8th, 8th, 8th) row 3 more times. 6 sts dec'd. 18 (20, 20, 22, 24, 24, 26) sts.

Leave pocket front on spare needle. Then join pocket lining.

Join Pocket Lining

Starting at base of pocket, where you left the 1st ball of yarn, with pocket lining behind your work and RS of pocket lining facing you, knit across pocket lining, and k62 (67, 67, 72, 77, 80, 85) to end of rnd.

K22 (22, 22, 30, 30, 30, 30) rnds. Then join pocket front and work body.

- -

Kangaroo Pocket Step by Step

1. Knit pocket lining. Set aside on spare needle.

2. Knit body to base of pocket openings.

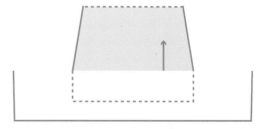

3. Join new ball of yarn, and knit front of pocket.

4. Join pocket lining, and continue body to top of pocket. Set aside on spare needle.

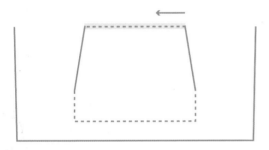

5. Join pocket front stitches to body stitches by knitting them together.

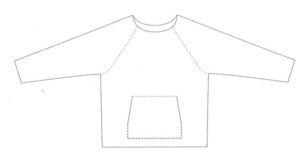

6. After knitting the sweater, sew pocket lining to wrong side of body.

- -

Join Pocket Front and Work Body

K16 (17, 17, 18, 19, 20, 21).

Arrange the spare needle with the pocket front sts on top of your work. Put the right needle through the next st on the spare needle *and* through the next st on your left needle, and knit together. Continue across the width of the pocket front, knitting each st tog with the st behind it.

K66 (71, 71, 76, 81, 84, 89) to the end of rnd.

Cont knitting every rnd until body measures 8¾ (8¾, 9, 9½, 11¼, 12¼, 13) inches (22 [22, 23, 24, 28.5, 31, 33] cm) from cast-on edge. Then join sleeves to body.

Join Body and Sleeves

K3 (3, 3, 4, 4, 4, 4) sts of current rnd, and set aside the sts just worked plus the last 3 (3, 3, 4, 4, 4, 4) sts of rnd on holder or scrap yarn (for left underarm).

Work 44 (48, 48, 50, 54, 56, 60) sts across front. Set aside next 6 (6, 6, 8, 8, 8, 8) sts of body (for right underarm), removing side marker.

PM, and work across sleeve, joining it to body. PM, and work across back. PM, and work across 2nd sleeve. 160 (176, 180, 188, 200, 212, 224) sts, 44 (48, 48, 50, 54, 56, 60) each front and back, 36 (40, 42, 44, 46, 50, 52) each sleeve, plus 4 sets of 6 (6, 6, 8, 8, 8, 8) sts set aside for underarms. Beg of rnd is at the left front underarm. Proceed with yoke.

Yoke

Knit 2 rnds.

Next rnd (dec): *K1, k2tog, knit to 3 sts before marker, ssk, k1, sm; rep from * 3 more times to end—8 sts dec'd. 152 (168, 172, 180, 192, 204, 216) sts, 42 (46, 46, 48, 52, 54, 58) each front and back, 34 (38, 40, 42, 44, 48, 50) each sleeve.

As the rnds get too short for your circular needles, switch to dpns (or your preferred method for working in the round).

Work a dec every 2nd rnd for 22 (24, 24, 24, 26, 28, 30) more rnds. 64 (72, 76, 84, 88, 92, 96) sts, 20 (22, 22, 24, 26, 26, 28) each front and back, 12 (14, 16, 18, 18, 20, 20) each sleeve.

Switch to smaller needles.

Work 6 rnds K2/P2 rib.

Bind (cast) off loosely.

Finishing

Block garment to measurements.

Pocket Lining

Stitch pocket lining to WS of front.

Underarms

(Work 1 underarm at a time.) Arrange sleeve underarm sts on 1 needle and body underarm sts on another. Working from the RS and using Kitchener stitch, graft the 2 sets of sts together.

Weave in ends.

kids' cabled
hoodie

● ● ● ● ●

This sweater is the perfect jacket for splashing in puddles or exploring the woods. With duffle-style closures and a tweedy yarn, it definitely has an old-fashioned feel. Richly textured cables, a cozy hood, and knit-in pockets—you'll love knitting this as much as they'll love wearing it.

Skills Needed

Knit/purl, cables, mattress stitch, picking up and knitting, 3-needle bind (cast) off

Finished Measurements

To fit 2 (3, 4, 6, 8, 10, 12) years

Choose a size 2 to 4 inches (5 to 10cm) larger than the actual chest measurement

Chest: 25 (27, 27, 29, 30, 32, 34) inches (63.5 [68.5, 68.5, 73.5, 76, 81.5, 86.5] cm)

Length: 13½ (14, 14½, 15½, 17½, 19, 20) inches (34.5 [35.5, 37, 39.5, 44.5, 48.5, 51] cm)

Yarn

4 (5, 5, 6, 6, 7, 8) balls bulky (chunky-weight) yarn, 100 grams/137 yards (125m) each. I used Knit Picks Wool of the Andes Superwash Bulky, 100 percent superwash wool, in Bamboo Heather.

Gauge (Tension)

16 stitches and 20 rows = 4 inches (10cm) in stockinette (stocking) stitch

Needles

1 set circular in the following sizes:

U.S. 10 (6mm/UK 4) or size needed to obtain gauge (tension)

U.S. 9 (5.5mm/UK 5) or 1 size smaller than gauge (tension) needle

Other Supplies

Cable needle, 3 stitch markers, stitch holders, scrap yarn, 3 medium buttons, 6 safety pins, blunt yarn needle, dpn in gauge size or smaller

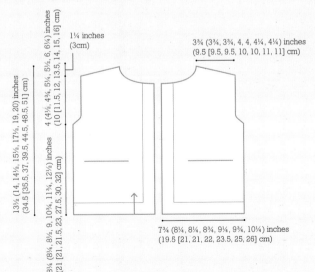

13½ (14, 14½, 15½, 17½, 19, 20) inches
(34.5 [35.5, 37, 39.5, 44.5, 48.5, 51] cm)
8¼ (8¼, 8½, 9, 10¾, 11¾, 12½) inches
(21 [21, 21.5, 23, 27.5, 30, 32] cm)
4 (4½, 4¾, 5¼, 5½, 6, 6¼) inches
(10 [11.5, 12, 13.5, 14, 15, 16] cm)
1¼ inches
(3cm)
3¾ (3¾, 3¾, 4, 4, 4¼, 4¼) inches
(9.5 [9.5, 9.5, 10, 10, 11, 11] cm)
7¾ (8¼, 8¼, 8¾, 9¼, 9¾, 10¼) inches
(19.5 [21, 21, 22, 23.5, 25, 26] cm)
4½ (5, 5, 5½, 5½, 6, 6½) inches
(11.5 [12.5, 12.5, 14, 14, 15, 16.5] cm)
13 (14, 14, 15, 15½, 16½, 17½) inches
(33 [35.5, 35.5, 38, 39.5, 42, 44.5] cm)
8 (9, 9½, 10½, 11, 12, 12½) inches
(20.5 [23, 24, 26.5, 28, 30.5, 32] cm)
6½ (6½, 7, 7½, 7½, 8, 8) inches
(16.5 [16.5, 18, 19, 19, 20.5, 20.5] cm)

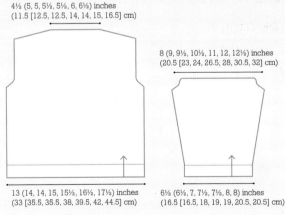

Construction Notes

This sweater is worked flat in five pieces and then sewed together at the shoulders, sides, and underarms. The knit cables run the length of the center back; cabled pockets and front bands are knit with the fronts; and the pocket linings, pocket edges, and hood are picked up and knit.

Tips for Modifying

- Add a little texture to the sleeves.
- Skip the pockets, and continue the cables up the fronts instead.
- Substitute a collar for the hood.

Stitch Patterns and Techniques

Cable 3 back (C3B): Hold 1 st to back on cable needle, k2, k1 from cable needle.

Cable 3 front (C3F): Hold 2 sts to front on cable needle, k1, k2 from cable needle.

Cable 4 back (C4B): Hold 2 sts to back on cable needle, k2, k2 from cable needle.

Cable 4 front (C4F): Hold 2 sts to front on cable needle, k2, k2 from cable needle.

Seed (moss) stitch (worked over even number of sts):

Row 1 (RS): *K1, p1; rep from * to end.

Row 2 (WS): *P1, k1; rep from * to end.

Rep Rows 1 and 2 for pattern.

Moss (double moss) stitch (worked over even number of sts):

Row 1 (RS): *K1, p1; rep from * to end.

Row 2 (WS): Rep Row 1.

Row 3: *P1, k1; rep from * to end.

Row 4: Rep Row 3.

Rep Rows 1 to 4 for pattern.

Stockinette (stocking) stitch (worked over any number of sts):

All RS rows: Knit all sts.

All WS rows: Purl all sts.

Back panel (worked over 38 sts; see chart):

Row 1 (RS): P1, k1-tbl, p1, C4B, C4F, p1, k1-tbl, p1, C4B, k2, C4B, p1, k1-tbl, p1, C4B, C4F, p1, k1-tbl, p1.

Row 2 (WS, and all WS rows): K1, p1-tbl, k1, p8, k1, p1-tbl, k1, p10, k1, p1-tbl, k1, p8, k1, p1-tbl, k1.

Row 3: P1, k1-tbl, p1, k8, p1, k1-tbl, p1, k2, C3F, C3B, k2, p1, k1-tbl, p1, k8, p1, k1-tbl, p1.

Row 5: P1, k1-tbl, p1, C4B, C4F, p1, k1-tbl, p1, k3, C4F, k3, p1, k1-tbl, p1, C4B, C4F, p1, k1-tbl, p1.

Row 7: P1, k1-tbl, p1, k8, p1, k1-tbl, p1, k2, C3B, C3F, k2, p1, k1-tbl, p1, k8, p1, k1-tbl, p1.

Rep Rows 1 to 8 for pattern.

Pocket front (worked over 18 sts; see chart):

Row 1 (RS): P4, C4B, k2, C4B, p4.

Row 2 (WS, and all WS rows): K4, p10, k4.

Row 3: P4, k2, C3F, C3B, k2, p4.

Row 5: P4, k3, C4F, k3, p4.

Row 7: P4, k2, C3B, C3F, k2, p4.

Rep Rows 1 to 8 for a total of 24 rows.

Chart

Back Panel (38 sts)

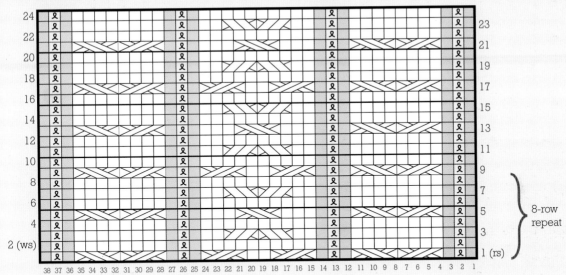

} 8-row repeat

Pocket Front (18 sts)

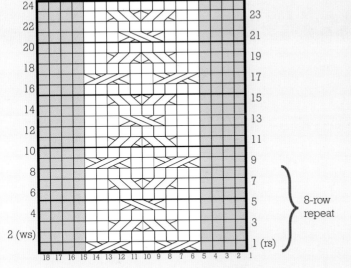

} 8-row repeat

Legend

Read WS rows left to right and RS rows from right to left.

☐	Knit on RS, purl on WS
☐ (grey)	Purl on RS, knit on WS
🇶	Knit through back loop (k-tbl) on RS, purl through back loop (p-tbl) on WS
⬜ C3B	Cable 3 Back (C3B): Hold 1 st to back on cable needle, k2, k1 from cable needle
⬜ C3F	Cable 3 Front (C3F): Hold 2 sts to front on cable needle, k1, k2 from cable needle
⬜ C4B	Cable 4 Back (C4B): Hold 2 sts to back on cable needle, k2, k2 from cable needle
⬜ C4F	Cable 4 Front (C4F): Hold 2 sts to front on cable needle, k2, k2 from cable needle

Kids' Cabled Hoodie

Back

With smaller needles, cast on 52 (56, 56, 60, 62, 66, 70) sts.

Work 8 rows seed (moss) stitch.

Switch to larger needles.

Next row (RS) (inc): K1, m1L, k6 (8, 8, 10, 11, 13, 15), pm, back panel (see "Stitch Patterns and Techniques") 38 sts, pm, knit to 1 st before end, m1R, k1. 2 sts inc'd. 54 (58, 58, 62, 64, 68, 72) sts.

Row 2 (WS): Purl to marker, sm, back panel to marker, sm, purl to end.

Cont as set by Rows 1 and 2, with stockinette (stocking) stitch either side of back panel, until piece measures 8¼ (8¼, 8½, 9, 10¾, 11¾, 12½) inches (21 [21, 21.5, 23, 27.5, 30, 32] cm) from cast-on edge, ending with a WS row. Then shape underarms.

Shape Underarms

Next 2 rows (dec): Bind (cast) off 1 (2, 2, 2, 2, 2, 3) st at beg of row, work to end. 52 (54, 54, 58, 60, 64, 66) sts.

Next 2 (2, 2, 2, 3, 3, 3) RS rows (dec): K2, k2tog, work to last 4 sts, ssk, k2. 2 sts dec'd each time. 48 (50, 50, 54, 54, 58, 60) sts.

Cont as set without shaping until back measures 12¾ (13, 13½, 14½, 16½, 17¾, 18¾)

inches (32.5 [33, 34.5, 37, 42, 45, 47.5] cm) from cast-on edge, ending with a WS row. Then shape shoulders.

Shape Shoulders

For easier finishing and smooth seams, use a sloped bind (cast) off for the shoulders and neck.

Next 4 rows (dec): Bind (cast) off 5 at beg of row, work to end. 28 (30, 30, 34, 34, 38, 40) sts.

Next 2 rows (dec): Bind (cast) off 5 (5, 5, 6, 6, 7, 7) at beg of row, work to end. 18 (20, 20, 22, 22, 24, 26) sts.

Set aside remaining sts on holder or scrap yarn.

Left Front

With smaller needles, cast on 30 (32, 32, 34, 36, 38, 40) sts.

Work 8 rows seed (moss) stitch.

Switch to larger needles.

Next row (RS) (inc): K1, m1L, k1 (2, 2, 3, 4, 5, 6), pm, pocket front 18 sts, pm, k2 (3, 3, 4, 5, 6, 7), pm, moss (double moss) 8 to end (front band). 1 st inc'd. 31 (33, 33, 35, 37, 39, 41) sts.

Row 2 (WS): Moss (double moss) to marker, sm, purl to marker, sm, pocket front to marker, sm, purl to end.

Cont as set by Rows 1 and 2 until you've worked all 24 rows of pocket front. Then mark left pocket.

Mark Left Pocket

Next row (RS): Knit to marker. Remove marker. With a 24-inch (60cm) piece of scrap yarn, k18 and remove 2nd marker. Slip all scrap yarn sts back to left needle. With working yarn, knit to final marker, sm, moss (double moss) to end. Tie ends of scrap yarn together to hold it in place.

Next row (WS): Moss (double moss) to marker, sm, purl to end.

Cont in stockinette (stocking) stitch and moss (double moss) until front measures 8¼ (8¼, 8½, 9, 10¾, 11¾, 12½) inches (21 [21, 21.5, 23, 27.5, 30, 32] cm) from cast-on edge, ending with a WS row. Then shape left underarm.

Shape Left Underarm

Next row (RS) (dec): Bind (cast) off 1 (2, 2, 2, 2, 2, 3) sts at beg of row, work to end. 30 (31, 31, 33, 35, 37, 38) sts.

Next 2 (2, 2, 2, 3, 3, 3) RS rows (dec): K2, k2tog, work to end. 1 st dec'd each time. 28 (29, 29, 31, 32, 34, 35) sts.

Cont as set without shaping until left front measures 10¾ (11¼, 11¾, 12¾, 14½, 16, 17) inches (27.5 [28.5, 30, 32.5, 37, 40.5, 43] cm) from cast-on edge, ending with a RS row. Then shape left neck.

Shape Left Neck

Next row (WS): Work 8 sts at beg of row, set these 8 sts aside on st holder or scrap yarn, work to end. 20 (21, 21, 23, 24, 26, 27) sts.

Next WS row: Bind (cast) off 3 (3, 3, 4, 4, 5, 5) sts at beg of row, work to end. 17 (18, 18, 19, 20, 21, 22) sts.

Next 2 (3, 3, 3, 4, 4, 5) RS rows: Work until 4 sts remain, ssk, k2. 1 st dec'd each time. 15 (15, 15, 16, 16, 17, 17) sts.

Cont as set without shaping until left front measures 12¾ (13, 13½, 14½, 16½, 17¾, 18¾) inches (32.5 [33, 34.5, 37, 42, 45, 47.5] cm) from cast-on edge, ending with a WS row. Then shape left shoulder.

Shape Left Shoulder

Nest 2 RS rows (dec): Bind (cast) off 5 at beg of row, work to end. 5 (5, 5, 6, 6, 7, 7) sts.

Next RS row (dec): Bind (cast) off remaining sts.

Right Front

With smaller needles, cast on 30 (32, 32, 34, 36, 38, 40) sts.

Work 8 rows seed (moss) stitch.

Switch to larger needles.

Next row (RS) (inc): Work 8 moss (double moss), pm, k2 (3, 3, 4, 5, 6, 7), pm, pocket front 18 sts, pm, k1 (2, 2, 3, 4, 5, 6), m1R, k1. 1 st inc'd. 31 (33, 33, 35, 37, 39, 41) sts.

Row 2 (WS): Purl to marker, sm, pocket front to marker, sm, purl to marker, sm, moss (double moss) to end.

Cont as set by Rows 1 and 2 until you've worked 24 rows of pocket front. Then mark right pocket.

Mark Right Pocket

Next row (RS): Moss (double moss) to marker, sm, knit to next marker, remove marker. With a 24-inch (60cm) piece of scrap yarn, k18 and remove 2nd marker. Slip all scrap yarn sts back to left needle. With working yarn, knit to end. Tie ends of scrap yarn together to hold it in place.

Next row (WS): Purl to marker, sm, moss (double moss) to end.

Cont in stockinette (stocking) stitch and moss (double moss) until front measures 8¼ (8¼, 8½, 9, 10¾, 11¾, 12½) inches (21 [21, 21.5, 23, 27.5, 30, 32] cm) from cast-on edge, ending with a RS row. Then shape right underarm.

Shape Right Underarm

Next row (WS) (dec): Bind (cast) off 1 (2, 2, 2, 2, 2, 3) sts at beg of row, work to end. 30 (31, 31, 33, 35, 37, 38) sts.

Next 2 (2, 2, 2, 3, 3, 3) RS rows (dec): Work to last 4 sts, ssk, k2. 1 st dec'd each time. 28 (29, 29, 31, 32, 34, 35) sts.

Cont as set without shaping until right front measures 10¾ (11¼, 11¾, 12¾, 14½, 16, 17) inches (27.5 [28.5, 30, 32.5, 37, 40.5, 43] cm) from cast-on edge, ending with a WS row. Then shape right neck.

Shape Right Neck

Next row (RS) (dec): Work 8 sts at beg of row, set these 8 sts aside on holder or scrap yarn, work to end. 20 (21, 21, 23, 24, 26, 27) sts.

Next RS row (dec): Bind (cast) off 3 (3, 3, 4, 4, 5, 5) sts at beg of row, work to end. 17 (18, 18, 19, 20, 21, 22) sts.

Next 2 (3, 3, 3, 4, 4, 5) RS rows (dec): K2, k2tog, work to end. 1 st dec'd each time. 15 (15, 15, 16, 16, 17, 17) sts.

Cont as set without shaping until right front measures 12¾ (13, 13½, 14½, 16½, 17¾, 18¾) inches (32.5 [33, 34.5, 37, 42, 45, 47.5] cm) from cast-on edge, ending with a RS row. Then shape right shoulder.

Shape Right Shoulder

Next 2 WS rows (dec): Bind (cast) off 5 at beg of row, work to end. 5 (5, 5, 6, 6, 7, 7) sts.

Next WS row (dec): Bind (cast) off remaining sts.

Sleeves

With smaller needles, cast on 28 (30, 30, 32, 32, 34, 34) sts.

Work 8 rows seed (moss stitch).

Switch to larger needles.

Row 1 (RS) (sleeve inc): K2, m1L, knit to 2 sts before end, m1R, k2. 2 sts inc'd. 30 (32, 32, 34, 34, 36, 36) sts.

Row 2 (WS): Purl all sts.

Working a sleeve inc every 9th (5th, 6th, 5th, 4th, 4th, 4th) RS 2 (4, 4, 5, 1, 4, 5) times and then every 0 (0, 0, 0, 5th, 5th, 5th) RS 0 (0, 0, 0, 5, 3, 3) times, cont in stockinette (stocking) stitch until sleeve measures 9½ (10½, 11½, 12½, 13½, 14½, 16) inches (24 [26.5, 29, 32, 34.5, 37, 40.5] cm) from cast-on edge, ending with a WS row. 34 (38, 40, 44, 46, 50, 52) sts. Then shape sleeve cap.

Shape Sleeve Cap

Begin with a RS row.

Next 2 rows (dec): Bind (cast) off 1 (2, 2, 2, 2, 2, 3) sts at beg of row, work to end. 32 (34, 36, 40, 42, 46, 46) sts.

Next 2 (2, 2, 2, 3, 3, 3) RS rows (dec): K2, k2tog, work to last 4 sts, ssk, k2. 2 sts dec'd each time. 28 (30, 32, 36, 36, 40, 40) sts.

Work 1 WS row.

Bind (cast) off.

Finishing

Pocket Linings

For help with pocket linings, see Baby Jacket.

With a dpn, pick up sts above pocket marker. Be sure you get all the sts anchored by the scrap yarn. You'll end up with 1 more st than the width of pocket marker. This is because you're picking up the bottom of the sts instead of the tops, and you're picking up 1 extra ½ st on either side.

Join yarn and work 24 rows stockinette (stocking) stitch. Bind (cast) off.

With a dpn, pick up sts below pocket marker. Be sure you get all the sts anchored by the scrap yarn. Carefully remove scrap yarn.

Join yarn, and work 3 rows seed (moss) stitch. Bind (cast) off.

Sew pocket linings to WS of fronts.

Block all pieces to schematic measurements.

Join shoulders. Set in sleeves. Join sleeve and side seams.

Hood

With RS of work facing and smaller circular needle, transfer 8 held sts from right front neck to spare needle. Join yarn and knit across the 8 sts, pm, and pick up and knit 12 (12, 12, 13, 13, 14, 14) sts along right neck edge to shoulder. Transfer held sts from back neck to spare needle, and k9 (10, 10, 11, 11, 12, 13), pm for center back of hood, k9 (10, 10, 11, 11, 12, 13) from other half of back neck, pick up and knit 12 (12, 12, 13, 13, 14, 14) sts along left neck edge, pm, and transfer and knit across the 8 held sts. 58 (60, 60, 64, 64, 68, 70) sts total.

Switch to larger needles.

Next row (WS): Knit to marker, purl to final marker, sm, knit to end.

Next row (RS): Knit all sts.

Work 1 WS row as set.

Next row (RS) (inc): Knit to 2 sts before center marker, m1R, k2, sm, k2, m1L, knit to end. 60 (62, 62, 66, 66, 70, 72) sts.

Working an inc row every 5th RS 3 (3, 3, 4, 4, 5, 5) times, continue until hood measures 3¾ (4½, 5½, 6¼, 7, 8¼, 8¼) inches (9.5 [11.5, 14, 16, 18, 21, 21] cm) from neck edge, ending with a WS row. 66 (68, 68, 74, 74, 80, 82) sts.

Next row (RS) (dec): Work to 3 sts before center marker, k2tog, k1, sm, k1, ssk, knit to end. 64 (66, 66, 72, 72, 78, 80) sts.

Working a dec row every RS 5 (5, 5, 6, 6, 7, 7) more times, cont for 10 (10, 10, 12, 12, 14, 14) rows. 54 (56, 56, 60, 60, 64, 66) sts.

Transfer half of sts to spare needle and with RS facing, and join top of hood with 3-needle bind (cast) off.

Button Loops and Buttons

On each front edge, starting at base of hood, mark 3 loop positions with safety pins 2½ inches (6.25cm) apart.

Loops: (Make 6.) With smaller needles, cable cast on 20 sts, and bind (cast) off, leaving a tail about 10 inches (25cm) long.

Fold each piece in half to join to RS of front band at marker with loop end 4 sts in from edge. On the right, anchor loops to fronts, leaving an opening large enough for buttons to pass through at folded end. On the left, anchor up to edge of band and sew buttons to loop end.

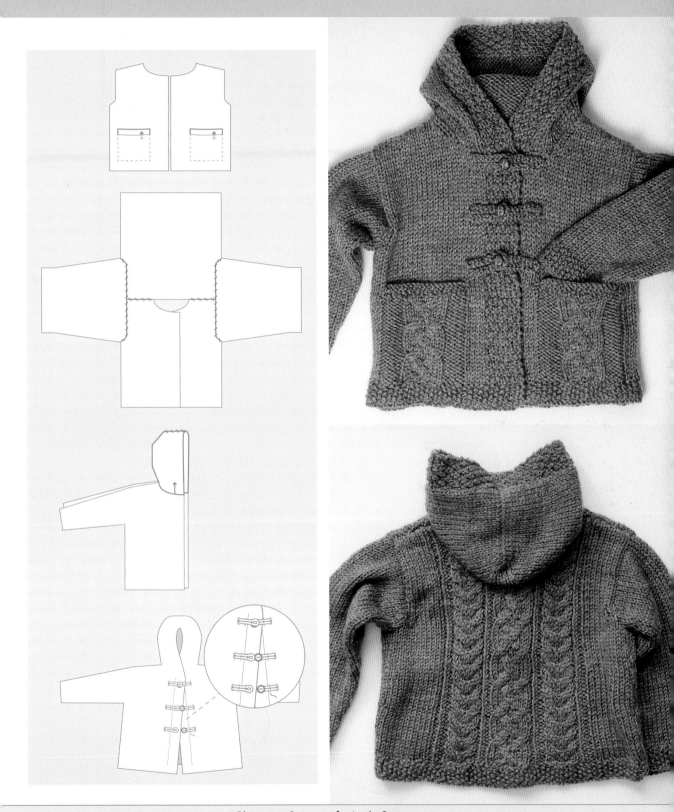

easy first sweaters

comfy drop shoulder
sweater

●○○○○

Even with a skill rating of 1, this is a very elegant sweater. One of the most basic types of sweaters, the drop shoulder, is transformed into a stylish, silky pullover you could throw on over a pair of leggings or a fitted skirt. The roomy body has a dropped back hem for a flattering line at the hip, and the fitted sleeves keep it from being too boxy.

Idiot's Guides: Knitting Sweaters

Skills Needed

Knit/purl, mattress stitch for joining pieces, 3-needle bind (cast) off for joining shoulders

Finished Measurements

Meant to be worn with 6 to 10 inches (15 to 25.5cm) of ease at the bust.

Bust: 36¾ (40¾, 44¾, 48¾, 52¾, 56¾, 60¾, 64¾, 68¾) inches (93.5 [103.5, 113.5, 124, 134, 144, 154.5, 164.5, 174.5] cm)

Length (measured at back): 23½ (23¾, 24, 24¼, 24½, 24¾, 25, 25¼, 25½) inches (59.5 [60.5, 61, 61.5, 62, 63, 63.5, 64, 65] cm)

Yarn

10 (11, 12, 13, 14, 15, 16, 17, 18) skeins DK (light) yarn, 50 grams/145 yards (133m) each. I used The Fibre Company Acadia, 60 percent merino wool, 20 percent baby alpaca, 20 percent silk, in Granite.

Gauge (Tension)

22 stitches and 32 rows = 4 inches (10cm) in stockinette (stocking) stitch

Needles

1 set circular or straight in each of the following sizes:

U.S. 6 (4mm/UK 8) or size needed to obtain gauge (tension)

U.S. 4 (3.5mm/UK 10) or 2 sizes smaller than gauge (tension) needle

Other Supplies

Blunt yarn needle, scrap yarn for holding stitches, 2 safety pins

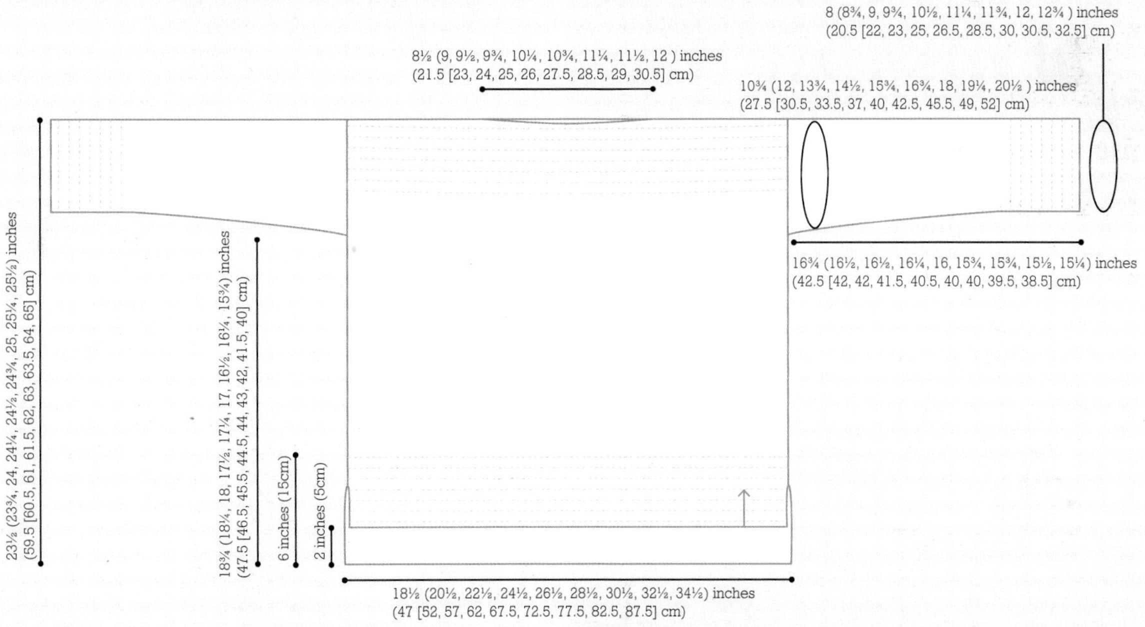
8 (8¾, 9, 9¾, 10½, 11¼, 11¾, 12, 12¾) inches
(20.5 [22, 23, 25, 26.5, 28.5, 30, 30.5, 32.5] cm)
8½ (9, 9½, 9¾, 10¼, 10¾, 11¼, 11½, 12) inches
(21.5 [23, 24, 25, 26, 27.5, 28.5, 29, 30.5] cm)
10¾ (12, 13¾, 14½, 15¾, 16¾, 18, 19¼, 20½) inches
(27.5 [30.5, 33.5, 37, 40, 42.5, 45.5, 49, 52] cm)
16¾ (16½, 16½, 16¼, 16, 15¾, 15¾, 15½, 15¼) inches
(42.5 [42, 42, 41.5, 40.5, 40, 40, 39.5, 38.5] cm)
23½ (23¾, 24, 24¼, 24½, 24¾, 25, 25¼, 25½) inches
(59.5 [60.5, 61, 61.5, 62, 63, 63.5, 64, 65] cm)
18¾ (18¼, 18, 17½, 17¼, 17, 16½, 16¼, 15¾) inches
(47.5 [46.5, 45.5, 44.5, 44, 43, 42, 41.5, 40] cm)
6 inches (15cm)
2 inches (5cm)
18½ (20½, 22½, 24½, 26½, 28½, 30½, 32½, 34½) inches
(47 [52, 57, 62, 67.5, 72.5, 77.5, 82.5, 87.5] cm)

Construction Notes

The front, back, and sleeves are worked separately. The shoulders are joined with a 3-needle bind (cast) off and then the pieces are sewn together.

Tips for Modifying

- Substitute a different stitch pattern for the garter stitch ridge.

- Work some stripes across the shoulders.

- Make the front and back the same length for a more conventional hemline.

Stitch Patterns and Techniques

Garter stitch (worked over any number sts):

All rows: Knit all sts.

Garter stitch ridge (worked over any number sts):

Rows 1 and 3 (RS): Knit all sts.

Row 2 (WS): Purl all sts.

Row 4: Knit all sts.

Rep Rows 1 to 4 for pattern.

Stockinette (stocking) stitch (worked over any number of sts):

All RS rows: Knit all sts.

All WS rows: Purl all sts.

Comfy Drop Shoulder Sweater

Back

With smaller needles, cast on 103 (114, 125, 136, 147, 158, 169, 180, 191) sts.

Work 4 rows garter stitch.

Switch to larger needles. Work 44 rows garter stitch ridge.

Work in stockinette (stocking) stitch until back measures 19½ (19¾, 20, 20¼, 20½, 20¾, 21, 21¼, 21¼) inches (49.5 [50, 51, 51.5, 52, 52.5, 53.5, 54, 54.5] cm) from cast-on edge.

Work 28 rows garter stitch ridge.

Switch to smaller needles, and work 4 rows garter stitch.

K28 (32, 36, 41, 45, 49, 53, 58, 62) for shoulder, bind (cast) off center 47 (50, 53, 54, 57, 60, 63, 64, 67), knit to end.

Do not bind (cast) off. Set aside shoulder sts on spare needle or scrap yarn.

Front

Cast on same as back.

Work 4 rows garter stitch.

Switch to larger needles. Work 28 rows garter stitch ridge.

Work in stockinette (stocking) stitch until back measures 17½ (17¾, 18, 18¼, 18½, 18¾, 19, 19¼, 19½) inches (44.5 [45, 45.5, 46.5, 47, 47.5, 48.5, 49, 49.5] cm) from cast-on edge.

Work 28 rows garter stitch ridge.

Switch to smaller needles, and work 4 rows garter stitch.

K28 (32, 36, 41, 45, 49, 53, 58, 62) for shoulder, bind (cast) off center 47 (50, 53, 54, 57, 60, 63, 64, 67), knit to end.

Do not bind (cast) off. Set aside shoulder sts on spare needle or scrap yarn.

Sleeves

With smaller needles, cast on 46 (50, 52, 56, 60, 64, 66, 68, 72) sts.

Work 4 rows garter stitch.

Switch to larger needles.

Work 28 rows garter stitch ridge.

Working a sleeve inc every 11th (7th, 5th, 4th, 4th, 3rd, 3rd, 2nd, 2nd) RS row 4 (6, 8, 10, 11, 12, 14, 17, 18) times, cont in stockinette (stocking) stitch until sleeve measures 16¾ (16½, 16½, 16¼, 16, 15¾, 15¾, 15½, 15¼) inches (42.5 [42, 42, 41.5, 40.5, 40, 40, 39.5, 38.5] cm) from cast-on edge. 54 (62, 68, 76, 82, 88, 94, 102, 108) sts.

Sleeve inc (RS) (inc): K2, m1L, knit to 2 sts before end, m1R, k2. 2 sts inc'd.

Bind (cast) off.

Finishing

Arrange front and back shoulder sts on 2 needles with RS facing each other. Using 3-needle
bind (cast) off, join shoulders.

With a safety pin, mark center of top edge of
each sleeve (fold sleeve lengthwise to find
center).

Line up safety pin with shoulder seam, and sew
sleeves to body.

Fold sweater at shoulder seams to line up sides
and sleeves. Sew sides and sleeves together.

Block sweater to measurements. Weave in
ends.

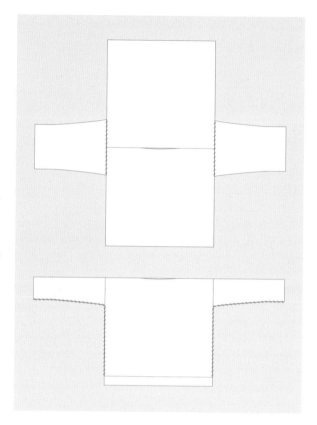

shrug

● ○ ○ ○ ○

A shrug can take many forms. It can be tailored and fitted high on the back or worn open and long. This interpretation is one of the simplest possible sweaters there is. A rectangle, folded and seamed with openings for armholes, transforms into an elegant, short-sleeved cardigan. Take your knitting upscale by treating yourself to a gorgeous yarn like this silvery baby alpaca and silk blend.

Skills Needed

Knit/purl, mattress stitch, picking up and knitting

Finished Measurements

Which size to knit? Shrugs can be worn loose or tight. Try a size that's about 75 percent of your bust measurement.

Cuff to cuff: 22¼ (24¾, 27¼, 29½, 32, 34½, 37, 39¾, 42¼) inches (56.5 [63, 69, 75, 81.5, 87.5, 94, 101, 107.5] cm)

Yarn

3 (4, 4, 5, 5, 6, 7, 8, 8) balls sport (light DK or 5-ply) yarn, 50 grams/147 yards (134m) each. I used Blue Sky Alpacas Metalico, 50 percent undyed baby alpaca, 50 percent silk, in Platinum.

Gauge (Tension)

22 stitches and 32 rows = 4 inches (10cm) in stockinette (stocking) stitch

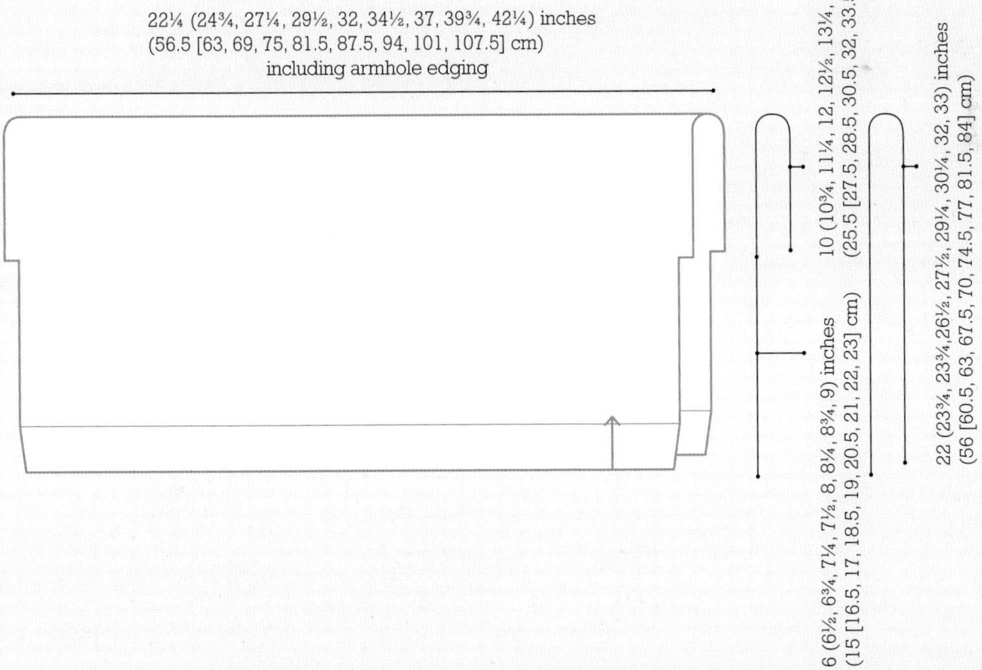

22¼ (24¾, 27¼, 29½, 32, 34½, 37, 39¾, 42¼) inches
(56.5 [63, 69, 75, 81.5, 87.5, 94, 101, 107.5] cm)
including armhole edging
10 (10¾, 11¼, 12, 12½, 13¼, 13¾, 14½, 15) inches
(25.5 [27.5, 28.5, 30.5, 32, 33.5, 35, 37, 38] cm)
6 (6½, 6¾, 7¼, 7½, 8, 8¼, 8¾, 9) inches
(15 [16.5, 17, 18.5, 19, 20.5, 21, 22, 23] cm)
22 (23¾, 23¾, 26½, 27½, 29¼, 30¼, 32, 33) inches
(56 [60.5, 63, 67.5, 70, 74.5, 77, 81.5, 84] cm)

Needles

1 set circular in each of the following sizes:

U.S. 6 (4mm/UK 8) or size needed to obtain gauge (tension)

U.S. 5 (3.75mm/UK 9) or 1 size smaller than gauge (tension) needle

Shrug is worked back and forth on circular needles.

Other Supplies

Blunt yarn needle, 2 stitch markers

Construction Notes

The shrug is worked as a large rectangle that's folded in half and seamed partway on both sides, leaving the bottom open. The bottom edge becomes the neck and front band.

Tips for Modifying

- Add some stripes, or use a self-striping yarn. The stripes curve around the neck for great visual impact.

- Add any stitch pattern you like to the body of the shrug.

Stitch Patterns and Techniques

K2/P2 rib (worked over a multiple of 4 plus 2 sts):

Row 1 (RS): P2, *k2, p2; rep from * to end.

Row 2 (WS): K2, *p2, k2; rep from * to end.

Rep Rows 1 and 2 for pattern.

Stockinette (stocking) stitch (worked over any number of sts):

All RS rows: Knit all sts.

All WS rows: Purl all sts.

Silver Shrug

Band

With smaller needles, cast on 106 (118, 134, 146, 158, 174, 186, 198, 210) sts.

Work 12 rows K2/P2 rib.

Switch to larger needles.

Part 1

Next row (inc) (RS): K4 (4, 4, 1, 2, 2, 5, 2, 0), [k10 (9, 13, 15, 13, 18, 15, 14, 13), kfb] 8 (10, 8, 8, 10, 8, 10, 12, 14) times, k14 (14, 18, 17, 16, 20, 21, 16, 14). 8 (10, 8, 8, 10, 8, 10, 12, 14) sts inc'd, 114 (128, 142, 154, 168, 182, 196, 210, 224) sts.

Work in stockinette (stocking) stitch until piece measures 6 (6½, 6¾, 7¼, 7½, 8, 8¼, 8¾, 9) inches (15 [16.5, 17, 18.5, 19, 20.5, 21, 22, 23] cm) from cast-on edge, ending on a WS row. Then add armhole edge.

Armhole Edge

Next row (RS): Cast on 4 sts at beg of row, k4, pm, knit to end.

Next row (WS): Cast on 4 sts at beg of row, k4, pm, purl to marker, sm, knit to end. 8 sts inc'd, 122 (136, 150, 162, 176, 190, 204, 218, 232) sts.

Next row: Knit all sts.

Next row: Knit to marker, sm, purl to last marker, sm, knit to end.

Cont rep the last 2 rows for about 78 (83, 88, 93, 98, 103, 108, 113, 118) more rows, or until armhole edge measures 10 (10¾, 11¼, 12, 12½, 13¼, 13¾, 14½, 15) inches (25.5 [27.5, 28.5, 30.5, 32, 33.5, 35, 37, 38] cm) from when you cast on the 4 sts either side.

Next row (RS) (end of armhole): Bind (cast) off 4 sts, removing marker, knit to end.

Next row (WS) (end of armhole): Bind (cast) off 4 sts, removing marker, purl to end.

Part 2

Work in stockinette (stocking) stitch until piece measures 20½ (22¼, 23¼, 25, 26, 27¾, 28¾, 30½, 31½) inches (52 [56.5, 59, 63.5, 66, 70.5, 73, 77.5, 80] cm) from cast-on edge, matching the number of rows you worked in Part 1, ending with a WS row.

Next row (dec) (RS): K4 (4, 4, 1, 2, 2, 5, 2, 0), [k10 (9, 13, 15, 13, 18, 15, 14, 13), k2tog] 8 (10, 8, 8, 10, 8, 10, 12, 14) times, k14 (14, 18, 17, 16, 20, 21, 16, 14). 8 (10, 8, 8, 10, 8, 10, 12, 14) sts dec'd. 106 (118, 134, 146, 158, 174, 186, 198, 210) sts. Then work band.

Band

Switch to smaller needles.

Work 12 rows K2/P2 rib.

Bind (cast) off.

Finishing

Block the piece.

Fold in half with wrong sides facing with cast-on edge lined up with bound (cast) off edge.

Starting at ribbing edge, join sides and underarms.

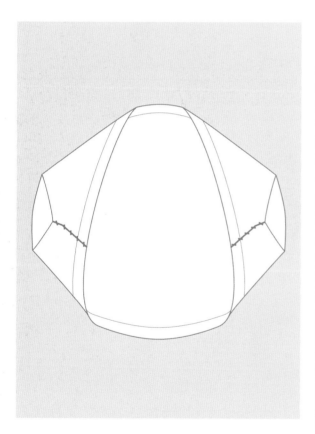

seamless
cardi

●●○○○

You'll adore the top-down seamless knitting in this romantic little cardigan. It's a very easy knit but has just enough details—short sleeves, A-line shaping, and little lace pockets—to keep it interesting. A pair of buttons hold it closed at the neck, and the fronts hang open, perfect for wearing over a dress.

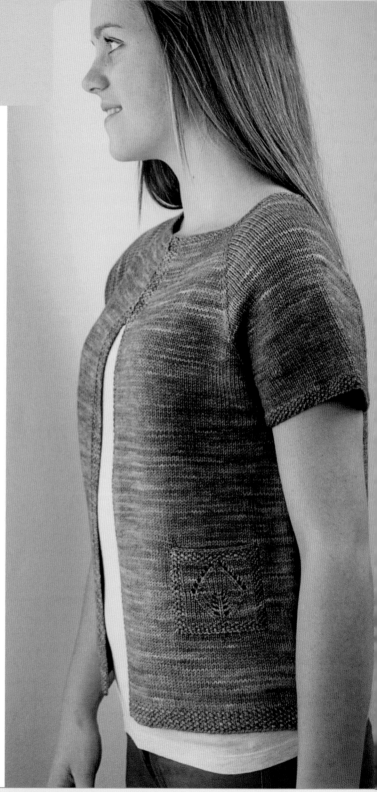

Skills Needed

Knit/purl, working in the round, picking up and knitting, stitching (for pockets)

Finished Measurements

Choose a size 1 to 3 inches (2.5 to 7.5cm) larger than the actual bust measurement

Bust: 29 (33½, 37½, 41¼, 43¾, 48¼, 52¼, 54¾) inches (73.5 [85, 95.5, 105, 111, 122.5, 132.5, 139] cm)

Length: 20½ (20¾, 21, 21¼, 21½, 21¾, 22, 22¼) inches (52 [52.5, 53.5, 54, 54.5, 55, 56, 56.5] cm)

Yarn

4 (4, 5, 5, 6, 6, 7, 7) skeins sport (fine) yarn, 50 grams/200 yards (185m) each. I used Malabrigo Finito, 100 percent superfine merino wool, in Archangel.

Gauge (Tension)

25 stitches and 37 rows = 4 inches (10cm) in stockinette (stocking) stitch

Needles

1 set circular long enough to accommodate a large number of stitches and 1 set for your preferred method of working in a small round in each of the following sizes:

U.S. 4 (3.5mm/UK 10) or size needed to obtain gauge (tension)

U.S. 2 or 3 (3.25mm/UK 11) or 1 or 2 sizes smaller than gauge (tension) needles

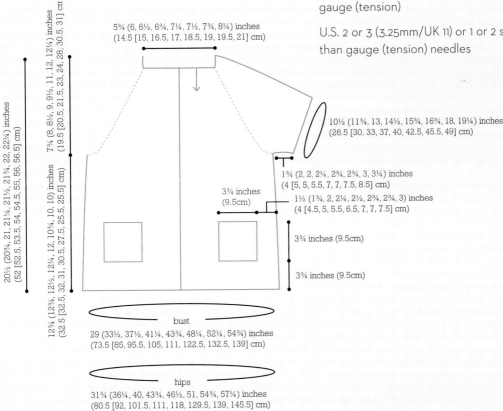

5¾ (6, 6½, 6¾, 7¼, 7½, 7¾, 8¼) inches (14.5 [15, 16.5, 17, 18.5, 19, 19.5, 21] cm)

7¾ (8, 8½, 9, 9½, 11, 12, 12¼) inches (19.5 [20.5, 21.5, 23, 24, 28, 30.5, 31] cm

20½ (20¾, 21, 21¼, 21½, 21¾, 22, 22¼) inches (52 [52.5, 53.5, 54, 54.5, 55, 56, 56.5] cm)

12¾ (12¾, 12¼, 12¼, 12, 10¾, 10, 10) inches (32.5 [32.5, 32, 31, 30.5, 27.5, 25.5, 25.5] cm)

10½ (11¾, 13, 14¼, 15¾, 16¾, 18, 19¼) inches (26.5 [30, 33, 37, 40, 42.5, 45.5, 49] cm)

1¾ (2, 2, 2¼, 2¾, 2¾, 3, 3¼) inches (4 [5, 5, 5.5, 7, 7, 7.5, 8.5] cm)

1½ (1¾, 2, 2¼, 2½, 2¾, 2¾, 3) inches (4 [4.5, 5, 5.5, 6.5, 7, 7, 7.5] cm)

3¾ inches (9.5cm)

3¾ inches (9.5cm)

3¾ inches (9.5cm)

bust
29 (33½, 37½, 41¼, 43¾, 48¼, 52¼, 54¾) inches (73.5 [85, 95.5, 105, 111, 122.5, 132.5, 139] cm)

hips
31¾ (36¼, 40, 43¾, 46½, 51, 54¾, 57¼) inches (80.5 [92, 101.5, 111, 118, 129.5, 139, 145.5] cm)

Other Supplies

6 stitch markers, blunt yarn needle, 2 safety pins, 2 small (about ⁷⁄₁₆- to ½-inch [11 to 12mm]) buttons

Construction Notes

The body is worked in one piece from the neck down to the underarms. The rest of the body is worked to the bottom edge with shaping at the sides. The sleeves are knit in the round from the underarms. The pockets are worked separately and sewn to the fronts, and the button loops are stitched on.

Tips for Modifying

- If A-line isn't your thing, skip the side increases for a straight silhouette.

- Change the motif on the pockets—or skip them entirely.

Stitch Patterns and Techniques

Seed (moss) stitch (worked flat over odd number of sts):

All rows: K1, *p1, k1; rep from * to end.

Seed (moss) stitch (worked in the round over even number of sts):

All odd-numbered rows: *K1, p1; rep from * to end.

All even-numbered rows: *P1, k1; rep from * to end.

Stockinette (stocking) stitch (worked flat over any number of sts):

All RS rows: Knit all sts.

All WS rows: Purl all sts.

Pocket Chart

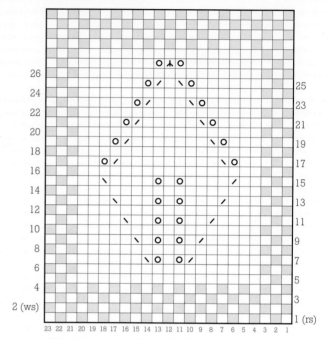

Read RS from right to left, WS from left to right

☐ Knit on RS, purl on WS

☐ Purl on RS, knit on WS

⊙ Yarn over

✓ Knit 2 together

✓ Slip, slip, knit 2 together

⅄ Slip 2 as if to k2tog, knit 1 pass 2 slipped sts over

Shaping Notes

Full raglan inc: *Work to 1 st before marker, m1R, k1, sm, k1, m1L; rep from * 3 times, work to end. 8 sts inc'd (2 sts each sleeve, 1 each front and 2 back).

Body only inc: Work to 1 st before marker, m1R, k1, sm, work to next marker, sm, m1L; rep from * once, work to end. 4 sts inc'd (1 st each front and 2 back).

Side inc: Work to 3 sts before side marker, yo, k3, sm, k3, yo; rep from * once. 4 sts inc'd (1 st each front and 2 back).

Sleeve dec: K1, k2tog, work to 3 sts before end, ssk, k1. 2 sts dec'd.

Seamless Cardi

Please read "Sweater Construction" for helpful tips.

Body

With smaller needles, cast on 109 (115, 117, 123, 139, 139, 141, 149) sts.

Raglan marker setup (WS): Seed stitch 5 (front band), pm, seed 17 (19, 19, 21, 23, 23, 23, 25) (front), pm, seed 14 (14, 14, 14, 18, 18, 18, 18) (sleeve), pm, seed 37 (39, 41, 43, 47, 47, 49, 53) (back), pm, seed 14 (14, 14, 14, 18, 18, 18, 18) (sleeve), pm, seed 17 (19, 19, 21, 23, 23, 23, 25) (front), pm, seed 5 (front band).

Work 4 more rows in seed stitch.

Switch to smaller needles. Then shape yoke.

Shape Yoke

Please read through yoke before proceeding.

Working the front bands in seed stitch and the yoke in stockinette (stocking) stitch, shape yoke over 58 (62, 66, 70, 72, 84, 92, 96) rows as follows:

Batch 1: Over the next 30 (46, 50, 54, 56, 52, 56, 68) rows, work a full raglan inc (see "Shaping Notes") every RS row 15 (23, 25, 27, 28, 26, 28, 34) times.

Work 37 (47, 49, 53, 56, 54, 56, 64) sts each front, 67 (85, 91, 97, 103, 99, 105, 121) sts back, 44 (60, 64, 68, 74, 70, 74, 86) sts each sleeve.

Then, over the next 28 (0, 0, 0, 0, 0, 0, 0) rows, work a full raglan inc *every other* RS row 7 (0, 0, 0, 0, 0, 0, 0) times.

Work 44 (47, 49, 53, 56, 54, 56, 64) sts each front, 81 (85, 91, 97, 103, 99, 105, 121) sts back, 58 (60, 64, 68, 74, 70, 74, 86) sts each sleeve.

Batch 2: Over the next 0 (0, 8, 16, 16, 32, 36, 28) rows, alt body and full raglan inc as follows:

*On the next RS, work a body only inc (see "Shaping Notes").

On the following RS, work a full raglan inc. Rep from * 0 (0, 1, 3, 3, 7, 8, 6) times.

Work 44 (47, 53, 61, 64, 70, 74, 78) sts each front, 81 (85, 99, 113, 119, 131, 141, 149) sts back, 58 (60, 68, 76, 82, 86, 92, 100) sts each sleeve.

Batch 3: Over the next 0 (16, 8, 0, 0, 0, 0, 0) rows, alt body and full raglan inc *every other* RS row as follows:

*On the 2nd RS, work a body only inc.

On the following 2nd RS, work a full raglan inc. Rep from * 0 (1, 0, 0, 0, 0, 0, 0) times.

Work 44 (51, 55, 61, 64, 70, 74, 78) sts each front, 81 (93, 103, 113, 119, 131, 141, 149) sts back, 58 (64, 70, 76, 82, 86, 92, 100) sts each sleeve.

Separate Sleeves from Body

Next row (RS): *Work to marker, remove marker. Transfer sleeve sts to scrap yarn or spare circular needle, remove next marker. Cast on 5 (6, 7, 8, 9, 10, 11, 11) (using backward loop), pm for side, cast on 5 (6, 7, 8, 9, 10, 11, 11). Rep from * once, work to end.

Work 49 (57, 62, 69, 73, 80, 85, 89) each front, 91 (105, 117, 129, 137, 151, 163, 171) back. Then work body and shape sides.

Work Body and Shape Sides

Working a side inc (see "Shaping Notes") every 12th (12th, 12th, 12th, 11th, 10th, 9th, 9th) *RS row* 4 times, cont in stockinette (stocking) stitch until work measures 11¾ (11¾, 11½, 11¼, 11, 9¾, 9, 9) inches (30 [30, 29, 28.5, 28, 25, 23, 23] cm) from underarm cast on, ending with a WS row.

Work 53 (61, 66, 73, 77, 84, 89, 93) each front, 99 (113, 125, 137, 145, 159, 171, 179) back.

Switch to smaller needles.

Work 8 rows seed stitch.

Bind (cast) off. Then work sleeves.

Sleeves

Transfer sleeve sts to needle. Rejoin yarn.

Pick up and knit 5 (6, 7, 8, 9, 10, 11, 11) from body underarm, pm, pick up and knit another 5 (6, 7, 8, 9, 10, 11, 11) sts, join in the round, being careful not to twist sts. 68 (76, 84, 92, 100, 106, 114, 122) sts.

Knit 8 (10, 12, 14, 17, 17, 19, 21) rnds.

Work 1 sleeve dec (see "Shaping Notes"). 66 (74, 82, 90, 98, 104, 112, 120) sts.

Switch to smaller needles.

Work 5 rnds seed stitch.

Bind (cast) off.

Finishing

Block garment to schematic measurements.

Button Loops and Buttons

Starting at top-right front edge, mark 2 button loop positions with safety pins 3 inches (7.5cm) apart.

With smaller needles, make 2 knitted strips as follows: cable cast on 18 sts and bind (cast) off, leaving a tail about 8 inches (20cm) long.

Fold each strip in half to form a loop, and stitch loop to WS of front band at marker. The portion of the loop that's visible on the RS should be just big enough to fit the button through.

Weave in ends on WS of band.

Sew buttons on left front band to match.

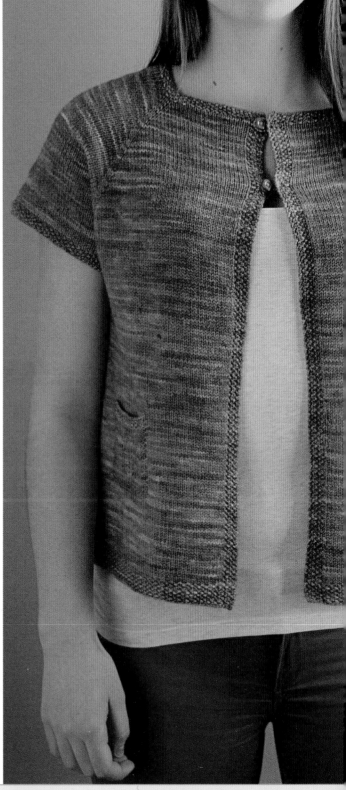

Pockets

(Make 2.) With larger needles, cast on 23.

Work from pocket chart.

Bind (cast) off.

Block.

Sew pockets to fronts following schematic for placement.

Weave in ends, closing gaps at underarms if necessary.

classic comfort

cabled cowl neck
sweater

● ● ● ○ ○

Cozy up in the luxurious rolled collar and cabled texture of this long-sleeve pullover. It knits up surprisingly fast in a medium-weight yarn, and the cables are simple to work. Traditional seamed construction and set-in sleeves give this sweater a flattering style, and the generous collar is slightly shaped for a relaxed fit around the neck.

Skills Needed

Knit/purl, basic cables, working in the round, picking up and knitting, mattress stitch, setting in sleeves

Finished Measurements

Choose a size 2 to 4 inches (5 to 10cm) larger than the actual bust measurement

Bust: 32 (36, 39¾, 43½, 48, 52, 55¾, 59½, 64) inches (81.5 [91.5, 101, 110.5, 122, 132, 141.5, 151, 162.5] cm)

Length: 24½ (24¾, 25, 25¼, 25½, 25¾, 26, 26¼, 26½) inches (62 [63, 63.5, 64, 65, 65.5, 66, 66.5, 67.5] cm)

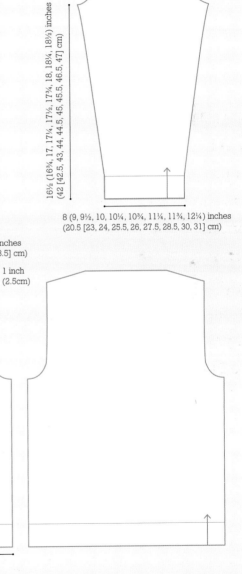

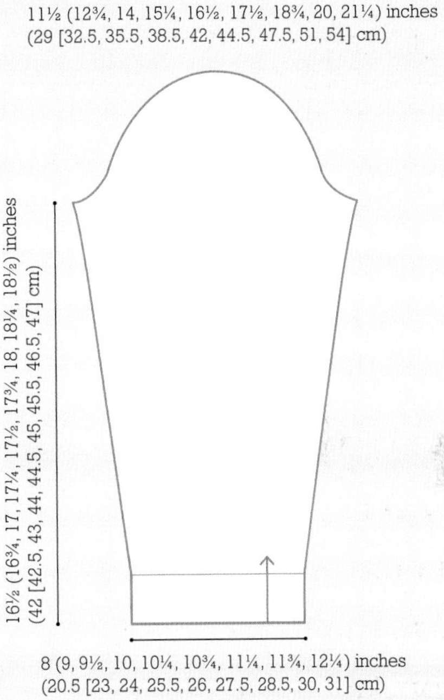
11½ (12¾, 14, 15¼, 16½, 17½, 18¾, 20, 21¼) inches
(29 [32.5, 35.5, 38.5, 42, 44.5, 47.5, 51, 54] cm)
16½ (16¾, 17, 17¼, 17½, 17¾, 18, 18¼, 18½) inches
(42 [42.5, 43, 44, 44.5, 45, 45.5, 46.5, 47] cm)
8 (9, 9½, 10, 10¼, 10¾, 11¼, 11¾, 12¼) inches
(20.5 [23, 24, 25.5, 26, 27.5, 28.5, 30, 31] cm)

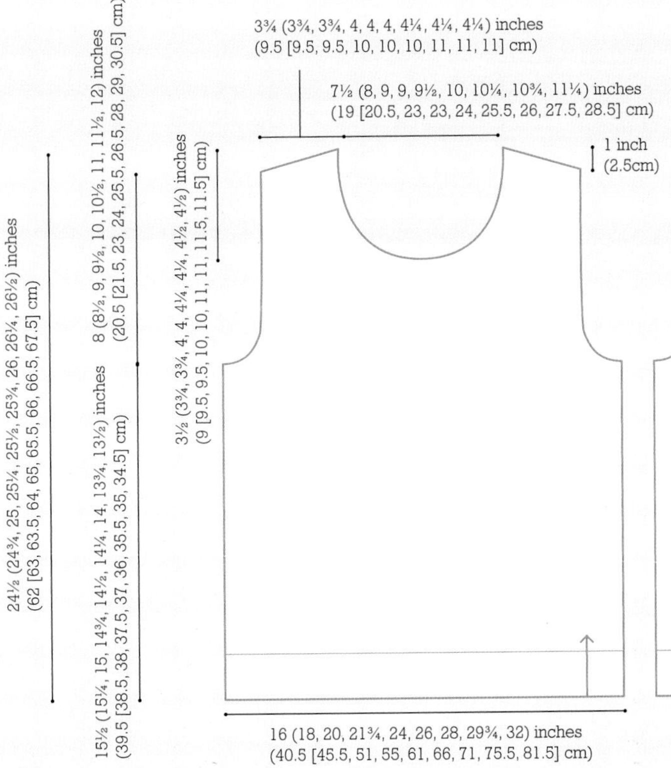
3¾ (3¾, 3¾, 4, 4, 4, 4¼, 4¼, 4¼) inches
(9.5 [9.5, 9.5, 10, 10, 10, 11, 11, 11] cm)
7½ (8, 9, 9, 9½, 10, 10¼, 10¾, 11¼) inches
(19 [20.5, 23, 23, 24, 25.5, 26, 27.5, 28.5] cm)
1 inch
(2.5cm)
24½ (24¾, 25, 25¼, 25½, 25¾, 26, 26¼, 26½) inches
(62 [63, 63.5, 64, 65, 65.5, 66, 66.5, 67.5] cm)
8 (8½, 9, 9½, 10, 10½, 11, 11½, 12) inches
(20.5 [21.5, 23, 24, 25.5, 26.5, 28, 29, 30.5] cm)
15½ (15¼, 15, 14¾, 14½, 14¼, 14, 13¾, 13½) inches
(39.5 [38.5, 38, 37.5, 37, 36, 35.5, 35, 34.5] cm)
3½ (3¾, 3¾, 4, 4, 4¼, 4¼, 4½, 4½) inches
(9 [9.5, 9.5, 10, 10, 11, 11, 11.5, 11.5] cm)
16 (18, 20, 21¾, 24, 26, 28, 29¾, 32) inches
(40.5 [45.5, 51, 55, 61, 66, 71, 75.5, 81.5] cm)

Yarn

9 (9, 10, 11, 12, 13, 14, 15, 16) skeins worsted (medium-weight) yarn, 50 grams/120 yards (110m) each. I used Quince & Co. Owl, 50 percent wool, 50 percent alpaca, in Abyssinian.

Gauge (Tension)

17 stitches and 24 rows = 4 inches (10cm) in stockinette (stocking) stitch

16 stitches in twin horseshoe cable pattern = 3 inches (7.5cm)

Needles

1 set straight or circular, plus 1 set for your preferred method of working in a small round:

U.S. 7 (4.5mm/UK 7) or size needed to obtain gauge (tension)

U.S. 6 (4mm/UK 8) or 1 size smaller than gauge (tension) needle

Other Supplies

6 stitch markers, blunt yarn needle, scrap yarn for holding stitches

Construction Notes

The front, back, and sleeves are worked in flat pieces, and the cables are worked on the front and back. The shoulders are joined, the sleeves are set in, and the sleeves and sides are joined. The collar is picked up and worked and can be worn folded to show the reverse stockinette (stocking) stitch side or draped casually.

Tips for Modifying

- Lengthen the body or sleeves to customize the fit.

- Add some shaping at the waist for a closer silhouette.

- Work a few rows of ribbing at the neck instead of a cowl for a traditional crew neck.

- To make a cardigan instead, work the front in two halves and add button bands.

- Design your own cable pattern.

Stitch Patterns and Techniques

Cable 4 back (C4B): Hold 2 sts to back on cable needle, k2, k2 from cable needle.

Cable 4 front (C4F): Hold 2 sts to front on cable needle, k2, k2 from cable needle.

K1/P1 rib (worked flat over a multiple of 2 plus 1 sts):

All RS rows: P1, *k1, p1; rep from * to end.

All WS rows: K1, *p1, k1; rep from * to end.

K1/P1 rib (worked in the round over a multiple of 2 sts):

All rnds: *K1, p1; rep from * to end.

Stockinette (stocking) stitch (worked flat over any number of sts):

All RS rows: Knit all sts.

All WS rows: Purl all sts.

Twin horseshoe cable (worked flat over 16 sts—see chart):

Row 1 (RS): [C4B, C4F] 2 times.

Row 2 and all WS rows: Purl all sts.

Row 3 and all RS rows except Row 1: Knit all sts.

Rep Rows 1 to 8 for pattern.

Shaping Notes

Sleeve dec (RS): K2, k2tog, knit to last 4, ssk, k2. 2
sts dec'd.

Chart

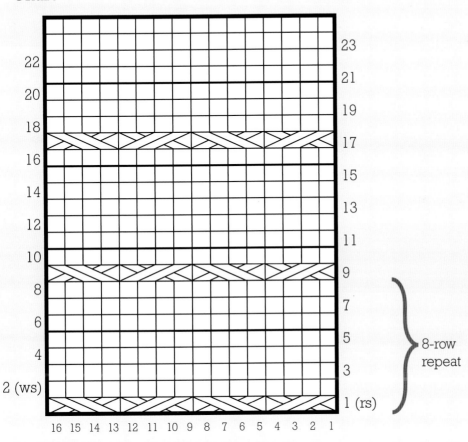

8-row repeat

Legend

Read WS rows left to right and RS rows right to left.

☐ Knit on RS, purl on WS

▨ Purl on RS, knit on WS

 Cable 4 Back (C4B): Hold 2 sts to back on
cable needle, k2, k2 from cable needle

Cable 4 Front (C4F): Hold 2 sts to front on
cable needle, k2, k2 from cable needle

Cabled Cowl Neck Sweater

Back

With smaller needles, cast on 70 (78, 86, 94, 104, 112, 120, 128, 138) sts.

Work 14 rows K1/P1 rib.

Switch to larger needles.

Next row (RS) (inc): K8 (7, 7, 6, 7, 6, 6, 5, 6), *m1L, k6 (7, 8, 9, 10, 11, 12, 13, 14); rep from * 8 more times, m1L, knit to end. 80 (88, 96, 104, 114, 122, 130, 138, 148) sts.

Next row (WS) (setup): P11 (14, 17, 20, 23, 26, 29, 32, 36), pm, p16, pm, p5 (6, 7, 8, 10, 11, 12, 13, 14), pm, p16, pm, p5 (6, 7, 8, 10, 11, 12, 13, 14), pm, p16, pm, purl to end.

Next row (RS): *Knit to marker, sm, twin horseshoe cable 16 to marker, sm; rep from * 2 more times, knit to end.

Cont as set, with 3 twin horseshoe cables on a background of stockinette (stocking) stitch, until work measures 15½ (15¼, 15, 14¾, 14½, 14¼, 14, 13¾, 13½) inches (39.5 [38.5, 38, 37.5, 37, 36, 35.5, 35, 34.5] cm) from cast-on edge, ending with a WS row. Then shape underarms.

Shape Underarms

Beg on a RS row. Maintain pattern as set.

Next 2 rows (dec): Bind (cast) off 3 (4, 4, 5, 7, 8, 8, 9, 11) sts at beg of row. 74 (80, 88, 94, 100, 106, 114, 120, 126) sts.

Next 2 rows (dec): Bind (cast) off 2 (3, 3, 4, 6, 7, 7, 8, 10) at beg of row. 70 (74, 82, 86, 88, 92, 100, 104, 106) sts.

Next 1 (2, 4, 5, 5, 6, 8, 9, 9) RS rows (dec): K2, k2tog, work to last 4 sts, ssk, k2. 68 (70, 74, 76, 78, 80, 84, 86, 88) sts.

Then dec on the 2nd RS once. 66 (68, 72, 74, 76, 78, 82, 84, 86) sts.

Cont until work measures 23½ (23¾, 24, 24¼, 24½, 24¾, 25, 25¼, 25½) inches (59.5 [60.5, 61, 61.5, 62, 63, 63.5, 64, 65] cm) from cast-on edge, ending with a WS row. Then shape shoulders.

Shape Shoulders

For easier finishing and smooth seams, use a sloped bind (cast) off for the shoulders and neck.

Work shoulders in stockinette (stocking) stitch.

Next 4 rows (dec): Bind (cast) off 6 (6, 6, 6, 7, 7, 7, 7, 7) sts at beg of row. 42 (44, 48, 50, 48, 50, 54, 56, 58) sts.

Next 2 rows (dec): Bind (cast) off 5 (5, 5, 6, 5, 5, 6, 6, 6) sts at beg of row. 32 (34, 38, 38, 38, 40, 42, 44, 46) sts.

Set aside remaining sts on holder or scrap yarn for neck.

Front

Work same as back until front measures 21 (21, 21¼, 21¼, 21½, 21½, 21¾, 21¾, 22) inches (53.5 [53.5, 54, 54, 54.5, 54.5, 55, 55, 56] cm) from cast-on edge, ending with a WS row. Then shape front neck.

Shape Front Neck

Next row (RS) (divide front): Maintaining cables as set, work 27 (28, 29, 30, 31, 32, 34, 34, 35), join new yarn and bind (cast) off center 12 (12, 14, 14, 14, 14, 14, 16, 16) sts, work to end. 27 (28, 29, 30, 31, 32, 34, 34, 35) sts each side of front.

Next 2 rows: Work across 1st set of sts, bind (cast) off 4 (4, 4, 4, 5, 5, 5, 5, 5) sts at beg of next set. 23 (24, 25, 26, 26, 27, 29, 29, 30) sts each side of front.

Next 2 rows: Work across 1st set of sts, bind (cast) off 2 (2, 3, 3, 3, 3, 3, 3, 4) sts at beg of next set. 21 (22, 22, 23, 23, 24, 26, 26, 26) sts each side of front.

Work 1 WS row.

Next 4 (5, 5, 5, 4, 5, 6, 6, 6) RS rows (dec): Work to 4 before end of 1st group of sts, ssk, k2. K2, k2tog at beg of 2nd group of sts, work to end. 17 (17, 17, 18, 19, 19, 20, 20, 20) sts each side.

Cont without shaping until front is same length as back, ending with a WS row. Then shape front shoulders.

Shape Front Shoulders

Next 4 rows: Bind (cast) off 6 (6, 6, 6, 6, 6, 7, 7, 7) sts at beg of 1st set of sts.

Next 2 rows: Bind (cast) off remaining 5 (5, 5, 6, 5, 5, 6, 6, 6) sts.

Sleeves

With smaller needles, cast on 34 (38, 40, 42, 44, 46, 48, 50, 52) sts.

Work 14 rows K1/P1 rib. Set aside on spare needle.

Switch to larger needles.

Work in stockinette (stocking) stitch 6 rows.

Next rnd (RS) (inc): K1, m1L, knit to 1 st before end, m1R, k1. 2 sts inc'd, 36 (40, 42, 44, 46, 48, 50, 52, 54) sts.

Working 1 inc every 5th (5th, 5th, 4th, 3rd, 3rd, 3rd, 3rd, 3rd) RS row 7 (5, 2, 6, 13, 12, 11, 8, 4) more times and then every 0 (4th, 4th, 3rd, 0, 2nd, 2nd, 2nd, 2nd) RS row 0 (3, 7, 5, 0, 2, 4, 9, 15) times, continue in stockinette (stocking) stitch until sleeve measures 16½ (16¾, 17, 17¼, 17½, 17¾, 18, 18¼, 18½) inches (42 [42.5, 43, 44, 44.5, 45, 45.5, 46.5, 47] cm) from cast-on edge, ending with a WS row. 50 (56, 60, 66, 72, 76, 80, 86, 92) sts. Then shape sleeve cap.

Shape Sleeve Cap

Next 2 rows (dec): Bind (cast) off 3 (4, 4, 5, 7, 7, 8, 8, 10) sts at beg of row. 44 (48, 52, 56, 58, 62, 64, 70, 72) sts.

Next 2 rows (dec): Bind (cast) off 2 (3, 3, 4, 5, 5, 6, 7, 8) sts at beg of row. 40 (42, 46, 48, 48, 52, 52, 56, 56) sts.

Work 0 (0, 0, 0, 4, 4, 4, 0, 4) rows, with a sleeve dec (see "Shaping Notes") on 2nd RS row. 40 (42, 46, 48, 46, 50, 50, 56, 54) sts.

*Work a sleeve dec on the next 2nd RS row, then the following RS, once. 36 (38, 42, 44, 42, 46, 46, 52, 50) sts.

Rep from * 2 (3, 3, 3, 3, 3, 4, 5, 4) times. 28 (26, 30, 32, 30, 34, 30, 32, 34) sts.

Then work a sleeve dec every RS 4 (2, 3, 3, 1, 3, 0, 0, 1) times. 20 (22, 24, 26, 28, 28, 30, 32, 32) sts.

Final 2 rows: Bind (cast) off 3 (4, 4, 4, 4, 4, 5, 5, 5) sts at beg of row. 14 (14, 16, 18, 20, 20, 20, 22, 22) sts.

Bind (cast) off remaining sts.

Finishing

Block all pieces to schematic measurements.

Sew shoulder seams together.

On smaller needles for working in a small round, place back neck sts from holder.

Note that, if folded, the collar will show the reverse side of the stockinette (stocking) stitch.

With RS of work facing and beginning at left shoulder, join yarn and pick up and knit 3 sts for every 4 rows along edge of left front neck, 1 st for every bound (cast) off st along center front neck, 3 sts for every 4 rows along right neck (matching number of sts picked up on left), knit across back neck sts. Arrange for working in the round.

Switch to larger needles.

Knit 12 rnds.

Next rnd (inc): Inc 8 (10, 10, 10, 10, 10, 10, 10, 10) sts evenly across rnd.

Knit until collar measures 7 inches (18cm).

Work in K1/P1 rib 8 rnds.

Bind (cast) off in pattern.

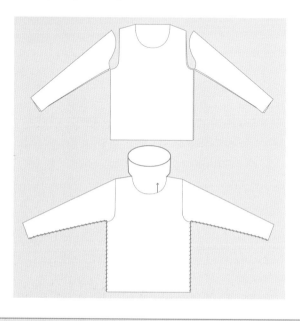

walking
jacket

● ● ● ○ ○

This sweater combines vintage styling with a hint of grandpa-cardigan comfort. Virtually seamless and knitted from the top down in medium-weight wool, it works up quite quickly. And with its pretty shawl collar and bracelet-length sleeves, this dressy little cardigan will be a new favorite for crisp autumn walks.

Skills Needed

Knit/purl, working in the round, picking up and knitting, basic sewing

Finished Measurements

Bust: 34 (38¼, 40¾, 45, 48½, 52¾, 56¾) inches (86.5 [97, 103.5, 114.5, 123, 134, 144] cm)

Length: 22½ (22¾, 23, 23¼, 23½, 23¾, 24) inches (57 [58, 58.5, 59, 59.5, 60.5, 61] cm)

Yarn

7 (8, 9, 9, 10, 11, 12) skeins worsted (medium-weight) yarn, 50 grams/128 yards (140m) each. I used Brooklyn Tweed Shelter, 100 percent wool, in Foothills.

Gauge (Tension)

19 stitches and 27 rows = 4 inches (10cm) in stockinette (stocking) stitch

Needles

1 circular and 1 set for your preferred method of working in a small round in each of the following sizes:

U.S. 8 (5mm/UK 6) or size needed to obtain gauge (tension)

U.S. 7 (4.5mm/UK 7) or 1 size smaller than gauge (tension) needle

Other Supplies

4 stitch markers, blunt yarn needle, scrap yarn for holding stitches, 6 medium (⅝-inch [15mm]) buttons

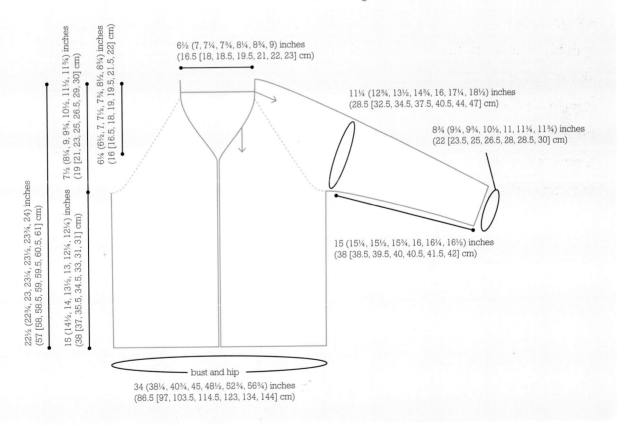

6½ (7, 7¼, 7¾, 8¼, 8¾, 9) inches (16.5 [18, 18.5, 19.5, 21, 22, 23] cm)

11¼ (12¾, 13½, 14¾, 16, 17¼, 18½) inches (28.5 [32.5, 34.5, 37.5, 40.5, 44, 47] cm)

8¾ (9¼, 9¾, 10½, 11, 11¼, 11¾) inches (22 [23.5, 25, 26.5, 28, 28.5, 30] cm)

15 (15¼, 15½, 15¾, 16, 16¼, 16½) inches (38 [38.5, 39.5, 40, 40.5, 41.5, 42] cm)

7½ (8¼, 9, 9¾, 10½, 11½, 11¾) inches (19 [21, 23, 25, 26.5, 29, 30] cm)

6¼ (6½, 7, 7½, 7¾, 8½, 8¾) inches (16 [16.5, 18, 19, 19.5, 21.5, 22] cm)

15 (14½, 14, 13½, 13, 12¼, 12¼) inches (38 [37, 35.5, 34.5, 33, 31, 31] cm)

22½ (22¾, 23, 23¼, 23½, 23¾, 24) inches (57 [58, 58.5, 59, 59.5, 60.5, 61] cm)

bust and hip
34 (38¼, 40¾, 45, 48½, 52¾, 56¾) inches (86.5 [97, 103.5, 114.5, 123, 134, 144] cm)

Construction Notes

The body is worked in one piece from the neck down to the underarms, and the rest of the body is worked to the bottom edge with no shaping at the sides. The sleeves are knit in the round from the underarms, the front bands and collar are picked up and worked together, and the collar is shaped with short rows.

Tips for Modifying

- Lengthen the sleeves for a warmer sweater.
- Increase the front neck more slowly for a deeper V shape.
- Modify the length of the body to suit your height.

Stitch Patterns and Techniques

Broken rib (worked flat over odd number sts):

All RS rows: Knit all sts.

All WS rows: P1, *k1, p1; rep from * to end.

Broken rib (worked in the round over even number sts):

Rnd 1: Knit all sts.

Rnd 2: *K1, p1; rep from * to end.

Rep Rnds 1 and 2 for pattern.

Stockinette (stocking) stitch (worked flat over any number of sts):

All RS rows: Knit all sts.

All WS rows: Purl all sts.

Stockinette (stocking) stitch (worked in the round over any number of sts):

All rnds: Knit all sts.

1-row buttonhole

Bring yarn to front, slip a st, take yarn to back, wrapping the st.

*Slip the next st, and pass the 1st slipped st over it. Rep from * twice.

Turn your work. Slip 1 st back to the right needle.

Using a cable cast on, cast on 4.

Turn your work. Slip 1 st purlwise. Pass 1 st over the slipped st.

Shaping Notes

Neck inc: K1, m1L at beg of row, m1R, k1 when you get to last st of row. 2 inc'd (1 each front).

Full raglan inc: *Work to 1 st before marker, m1R, k1, sm, k1, m1L; rep from * 3 times, work to end. 8 inc'd (2 sts each sleeve, 1 each front and 2 back).

Body-only inc: Work to 1 st before marker, m1R, k1, sm, work to next marker, sm, k1, m1L; rep from * once, work to end. 4 inc'd (1 st each front and 2 back).

Side dec: Work to 3 sts before side marker, ssk, k1, sm, k1, k2tog; rep from * once. 4 dec'd (1 st each front and 2 back).

Sleeve dec: K1, k2tog, work to 3 sts before end, ssk, k1. 2 sts dec'd.

Short rows: Short rows are partial rows: before reaching the end of a row or rnd, turn your work and begin the next one. To avoid creating a gap at the turning point, *wrap* the next st before turning. To do this, move the yarn to the opposite side (i.e., if the yarn is at the back, bring it to the front, and vice versa), slip the next st pwise, move the yarn back to its original position, slip the st back to the left needle, and turn your work. This is called a *wrap and turn* (w&t). The wraps are camouflaged in the garter stitch of the collar so they don't need any special handling on the following row.

Walking Jacket

Please read "Sweater Construction" for helpful tips.

Yoke (starting at neck and working down)

With gauge (tension) needles, cast on 67 (69, 71, 73, 79, 81, 83) sts.

Raglan marker setup (WS): P2 (front), pm, p16 (16, 16, 16, 18, 18, 18) (sleeve), pm, p31 (33, 35, 37, 39, 41, 43) (back), pm, p16 (16, 16, 16, 18, 18, 18) (sleeve), pm, p2 (front).

Please read "Shaping Notes" before working yoke.

Work yoke in stockinette (stocking) stitch over 42 (48, 52, 58, 62, 68, 70) rows, as follows:

Batch 1: Over the next 12 rows, work a full raglan inc every RS row and a neck inc (see "Shaping Notes") *every other* RS row. 11 sts each front, 43 (45, 47, 49, 51, 53, 55) sts back, 28 (28, 28, 28, 30, 30, 30) sts each sleeve.

Then over the next 6 (8, 12, 14, 14, 16, 14) rows, work a full raglan inc and a neck inc *every* RS row 3 (4, 6, 7, 7, 8, 7) times. 17 (19, 23, 25, 25, 27, 25) sts each front, 49 (53, 59, 63, 65, 69, 69) sts back, 34 (36, 40, 42, 44, 46, 44) sts each sleeve.

Batch 2: Over the next 12 (12, 12, 12, 12, 16, 20) rows, cont increasing at the neck edge every RS, and *at the same time,* alternate body-only inc and full raglan inc as follows:

*On the next RS, work a body-only inc and neck inc (see "Shaping Notes").

On the following RS, work a full raglan inc and a neck inc.

Rep from * 5 (5, 5, 5, 5, 7, 9) times more. 6 (6, 6, 6, 6, 8, 10) neck inc worked. 29 (31, 35, 37, 37, 43, 45) sts each front, 61 (65, 71, 75, 77, 85, 89) sts back, 40 (42, 46, 48, 50, 54, 54) sts each sleeve.

Batch 3: Over the next 8 (8, 16, 20, 24, 24, 24) rows, cont alternating body-only inc and full raglan inc 2 (2, 4, 5, 6, 6, 6) times. 33 (35, 43, 47, 49, 55, 57) sts each front, 69 (73, 87, 95, 101, 109, 113) sts back, 44 (46, 54, 58, 62, 66, 66) sts each sleeve.

Batch 4: Over the next 4 (8, 0, 0, 0, 0, 0) rows, alternate body-only inc and full raglan inc *every other* RS row, as follows:

*On the 2nd RS, work a body-only inc.

On the following 2nd RS, work a full raglan inc.

Rep from * 0 (1, 0, 0, 0, 0, 0, 0) times. 35 (39, 43, 47, 49, 55, 57) sts each front, 73 (81, 87, 95, 101, 109, 113) sts back, 46 (50, 54, 58, 62, 66, 66) sts each sleeve.

Separate Sleeves from Body

Separate sleeves, and begin body as follows:

Next row (RS): *Work to marker, remove marker. Transfer sleeve sts to scrap yarn or spare circular needle, remove next marker. Cast on 8 (10, 10, 12, 14, 16, 22) (using backward loop). Rep from * once, work to end. 159 (179, 193, 213, 227, 251, 271) sts body.

Body

Cont in stockinette (stocking) stitch until piece measures 12½ (12, 11½, 11, 10½, 9½, 9½) inches (32 [30.5, 29, 28, 26.5, 25, 25] cm) from underarm cast on, ending with a WS row.

Switch to smaller needles.

Work in broken rib (flat) until rib measures 2½ inches (6.5cm), ending with a WS row.

Bind (cast) off.

Sleeves

Transfer sleeve sts to needle. Rejoin yarn.

Pick up and knit 4 (5, 5, 6, 7, 8, 11) from body underarm, pm, pick up and knit another 4 (5, 5, 6, 7, 8, 11) sts, join in the round, being careful not to twist sts. 54 (60, 64, 70, 76, 82, 88) sts.

Working a sleeve dec (see "Shaping Notes") every 14th (10th, 9th, 8th, 7th, 6th, 5th) rnd 6 (8, 9, 10, 12, 14, 16) times, cont in stockinette (stocking) stitch until sleeve measures 12½ (12¾, 13, 13¼, 13½, 13¾, 14) inches (32 [32.5, 33, 33.5, 34.5, 35, 35.5] cm) from underarm. 44 (44, 48, 48, 52, 52, 56) sts.

Switch to smaller needles.

Work in broken rib (in the round) until rib measures 2½ inches (6.5cm), ending with a WS row.

Bind (cast) off.

Finishing

Block to finished measurements. Then work front bands and collar.

Front Bands and Collar

With safety pins, mark 6 evenly spaced buttonhole positions along the right front edge, starting at base of neck shaping.

With RS of work facing and using smaller needles, join yarn and, starting at top of bottom right front edge, pick up and knit 3 sts for every 4 rows to base of neck, pm, pick up and knit 1 st for every st of right neck and sleeve, pm, pick up and knit 1 st for every st of back neck, pm, pick up and knit along left sleeve, neck, and front, placing a marker at the base of left neck to mirror the one on the right neck. You should have 4 markers, 2 at the base of the neck and 2 either side of the back neck.

Knit 1 row.

Short row 1 (RS): Knit to 3rd marker, sm, wrap next st, and turn work.

Short row 2 (WS): Knit to marker on far side of back neck, sm, wrap next st, and turn work.

Short rows 3 and 4: Work the same as preceding two rows, except knit 2 sts past previous wrap.

Cont working pairs of short rows, going 2 sts past the previous wrap each time, until you reach the markers at the base of the neck.

Next row (RS): Knit to end.

Knit 2 rows.

Buttonhole row (WS): Knit, making a 1-row buttonhole (see "Stitch Patterns and Techniques") at each safety pin.

Knit 3 rows.

Bind (cast) off on WS.

Sew buttons onto the left front button band, being careful to line them up with the buttonholes.

Weave in remaining ends, closing any gaps at the underarms if necessary. Block front bands and collar if desired.

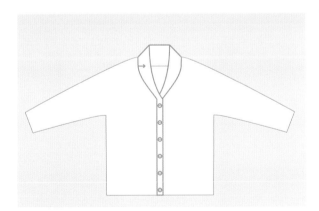

funnel neck
vest

●●○○○

A sleeveless sweater is a great way to layer on a little winter style. And it knits up extra quick—no sleeves! This comfortable, funnel neck vest contrasts the deep texture of garter stitch rib with plain knitting, making it a wonderful way to feature a hand-dyed yarn, as done here. The high-low hem and deep side vents make a flattering outline at the hip, while the armhole edging and neck are worked with the vest for a quick finish.

Skills Needed

Knit/purl, working in the round, mattress stitch

Finished Measurements

Choose a size 3 to 5 inches (7.5 to 13cm) larger than the actual bust measurement

Bust: 29½ (33¾, 38, 42, 46¼, 50½, 54½, 58¾) inches (75 [85.5, 96.5, 106.5, 117.5, 128.5, 138.5, 149] cm)

Length (back): 22 (22¾, 23, 23¼, 23½, 23¾, 24, 24¼) inches (56 [58, 58.5, 59, 59.5, 60.5, 61, 61.5] cm)

Yarn

3 (3, 4, 4, 4, 4, 5, 5) skeins sport (fine) yarn, 125 grams/270 yards (247m) each. I used Madelinetosh Tosh Sport, 100 percent superfine merino wool, in Georgia O'Keefe.

Gauge (Tension)

23 stitches and 32 rows = 4 inches (10cm) in garter stitch 1/2 rib

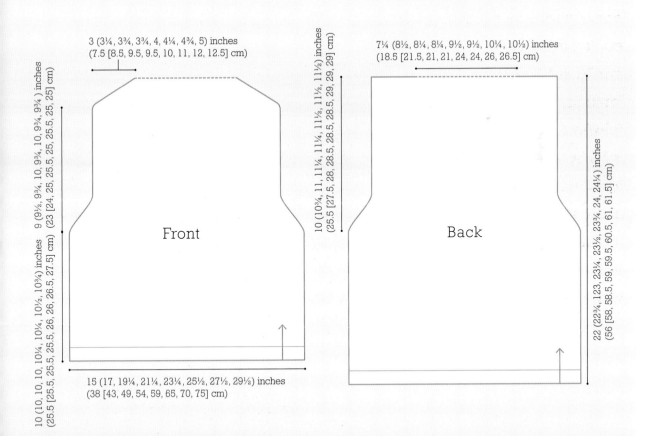

Needles

1 set circular or straight in the following sizes, plus 1 set for your preferred method of working in a small round in the smaller size:

U.S. 6 (4mm/UK 8) or size needed to obtain gauge (tension)

U.S. 4 (3.5mm/UK 10) or 2 sizes smaller than gauge (tension) needle

Other Supplies

Blunt yarn needle

Construction Notes

The back and front are worked flat and joined at the shoulders and sides. The back is longer than the front to create a dropped, high-low hem. The back shoulders are straight while the front shoulders are shaped so the seams sit slightly on the front of the shoulder. The funnel neck is worked in the round directly from live stitches from the center front and back. The side seams start above the cast-on edge to create side vents.

Tips for Modifying

- Skip the side vents, and sew the side seams to the cast-on edges.

- Make the front and back shorter for a cropped vest.

- Substitute a different neckline for the funnel neck.

- For a more conventional shoulder seam that lies toward the back, swap the front and back shoulder shaping.

Stitch Patterns and Techniques

K1/P2 rib (worked over multiple 3 plus 2 sts):

All RS rows: P2, *k1, p2; rep from * to end.

All WS rows: K2, *p1, k2; rep from * to end.

Garter stitch 1/2 rib (worked over multiple 3 plus 2 sts):

All RS rows: Knit all sts.

All WS rows: K2, *p1, k2; rep from * to end.

Check your work often from the RS to ensure you're keeping the pattern correct.

Stockinette (stocking) stitch (worked flat over any number of sts):

All RS rows: Knit all sts.

All WS rows: Purl all sts.

Double decreases:

Ssk-slL-psso-slR (right-leaning double decrease): Ssk, slip st just worked back to left needle, pass next st over it and off needle, slip st (purlwise) back to right needle. 2 dec'd.

Sl-k2og-psso (left-leaning double decrease): Slip 1 st knitwise, k2tog, pass slip st over and off needle. 2 dec'd.

Funnel Neck Vest

Back

With smaller needles, cast on 86 (98, 110, 122, 134, 146, 158, 170) sts.

Work 8 rows K1/P2 rib.

Switch to larger needles.

Work in garter stitch 1/2 rib until back measures 12 (12, 12, 12, 12¼, 12¼, 12½, 12¾) inches (30.5 [30.5, 30.5, 30.5, 31, 31, 32, 32.5] cm) from cast-on edge, ending with a WS row. Then shape underarms.

Shape Underarms

Next row (RS) (dec): K8, ssk, knit to 10 sts before end, k2tog, k8. 2 dec'd. 84 (96, 108, 120, 132, 144, 156, 168) sts.

Cont, *keeping pattern correct on the WS,* with a dec on the next 4 (5, 9, 15, 16, 20, 21, 25) *RS* rows. 76 (86, 90, 90, 100, 104, 114, 118) sts.

Cont without shaping, *keeping pattern correct* (you can place a marker 9 sts in from each edge to help you remember), until back measures 22 (22¾, 23, 23¼, 23½, 23¾, 24, 24¼) inches (56 [58, 58.5, 59, 59.5, 60.5, 61, 61.5] cm) from cast-on edge, ending with a WS row.

Next 2 rows: Bind (cast) off 17 (19, 21, 21, 23, 25, 27, 29) at beg of row, work to end.

Transfer remaining 42 (48, 48, 48, 54, 54, 60, 60) sts to scrap yarn or holder.

"Keeping pattern correct" is a signal that the stitch count has changed and a stitch pattern has been interrupted. When you see this instruction, you need to work the stitch pattern a little differently so it continues to flow visually. In this case, on the first wrong side following the underarm decrease, do this: K2, [p1, k2] twice, p1. (The 1st and 9 sts are uninterrupted.) Then *k1 instead of k2* to adjust for the dec on the previous row and keep the pattern correct. P1, k2, p1, … until 9 sts remain and then k1, p1, [k2, p1] 2 times, k2.

Front

Cast on and work first 8 rows same as back.

Switch to larger needles.

Next row (marker setup): K8, pm, knit to last 8 sts, pm, k8 to end.

Next row (WS): Garter stitch 1/2 rib to marker, sm, purl to marker, sm, garter stitch 1/2 rib to end.

Cont as set by these 2 rows until front measures 10 (10, 10, 10, 10¼, 10¼, 10½, 10¾) inches (25.5 [25.5, 25.5, 25.5, 26, 26, 26.5, 27.5] cm) from cast-on edge. Then shape underarms.

Shape Underarms

Next row (RS) (dec): K8, sm, ssk, knit to 10 sts before end, k2tog, sm, k8. 2 dec'd. 84 (96, 108, 120, 132, 144, 156, 168) sts.

Cont, working garter stitch 1/2 rib over 1st and last 8 sts, with a dec on the next 4 (5, 9, 15, 16, 20, 21, 25) *RS* rows. 76 (86, 90, 90, 100, 104, 114, 118) sts.

Cont as set without shaping until front measures 19 (19½, 19¾, 20, 20, 20¼, 20¼, 20½) inches (48.5 [49.5, 50, 51, 51, 51.5, 51.5, 52] cm) from cast-on edge, ending with a WS row. Then shape front shoulders.

Shape Front Shoulders

Next row (RS) (double dec): K8, sl-k2og-psso (see "Stitch Patterns and Techniques"), knit to last 11 sts, ssk-slL-psso-slR (see "Stitch Patterns and Techniques"), k8. 72 (82, 86, 86, 96, 100, 110, 114) sts.

Cont working garter stitch 1/2 rib over 1st and last 8 sts, with a double dec on the next 7 (8, 9, 9, 10, 11, 12, 13) *RS* rows. 44 (50, 50, 50, 56, 56, 62, 62) sts.

Work 1 WS row. Then work neck.

Neck

Transfer front sts and held back sts to needles for working in a small round. Starting at left shoulder, join for working in the round, being careful not to twist sts. 86 (98, 98, 98, 110, 110, 122, 122) sts.

Rnd 1 (dec): K2tog, knit to 2 sts before end of front, ssk, knit to end. 84 (96, 96, 96, 108, 108, 120, 120) sts. (At this point, you should have a multiple of 3 sts. If you've missed a dec along the way, adjust on the next rnd.)

Rnd 2: Starting and ending with p1, reestablish garter stitch 1/2 rib.

Work 31 more rnds garter stitch 1/2 rib.

Bind (cast) off.

Finishing

Block garment to schematic measurements. A thorough blocking is essential for the shoulder seam in this sweater.

Join shoulders.

Join sides from 2 inches (5cm) above front edge to underarms.

Weave in ends.

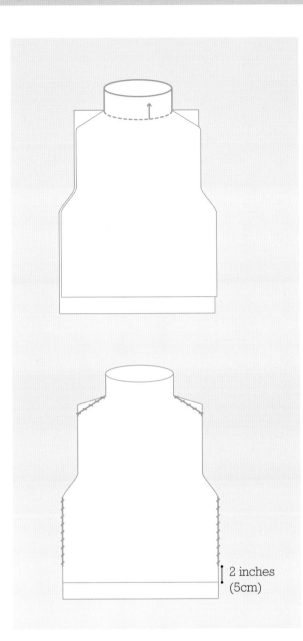

2 inches
(5cm)

funky knits

IN THIS CHAPTER

Charming Sweetheart Cardigan

Lovely Lace Panel Sweater

Comfortable Rounded Hem Pullover

sweetheart
cardigan

▪ ▪ ▪ ▪ ▪

This sweetly old-fashioned cardigan, perfect for pairing with either jeans or a vintage skirt, will charm any funky dresser. Fine-weight wool, bracelet sleeves, and a ring of hearts give it a sophisticated femininity, while the seamless construction and minimal details make it a straightforward knit. Even if you're new to color knitting, the heart motif is within your grasp.

Skills Needed

Knit/purl, working in the round, picking up and knitting, basic color knitting

Finished Measurements

Bust: 30½ (32¾, 35¼, 36¾, 38½, 40¼, 42, 44¼, 46½, 48¼, 50¾, 52½) inches (77.5 [83, 89.5, 93.5, 98, 102, 106.5, 112.5, 118, 122.5, 129, 133.5] cm)

Length: 20½ (20¾, 20¾, 21¼, 21¼, 21½, 21½, 21½, 21½, 21¾, 22, 22¼) inches (52 [52.5, 52.5, 54, 54, 54.5, 54.5, 54.5, 54.5, 55, 56, 56.5] cm)

Yarn

6 (7, 7, 8, 8, 9, 9, 9, 10, 10, 11, 11) skeins Main Color (MC), 1 skein Contrast Color (CC) sport (fine) yarn, 50 grams/145 yards (133m) each. I used Berroco Ultra Alpaca Light, 50 percent alpaca, 50 percent wool, in Boysenberry (MC) and Orchid (CC).

Gauge (Tension)

23 stitches and 27 rows = 4 inches (10cm) in stockinette (stocking) stitch

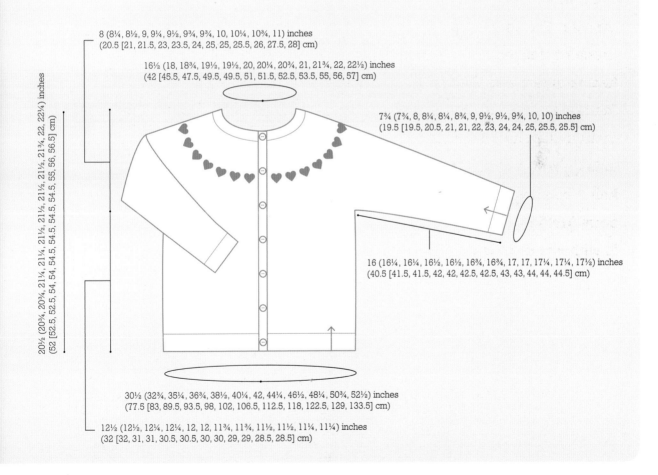

8 (8¼, 8½, 9, 9¼, 9½, 9¾, 9¾, 10, 10¼, 10¾, 11) inches (20.5 [21, 21.5, 23, 23.5, 24, 25, 25, 25.5, 26, 27.5, 28] cm)

16½ (18, 18¾, 19½, 19½, 20, 20¼, 20¾, 21, 21¾, 22, 22½) inches (42 [45.5, 47.5, 49.5, 49.5, 51, 51.5, 52.5, 53.5, 55, 56, 57] cm)

7¾ (7¾, 8, 8¼, 8¼, 8¾, 9, 9½, 9½, 9¾, 10, 10) inches (19.5 [19.5, 20.5, 21, 21, 22, 23, 24, 24, 25, 25.5, 25.5] cm)

20½ (20¾, 20¾, 21¼, 21¼, 21½, 21½, 21½, 21½, 21¾, 22, 22¼) inches (52 [52.5, 52.5, 54, 54, 54.5, 54.5, 54.5, 54.5, 55, 56, 56.5] cm)

16 (16¼, 16¼, 16½, 16½, 16¾, 16¾, 17, 17, 17¼, 17¼, 17½) inches (40.5 [41.5, 41.5, 42, 42, 42.5, 42.5, 43, 43, 44, 44, 44.5] cm)

30½ (32¾, 35¼, 36¾, 38½, 40¼, 42, 44¼, 46½, 48¼, 50¾, 52½) inches (77.5 [83, 89.5, 93.5, 98, 102, 106.5, 112.5, 118, 122.5, 129, 133.5] cm)

12½ (12½, 12¼, 12¼, 12, 12, 11¾, 11¾, 11½, 11½, 11¼, 11¼) inches (32 [32, 31, 31, 30.5, 30.5, 30, 30, 29, 29, 28.5, 28.5] cm)

Needles

1 set circular, plus 1 set for your preferred method of working in a small round, in each of the following sizes:

U.S. 5 (3.75mm/UK 9) or size needed to obtain gauge (tension)

U.S. 3 (3.25mm/UK 11) or 2 U.S. sizes smaller than gauge (tension) needle

Other Supplies

Blunt yarn needle, 7 small (about ⁷⁄₁₆- to ½-inch [11 or 12mm]) buttons

Construction Notes

The body is worked flat from the bottom up to the underarms. The sleeves are worked in the round to the underarms. The sleeves and body are joined, and the yoke is shaped with a few rows of decreases. The button bands are picked up and knit.

Tips for Modifying

- Seed (moss) stitch would look pretty in place of the rib.
- Substitute your own motif for the hearts.
- Add shaping at the sides for the waist.
- Work in the round for a pullover.

Stitch Patterns and Techniques

K1/P1 rib (worked flat over a multiple of 2 plus 1 sts):

All RS rows: P1, *k1, p1; rep from * to end.

All WS rows: K1, *p1, k1; rep from * to end.

K1/P1 rib (worked in the round over a multiple of 2 sts):

All rnds: *K1, p1; rep from * to end.

Stockinette (stocking) stitch (worked over any number of sts):

All RS rows: Knit all sts.

All WS rows: Purl all sts.

Chart

Multiple of 10 plus 3, plus 2 selvedge sts

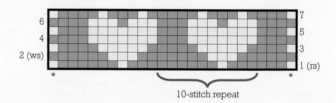

10-stitch repeat

Knit on right side, purl on wrong side

- Main Color (MC)
- Contrast Color (CC)
- * Selvedge

Sweetheart Cardigan

Sleeves

With smaller needles for working in a small round, cast on 44 (46, 46, 48, 48, 50, 52, 54, 54, 56, 60, 60) sts. Arrange for working in the round.

Work 14 rnds K1/P1 rib.

Switch to larger needles.

Knit 8 rnds.

Next rnd (RS) (inc): K3, m1L, knit to last 3, m1R, k3. 2 inc'd. 46 (48, 48, 50, 50, 52, 54, 56, 56, 58, 62, 62) sts.

Cont in stockinette (stocking) stitch with an inc every 10th (8th, 7th, 7th, 6th, 6th, 6th, 5th, 5th, 5th, 5th, 4th) rnd 8 (10, 12, 12, 14, 14, 14, 16, 18, 18, 18, 20) more times until sleeve measures 16 (16¼, 16¼, 16½, 16½, 16¾, 16¾, 17, 17, 17¼, 17¼, 17½) inches (40.5 [41.5, 41.5, 42, 42, 42.5, 42.5, 43, 43, 44, 44, 44.5] cm) from cast-on edge, ending on a WS row. 62 (68, 72, 74, 78, 80, 82, 88, 92, 94, 98, 102) sts.

Transfer 1st and last 5 (5, 6, 6, 7, 7, 7, 7, 8, 8, 9, 10) sts of final round onto holder or scrap yarn, and set sleeves aside on spare circular needle.

Body

With smaller circular needles, cast on 167 (181, 195, 203, 217, 225, 235, 249, 261, 271, 283, 297) sts.

Work 14 rows K1/P1 rib.

Switch to larger needles.

Next row (WS) (inc 1 st for some sizes): P1, m1L 1 (1, 0, 1, 0, 1, 0, 0, 1, 0, 1, 0) times, purl to end. 168 (182, 195, 204, 217, 226, 235, 249, 262, 271, 284, 297) sts.

Work in stockinette (stocking) stitch until body measures 12½ (12½, 12¼, 12¼, 12, 12, 11¾, 11¾, 11½, 11½, 11¼, 11¼) inches (32 [32, 31, 31, 30.5, 30.5, 30, 30, 29, 29, 28.5, 28.5] cm) from cast-on edge, ending with a WS row. Then join sleeves to body.

Join Sleeves to Body

(RS): K35 (39, 41, 43, 46, 48, 50, 54, 56, 58, 60, 63) across front, slip next 10 (10, 12, 12, 14, 14, 14, 14, 16, 16, 18, 20) onto holder or scrap yarn for underarm, k52 (58, 60, 62, 64, 66, 68, 74, 76, 78, 80, 82) across sleeve, k78 (84, 89, 94, 97, 102, 107, 113, 118, 123, 128, 131) across back, slip next 10 (10, 12, 12, 14, 14, 14, 14, 16, 16, 18, 20) onto holder or scrap yarn for other underarm, knit across 2nd sleeve, k35 (39, 41, 43, 46, 48, 50, 54, 56, 58, 60, 63) to end. 252 (278, 291, 304, 317, 330, 343, 369, 382, 395, 408, 421) sts total. Then proceed with yoke.

Yoke

Starting on WS row, work 15 (17, 19, 19, 19, 19, 21, 21, 23, 23, 25, 25) rows stockinette (stocking) stitch.

In very traditional knitting, a color yoke like this would be worked in the round and then sliced up the center in a process called steeking. With steeking, all the color knitting is done from the right, knit, side of the fabric. However, because the hearts are worked over only 7 rows, this pattern uses the less-advanced method of working back and forth on both the knit and purl sides.

Keep it relaxed: As you work, spread out the stitches on your right needle every 10 stitches or so. The goal is to have the loose strands lie flat against the back of the work without any added tension.

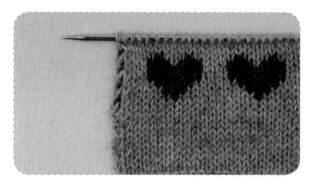

Color your selvedge: You'll see from the chart that the first and last stitch of each row alternates between the Main and Contrast Colors. This helps maintain an even stitch size in the hearts near the front edges.

Long floats: If this were an allover color pattern, you'd weave in the yarn strands (or floats) every 3 to 5 stitches on the back of the work. However, to ensure the sweater lies smoothly around the shoulders, don't weave in the long strands.

Under and over: For the best results, try to always bring the Contrast Color yarn under the Main Color strand, and the Main Color over the Contrast Color.

Swatch it! Before you tackle colorwork in the yoke itself, where the rows are very long, try a practice swatch of hearts. Cast on 35 stitches, work a few rows plain, and then work from the chart.

1st yoke dec row (RS): K1, *k3, k2tog, k2, k2tog, k2, k2tog; rep from * until 4 sts remain, k4. 195 (215, 225, 235, 245, 255, 265, 285, 295, 305, 315, 325) sts.

Work 15 (15, 15, 17, 19, 21, 21, 21, 21, 23, 23, 25) rows stockinette (stocking) stitch.

Work 7 rows from chart, beginning and ending with RS row.

Work 3 rows stockinette (stocking) stitch.

2nd yoke dec row (RS): K2 (3, 2, 2, 3, 2, 2, 2, 2, 3, 2, 2), k2tog, *k1, k2tog; rep from * 62 (68, 72, 75, 78, 82, 85, 92, 95, 98, 102, 105) more times, k2 (3, 2, 3, 3, 2, 3, 2, 3, 3, 2, 3). 131 (145, 151, 158, 165, 171, 178, 191, 198, 205, 211, 218) sts.

Work 7 rows stockinette (stocking) stitch.

3rd yoke dec row (RS): K3 (2, 2, 3, 2, 2, 2, 3, 2, 2, 2, 3), k2tog, *k1, k2tog; rep from * 40 (45, 47, 49, 52, 54, 56, 60, 63, 65, 67, 69) more times, k3 (3, 3, 3, 2, 2, 3, 3, 2, 3, 3, 3). 89 (98, 102, 107, 111, 115, 120, 129, 133, 138, 142, 147) sts.

Work 3 rows stockinette (stocking) stitch.

Final yoke dec row (RS) 38½ (40¼, 42, 44¼, 46½, 48¼, 50¾, 52½) sizes only, 1st 4 sizes, knit across): K10 (9, 7, 3, 6, 5, 10, 3), k2tog, *k20 (17, 11, 6, 5, 5, 4, 4), k2tog; rep from * 3 (4, 7, 14, 16, 17, 19, 22) more times, k11 (9, 7, 6, 5, 5, 4, 4). 89 (98, 102, 107, 106, 109, 111, 113, 115, 119, 121, 123) sts.

Switch to smaller needles.

Work 9 rows K1/P1 rib.

Bind (cast) off.

Finishing

Block garment to schematic measurements.

Underarms

(Work 1 underarm at a time.) Arrange sleeve underarm sts on 1 needle and body underarm sts on another. Working from the RS and using Kitchener stitch, graft the 2 sets of sts together.

Button Band

With RS of work facing and smaller needles, join MC and starting at top of left front edge, pick up and knit 3 sts for every 4 rows.

Work 10 rows garter stitch.

Bind (cast) off.

Buttonhole Band

With safety pins, mark 7 evenly spaced button-hole positions along right front edge.

With RS of work facing and smaller needles, join MC and starting at bottom right front edge, pick up and knit the same number of sts for button band.

Work 5 rows garter stitch.

Buttonhole row (RS): Knit to 1st safety pin marker, k2tog, yo; repeat for each marker, knit to end.

Work 4 more rows garter stitch.

Bind (cast) off.

Weave in remaining ends. Block front bands if desired.

lace panel
sweater

● ● ● ● ○

I love the easy lace and deliciously soft baby alpaca blend in this vibrant blue pullover. Seamless construction means easy finishing, while the gentle side shaping and cute turtle neck make this adorable to throw on with jeans on a brisk winter day.

Skills Needed

Knit/purl, basic lace, working in the round, basic lace, picking up and knitting

Finished Measurements

Bust: 32½ (34¼, 36, 37¾, 40½, 42¼, 45¾, 50¼, 53¾) inches (82.5 [87, 91.5, 96, 103, 107.5, 116, 127.5, 136.5] cm)

Length: 21½ (21¾, 22, 22¼, 23¼, 23¼, 23¼, 24¼, 24¾) inches (54.5 [55, 56, 56.5, 59, 59, 59, 61.5, 63] cm)

Yarn

8 (9, 9, 10, 10, 11, 12, 12, 13) skeins worsted (medium-weight) yarn, 50 grams/183 yards (167m) each. I used HiKoo Simplinatural, 40 percent baby alpaca, 40 percent fine merino wool, 20 percent mulberry silk, in Bright Blue.

Gauge (Tension)

18 stitches and 22 rows = 4 inches (10cm) in stockinette (stocking) stitch

Needles

1 set circular, plus 1 set in your preferred method of working in a small round:

U.S. 8 (5mm/UK 6) or size needed to obtain gauge (tension)

U.S. 7 (4.5mm/UK 7) or 1 size smaller than gauge (tension) needles

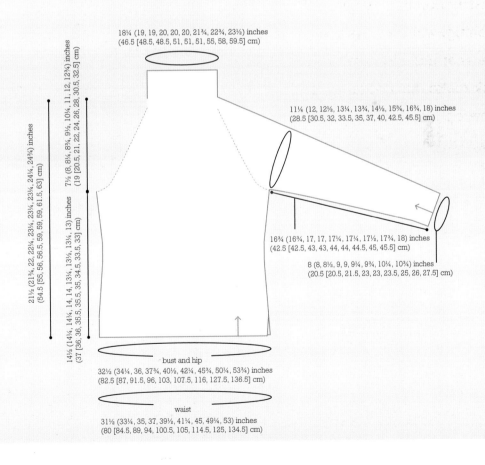

18¼ (19, 19, 20, 20, 20, 21¾, 22¾, 23½) inches
(46.5 [48.5, 48.5, 51, 51, 51, 55, 58, 59.5] cm)

11¼ (12, 12½, 13¼, 13¾, 14½, 15¾, 16¾, 18) inches
(28.5 [30.5, 32, 33.5, 35, 37, 40, 42.5, 45.5] cm)

21½ (21¾, 22, 22¼, 23¼, 23¼, 23¼, 24¼, 24¾) inches
(54.5 [55, 56, 56.5, 59, 59, 59, 61.5, 63] cm)

14½ (14¼, 14¼, 14, 14, 13¾, 13½, 13¼, 13) inches
(37 [36, 36, 35.5, 35, 34.5, 33.5, 33.5, 33] cm)

7½ (8, 8¼, 8¾, 9¼, 10¼, 11, 12, 12¾) inches
(19 [20.5, 21, 22, 24, 26, 28, 30.5, 32.5] cm)

16¾ (16¾, 17, 17, 17¼, 17¼, 17½, 17¾, 18) inches
(42.5 [42.5, 43, 43, 44, 44, 44.5, 45, 45.5] cm)

8 (8, 8½, 9, 9, 9¼, 9¾, 10¼, 10¾) inches
(20.5 [20.5, 21.5, 23, 23, 23.5, 25, 26, 27.5] cm)

bust and hip
32½ (34¼, 36, 37¾, 40½, 42¼, 45¾, 50¼, 53¾) inches
(82.5 [87, 91.5, 96, 103, 107.5, 116, 127.5, 136.5] cm)

waist
31½ (33¼, 35, 37, 39½, 41¼, 45, 49¼, 53) inches
(80 [84.5, 89, 94, 100.5, 105, 114.5, 125, 134.5] cm)

Other Supplies

4 stitch markers, blunt yarn needle, spare circular needle in gauge size or smaller, scrap yarn for holding stitches

Construction Notes

The body and sleeves are worked in the round to the underarms and then joined. The yoke is shaped to form raglan sleeves. The collar is worked in the round from the top of the yoke.

Tips for Modifying

- Skip the lace panel, or substitute a different texture on the front.

- For a dropped hem, make the back longer before joining.

- Tailor the neck to suit your figure. You can easily modify the mock neck into a V neck, cowl, or boat neck.

Stitch Patterns and Techniques

K1/P1 rib (worked in the round over a multiple of 2 sts):

All rnds: *K1, p1; rep from * to end.

K1/P1 rib (worked flat over odd number sts):

All RS rows: K1, *p1, k1; rep from * to end.

All WS rows: P1, *k1, p1; rep from * to end.

Stockinette (stocking) stitch (worked in the round over any number of sts):

All rnds: Knit all sts.

Stockinette (stocking) stitch (worked flat over any number of sts):

All RS rows: Knit all sts.

All WS rows: Purl all sts.

Shetland stitch (worked in the round over a multiple of 8 plus 1 sts):

Rnds 1 through 4, 6, and 8: Knit all sts.

Rnds 5 and 7: K1, *yo, k2, sl2-k1-p2sso, k2, yo, k1; rep from * to end.

Rep Rnds 1 to 8 for pattern.

Shetland stitch (worked in flat over a multiple of 8 plus 1 sts):

Work the same as Shetland stitch in the round, except purl all WS rows.

Full dec: *K1, ssk, work to 3 sts before marker, k2tog, k1, sm; rep from * 3 more times to end. 8 sts dec'd.

Body-only dec: *Knit across sleeve to marker, sm, k1, ssk, work to 3 sts before marker, k2tog, k1, sm; rep from * once. 4 sts dec'd.

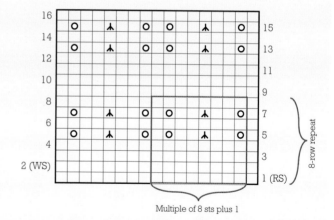

Read RS from right to left, WS from left to right

☐ Knit on RS, purl on WS

Ⓞ Yarn over

⅄ Slip 2 as if to k2tog, knit 1, pass 2 slipped sts over

Lace Panel Sweater

Please read "Sweater Construction" for helpful tips.

Sleeves

With smaller needles for working in a small round, cast on 36 (36, 38, 40, 40, 42, 44, 46, 48) sts.

Join in round, being careful not to twist sts, and work 12 rnds K1/P1 rib.

Switch to larger needles.

Work in stockinette (stocking) stitch 8 (7, 6, 6, 6, 5, 4, 4, 4) rnds.

Next round (inc): K1, m1L, knit to 1 st before end, m1R, k1. 2 sts inc'd. 38 (38, 40, 42, 42, 44, 46, 48, 50) sts.

Working an inc every 9th (8th, 7th, 7th, 7th, 6th, 5th, 5th, 5th) rnd 7 (8, 9, 9, 10, 11, 13, 14, 16) more times, cont in stockinette (stocking) stitch until sleeve measures 16¾ (16¾, 17, 17, 17¼, 17¼, 17½, 17¼, 18) inches (42.5 [42.5, 43, 43, 44, 44, 44.5, 45, 45.5] cm) from cast-on edge. 52 (54, 58, 60, 62, 66, 72, 76, 82) sts. Cut yarn.

Underarms

Set aside 1st and last 4 (4, 5, 5, 6, 6, 8, 9, 10) sts of round (total of 8 [8, 10, 10, 12, 12, 16, 18, 20] sts) on scrap yarn or holder. 44 (46, 48, 50, 50, 54, 56, 58, 62) each sleeve.

Set aside sleeves on spare circular needle or scrap yarn. Then work body.

Body

Back and front are worked flat for the ribbing and then joined to work the body in the round.

Back

With smaller needles, cast on 73 (77, 81, 85, 91, 95, 103, 113, 121) sts.

Work 12 rows K1/P1 rib. Set aside on spare needle.

Front

Work same as back, and leave on needle. Then join front and back.

Join Front and Back

With larger circular needle, knit across front. PM for side, knit across back, and join for working in the round, being careful not to twist sts. 146 (154, 162, 170, 182, 190, 206, 226, 242) sts.

Marker setup rnd: K20 (18, 20, 22, 25, 27, 27, 28, 32), pm, k33 (41, 41, 41, 41, 41, 49, 57, 57), pm, knit to end.

Rnd 1: Knit to marker, sm, Shetland stitch to marker, sm, knit to end.

Cont as set by Rnd 1 for 14 more rounds. Then shape waist.

Shape Waist

Next rnd (dec): K1, k2tog, work across front (maintaining Shetland stitch at center) to 3 sts before side marker, ssk, k1, sm, k1, k2tog, knit to 3 before end, ssk, k1. 4 sts dec'd. 142 (150, 158, 166, 178, 186, 202, 222, 238) sts.

Cont until work measures 9 inches (23cm) from cast-on edge. Then shape bust.

Shape Bust

Next rnd (inc): *K1, m1L, work to 1 st before side marker, m1R, k1, sm; rep from * once. 4 sts inc'd. 146 (154, 162, 170, 182, 190, 206, 226, 242) sts.

Stopping 4 (4, 5, 5, 6, 6, 8, 9, 10) sts from end on final round, cont until work measures 14½ (14¼, 14¼, 14, 14, 13¾, 13½, 13¼, 13) inches (37 [36, 36, 35.5, 35.5, 35, 34.5, 33.5, 33] cm) from cast-on edge. Then join body and sleeves.

Join Body and Sleeves

Set aside last 4 (4, 5, 5, 6, 6, 8, 9, 10) sts of current round and 1st 4 (4, 5, 5, 6, 6, 8, 9, 10) sts of next round on holder or scrap yarn.

Work across one sleeve, joining it to the body. PM and work across front to 4 (4, 5, 5, 6, 6, 8, 9, 10) sts before side marker. Set aside next 8 (8, 10, 10, 12, 12, 16, 18, 20) sts of body, removing side marker.

PM and work across other sleeve, joining it to body.

PM and work across back. 218 (230, 238, 250, 258, 274, 286, 306, 326) sts, 65 (69, 71, 75, 79,

83, 87, 95, 101) each front and back, 44 (46, 48, 50, 50, 54, 56, 58, 62) each sleeve, plus 4 sets of 8 (8, 10, 10, 12, 12, 16, 18, 20) sts set aside for underarms. Beginning of round is at the left back. Proceed with yoke.

Yoke

Please read ahead to familiarize yourself with the yoke shaping.

Knit 2 rnds.

Following the "Yoke Shaping Schedule," work yoke for 36 (38, 40, 42, 46, 50, 52, 58, 62) rnds in pattern as established.

Yoke Shaping Schedule

Over the next 0 (0, 0, 0, 16, 16, 20, 28, 28) rnds, work a body-only dec every 2nd and a full dec every 4th rnd 0 (0, 0, 0, 4, 4, 5, 7, 7) times. 65 (69, 71, 75, 63, 67, 67, 67, 73) sts each front and back, 44 (46, 48, 50, 42, 46, 46, 44, 48) sts each sleeve.

Over the next 28 (30, 32, 34, 30, 34, 32, 30, 34) rnds, work a full dec every 2nd rnd 14 (15, 16, 17, 15, 17, 16, 15, 17) times. 37 (39, 39, 41, 33, 33, 35, 37, 39) sts each front and back, 16 (16, 16, 16, 12, 12, 14, 14, 14) sts each sleeve.

Over the next 8 (8, 8, 8, 0, 0, 0, 0, 0) rnds, work a body-only dec every 2nd and a full dec every 4th rnd 2 (2, 2, 2, 0, 0, 0, 0, 0) times. 29 (31, 31, 33, 33, 33, 35, 37, 39) sts each front and back, 12 (12, 12, 12, 12, 12, 14, 14, 14) sts each sleeve, 82 (86, 86, 90, 90, 90, 98, 102, 106) sts total.

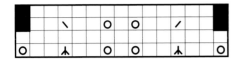

To keep the lace pattern correct while you shape the yoke, and when you have partial multiples at the right and left of the lace panel, only work a yo when you have a minimum of 5 sts in the partial repeat. Substitute the sl2-k1-p2sso with k2tog on right, ssk on left. When you have fewer than 5 sts remaining in the partial repeat, knit the sts.

Neck

Work K1/P1 rib until neck measures 7 or 8 inches (17.5 to 20cm).

Bind (cast) off loosely.

Finishing

Block sweater to schematic measurements.

Underarms

(Work one underarm at a time.) Arrange sleeve underarm sts on one needle and body underarm sts on another. Working from the RS and using Kitchener stitch, graft the two sets of sts together.

Weave in ends, closing any gaps either side of underarm if necessary.

rounded hem
pullover

● ● ● ● ○

This layering pullover makes a lovely addition to your wardrobe. Worked in a fine, soft yarn like this baby alpaca and silk blend, the result is both comfortable and elegant. Simple, straight lines and easy construction are offset by the rounded hem and the geometric lines at the yoke. Make it as written, or use the pattern as a blank canvas for your own modifications.

Skills Needed

Knit/purl, working in the round, picking up and knitting, mattress stitch, reading from chart

Finished Measurements

Meant to be worn 3 to 5 inches (7.5 to 13cm) of ease at the bust.

Bust: 33¾ (36, 38¼, 39¾, 41¾, 44, 46¼, 47¾, 49¾, 52, 54¼, 55¾) inches (85.5 [91.5, 97, 101, 106, 112, 117.5, 121.5, 126.5, 132, 138, 141.5] cm)

Length (at longest point): 22¾ (22¾, 23, 23, 23¼, 23¼, 23½, 23½, 23¾, 23¾, 24, 24) inches (58 [58, 58.5, 58.5, 59, 59, 59.5, 59.5, 60.5, 60.5, 61, 61] cm)

Yarn

6 (6, 7, 7, 7, 8, 8, 8, 9, 9, 9, 10) skeins sport (fine) yarn, 100 grams/275 yards (251m) each. I used Lorna's Laces Honor, 70 percent baby alpaca, 30 percent silk, in Waistcoat.

Gauge (Tension)

22 stitches and 30 rows = 4 inches (10cm) in stockinette (stocking) stitch

Needles

2 sets circular and 1 set for your preferred method of working in a small round in each of the following sizes:

U.S. 6 (4mm/UK 8) or size needed to obtain gauge (tension)

U.S. 4 (3.5mm/UK 10) or 2 sizes smaller than gauge (tension) needles

Other Supplies

2 stitch markers, blunt yarn needle

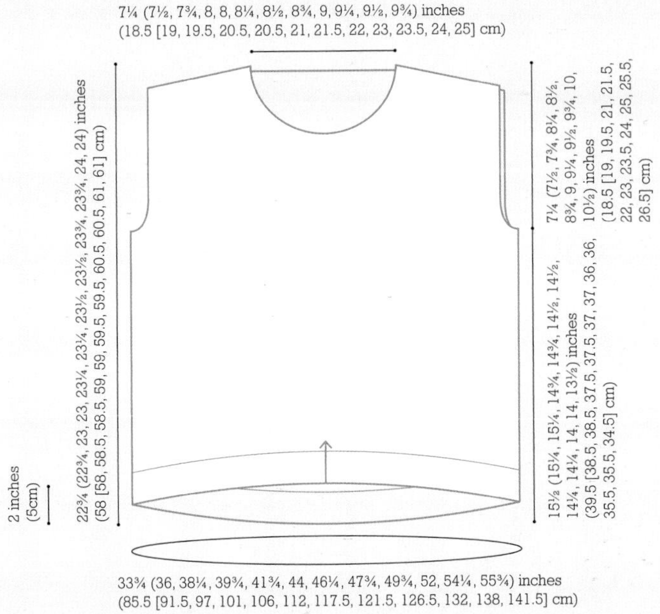
7¼ (7½, 7¾, 8, 8, 8¼, 8½, 8¾, 9, 9¼, 9½, 9¾) inches
(18.5 [19, 19.5, 20.5, 20.5, 21, 21.5, 22, 23, 23.5, 24, 25] cm)
2 inches (5cm)
22¾ (22¾, 23, 23, 23¼, 23¼, 23½, 23½, 23¾, 23¾, 24, 24) inches (58 [58, 58.5, 58.5, 59, 59, 59.5, 59.5, 60.5, 60.5, 61, 61] cm)
7¼ (7½, 7¾, 8¼, 8½, 8¾, 9, 9¼, 9½, 9¾, 10, 10½) inches (18.5 [19, 19.5, 21, 21.5, 22, 23, 23.5, 24, 25, 25.5, 26.5] cm)
15½ (15¼, 15¼, 14¾, 14¾, 14½, 14½, 14¼, 14¼, 14, 14, 13½) inches (39.5 [38.5, 38.5, 37.5, 37.5, 37, 37, 36, 36, 35.5, 35.5, 34.5] cm)
33¾ (36, 38¼, 39¾, 41¾, 44, 46¼, 47¾, 49¾, 52, 54¼, 55¾) inches
(85.5 [91.5, 97, 101, 106, 112, 117.5, 121.5, 126.5, 132, 138, 141.5] cm)

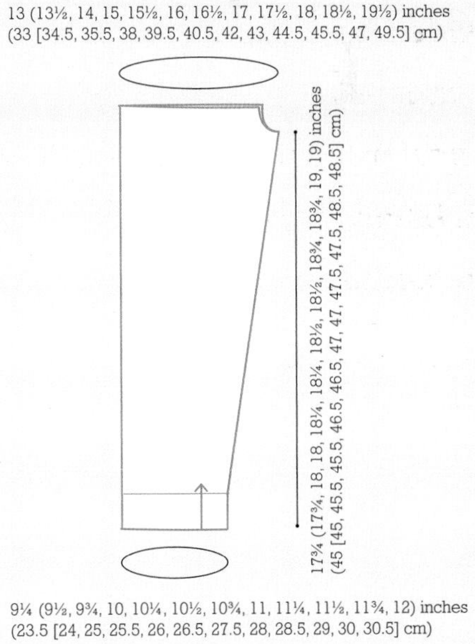
13 (13½, 14, 15, 15½, 16, 16½, 17, 17½, 18, 18½, 19½) inches
(33 [34.5, 35.5, 38, 39.5, 40.5, 42, 43, 44.5, 45.5, 47, 49.5] cm)
17¾ (17¾, 18, 18, 18¼, 18¼, 18½, 18½, 18¾, 18¾, 19, 19) inches (45 [45, 45.5, 45.5, 46.5, 46.5, 47, 47, 47.5, 47.5, 48.5, 48.5] cm)
9¼ (9½, 9¾, 10, 10¼, 10½, 10¾, 11, 11¼, 11½, 11¾, 12) inches
(23.5 [24, 25, 25.5, 26, 26.5, 27.5, 28, 28.5, 29, 30, 30.5] cm)

Construction Notes

The body and sleeves are worked in the round from the bottom up to the underarms. The rounded hem is shaped with short rows. The front, back, and sleeves are worked flat from the underarms. To finish, the shoulders are joined, the sleeves are set in, and the neck band is picked up and knit.

Tips for Modifying

- Change the length of the sleeve or body for a totally different fit.

- Make it even easier by skipping the short rows for the rounded hem.

- Try charting your own motif for the yoke.

Stitch Patterns and Techniques

Garter stitch 1/1 rib (worked in the round over even number of sts):

> **All odd-numbered rnds:** Knit all sts.

> **All even-numbered rnds:** *K1, p1; rep from * to end.

Stockinette (stocking) stitch (worked in the round over any number of sts):

> **All rnds:** Knit all sts.

Stockinette (stocking) stitch (worked flat over any number of sts):

> **All RS rows:** Knit all sts.

> **All WS rows:** Purl all sts.

Short rows: Short rows are partial rows: before reaching the end of a row or round, turn your work and begin the next one. To avoid creating a gap at the turning point, *wrap* the next stitch before turning. To do this, stop where instructed by the pattern, move the yarn to the opposite side (i.e., if the yarn is at the back, bring it to the front, and vice versa), slip the next stitch purlwise, move the yarn back to its original position, slip the stitch back to the left needle, and turn your work. This is called a *wrap and turn* (w&t).

The wraps are visible in stockinette (stocking) stitch, and most of the time they need to be picked up and worked together with the wrapped stitch to hide them. However, this pattern camouflages the wraps by placing them next to a purl bump, so they don't need to be picked up. I call that a short row shortcut!

Chevron pattern (worked flat with multiple of 6 sts either side of center st):

Read RS from right to left, WS from left to right

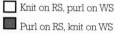

Knit on RS, purl on WS

Purl on RS, knit on WS

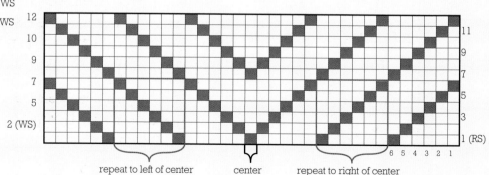

repeat to left of center   center   repeat to right of center

Rounded Hem Pullover

Body

With smaller circular needles, cast on 186 (198, 210, 218, 230, 242, 254, 262, 274, 286, 298, 306) sts. Arrange for working in the round, being careful not to twist sts, and pm for beginning of rnd.

Work 12 rnds garter stitch 1/1 rib. Then shape hem.

Shape Hem

Switch to larger needles.

The rounded hem is shaped by working short rows (see "Stitch Patterns and Techniques"). Pay close attention to the wrapping points; the st you wrap should be a *purl* st from the previous round of garter stitch 1/1 rib.

Short row 1: K15 (15, 17, 17, 19, 19, 19, 19, 21, 23, 23, 25) sts, wrap next st, and turn work.

Short row 2: P29 (29, 33, 33, 37, 37, 37, 37, 41, 45, 45, 49) sts, wrap, and turn.

Short row 3: K39 (39, 45, 45, 49, 51, 51, 51, 57, 61, 61, 65) sts—9 (9, 11, 11, 11, 13, 13, 13, 15, 15, 15, 15) sts past previous wrap—wrap, and turn.

Short row 4: P49 (49, 57, 57, 61, 65, 65, 65, 73, 77, 77, 81) sts—9 (9, 11, 11, 11, 13, 13, 13, 15, 15, 15, 15) sts past previous wrap—wrap, and turn.

Short rows 5 and 6: Work 7 (9, 9, 9, 9, 11, 11, 11, 11, 13, 13, 13) sts past previous wrap, wrap, and turn.

Short rows 7 and 8: Work 5 (7, 7, 7, 7, 7, 9, 9, 9, 9, 9, 11) sts past previous wrap, wrap, and turn.

Short rows 9 and 10: Work 5 (7, 7, 7, 7, 7, 9, 9, 9, 9, 9, 11) sts past previous wrap, wrap, and turn.

Short rows 11 and 12: Work 5 (7, 7, 7, 7, 7, 9, 9, 9, 9, 9, 11) sts past previous wrap, wrap, and turn.

Short rows 13 and 14: Work 7 (9, 9, 9, 9, 11, 11, 11, 11, 13, 13, 13) sts past previous wrap, wrap, and turn.

Short rows 15 and 16: Work 9 (9, 11, 11, 11, 13, 13, 13, 15, 15, 15, 15) sts past previous wrap, wrap, and turn.

Rnd 1 (reset beginning of rounds, marker setup): K68 (78, 84, 84, 86, 94, 100, 100, 106, 112, 112, 120) to beg of rnd marker and remove it. K46 (49, 52, 54, 57, 60, 63, 65, 68, 71, 74, 76), pm. (This marks the left side of body and new beg of rnd.) K93 (99, 105, 109, 115, 121, 127, 131, 137, 143, 149, 153), pm for right side of body, knit to end.

Work in stockinette (stocking) stitch until back measures 15½ (15¼, 15¼, 14¾, 14¾, 14½, 14½, 14¼, 14¼, 14, 14, 13½) inches (39.5 [38.5, 38.5, 37.5, 37.5, 37, 37, 36, 36, 35.5, 35.5,

34.5] cm) from cast-on edge. *At the same time,* on the final row, stop 2 (2, 3, 3, 3, 3, 3, 3, 3, 4, 4, 4) sts short of the end of rnd. Proceed to front.

Front

Begin 2 (2, 3, 3, 3, 3, 3, 3, 3, 4, 4, 4) sts before end of round.

Next row (RS) (dec): With 2nd larger circular needle, bind (cast) off 4 (4, 6, 6, 6, 6, 6, 6, 6, 8, 8, 8) sts for underarm, removing marker, knit to 2 (2, 3, 3, 3, 3, 3, 3, 3, 4, 4, 4) sts before other side marker. 89 (95, 99, 103, 109, 115, 121, 125, 131, 135, 141, 145) sts front.

Leave the back on its needle, turn work, and cont front.

Next row (WS): Purl across.

Next row (RS) (dec): K2, k2tog, knit to 4 sts before end, ssk, k2. 2 sts dec'd. 87 (93, 97, 101, 107, 113, 119, 123, 129, 133, 139, 143) sts.

Work a dec on the next 2 (3, 3, 3, 3, 4, 5, 5, 5, 5, 6, 6) RS rows. 83 (87, 91, 95, 101, 105, 109, 113, 119, 123, 127, 131) sts.

Next row (RS) (mark center): K41 (43, 45, 47, 50, 52, 54, 56, 59, 61, 63, 65), pm, k1, pm, knit to end.

Purl 1 row. Then begin yoke.

Yoke

Yoke row 1 (RS): Reading from right to left, starting on st 1 (5, 3, 1, 4, 2, 6, 4, 1, 5, 3, 1) of Row 1, work in chevron pattern across, being careful to keep the pattern correct either side of center st.

Yoke row 2 (WS): Reading from left to right, starting on st 1 (5, 3, 1, 4, 2, 6, 4, 1, 5, 3, 1) of Row 2, work in chevron pattern across.

Cont in chevron pattern until front measures 3¾ (3¾, 4, 4½, 4¾, 4¾, 5, 5¼, 5½, 5½, 5¾, 6¼) inches (9.5 [9.5, 10, 11.5, 12, 12, 12.5, 13.5, 14, 14, 14.5, 16] cm) from underarm bind (cast) off. Then shape front neck.

Shape Front Neck

For easier finishing and smooth seams, use a sloped bind (cast) off for the front neck and shoulders.

Keep chevron pattern correct throughout. Instructions are given to work left and right side of front at the same time.

Next row (RS) (dec): Work 34 (36, 38, 40, 43, 44, 46, 48, 51, 53, 54, 56), join new ball, bind (cast) off center 15 (15, 15, 15, 15, 17, 17, 17, 17, 17, 19, 19), work to end.

Next row (WS) (dec): Purl across 1st set of sts. On next set, bind (cast) off 6 (6, 6, 6, 6, 6, 6, 7, 7, 7, 7, 8) at neck edge, purl to end.

Next row (RS) (dec): Knit across 1st set of sts. On next set, bind (cast) off 6 (6, 6, 6, 6, 6, 6, 7, 7, 7, 7, 8) at neck edge, knit to end. 28 (30, 32, 34, 37, 38, 40, 41, 44, 46, 47, 48) sts each side of front neck.

Over the next 2 rows, bind (cast) off 3 each neck edge. 25 (27, 29, 31, 34, 35, 37, 38, 41, 43, 44, 45) sts each side.

Over the next 2 rows, bind (cast) off 2 each neck edge. 23 (25, 27, 29, 32, 33, 35, 36, 39, 41, 42, 43) sts each side.

Next 2 (3, 3, 4, 4, 4, 4, 4, 5, 5, 5, 5) RS rows (dec): On 1st set of sts, knit to 4 sts before neck edge, ssk, k2. On the next set, k2, k2tog, knit to end. 21 (22, 24, 25, 28, 29, 31, 32, 34, 36, 37, 38) sts each side.

Cont without shaping for a few more rows if necessary until armhole measures 6½ (6¾, 7, 7½, 7¾, 8, 8¼, 8½, 8¾, 9, 9¼, 9¾) inches (16.5 [17, 18, 19, 19.5, 20.5, 21, 21.5, 22, 23, 23.5, 25] cm) from underarm bind (cast) off, ending on a WS row. Then shape front shoulders.

Shape Front Shoulders

Next 6 rows (dec): Bind (cast) off 5 (6, 6, 6, 7, 7, 8, 8, 9, 9, 9, 10) at beg of row (armhole edge). 6 (4, 6, 7, 7, 8, 7, 8, 7, 9, 10, 8) sts.

Next 2 rows (dec): Bind (cast) off remaining sts.

Back

Rejoin yarn.

Bind (cast) off 4 (4, 6, 6, 6, 6, 6, 6, 6, 8, 8, 8) for underarm, and knit to end. 89 (95, 99, 103, 109, 115, 121, 125, 131, 135, 141, 145) sts.

Next row (WS): Purl across.

Next row (RS) (dec): K2, k2tog, knit to 4 sts before end, ssk, k2. 2 sts dec'd. 87 (93, 97, 101, 107, 113, 119, 123, 129, 133, 139, 143) sts.

Work a dec on the next 2 (3, 3, 3, 3, 4, 5, 5, 5, 5, 6, 6) RS rows. 83 (87, 91, 95, 101, 105, 109, 113, 119, 123, 127, 131) sts.

Next row (RS) (mark center): K41 (43, 45, 47, 50, 52, 54, 56, 59, 61, 63, 65), pm, k1, pm, knit to end.

Purl 1 row. Then work yoke pattern (same as front) until armhole measures 6½ (6¾, 7, 7½, 7¾, 8, 8¼, 8½, 8¾, 9, 9¼, 9¾) inches (16.5 [17, 18, 19, 19.5, 20.5, 21, 21.5, 22, 23, 23.5, 25] cm) from underarm bind (cast) off, ending with a WS row. Then shape back shoulders.

Shape Back Shoulders

Next 6 rows (dec): Bind (cast) off 5 (6, 6, 6, 7, 7, 8, 8, 9, 9, 9, 10) at beg of row (armhole edge). 53 (51, 55, 59, 59, 63, 61, 65, 65, 69, 73, 71) sts.

Next 2 rows (dec): Bind (cast) off 6 (4, 6, 7, 7, 8, 7, 8, 7, 9, 10, 8) at beg of row. 41 (43, 43, 45, 45, 47, 47, 49, 51, 51, 53, 55) sts.

Bind (cast) off remaining sts for back neck.

Sleeves

With smaller needles for working in a small round, cast on 52 (54, 54, 56, 58, 58, 60, 62, 62, 64, 66, 66) sts. Arrange for working in the round, being careful not to twist sts.

Work 12 rnds garter stitch 1/1 rib.

Switch to larger needles. Work 5 rnds stockinette (stocking) stitch.

Next round (RS) (inc): K3, m1L, knit to last 3, m1R, k3. 2 inc'd. 54 (56, 56, 58, 60, 60, 62, 64, 64, 66, 68, 68) sts.

Cont in stockinette (stocking) stitch, working an inc every 12th (10th, 10th, 8th, 8th, 8th, 7th, 7th, 6th, 6th, 6th, 5th) rnd 9 (2, 11, 7, 5, 14, 6, 6, 3, 3, 1, 2) times, then every 0 (11th, 0, 9th, 9th, 0, 8th, 8th, 7th, 7th, 7th, 6th) rnd 0 (8, 0, 6, 8, 0, 9, 9, 14, 14, 16, 18) times. 72 (76, 78, 84, 86, 88, 92, 94, 98, 100, 102, 108) sts.

Work without shaping until sleeve measures 17¾ (17¾, 18, 18, 18¼, 18¼, 18½, 18½, 18¾, 18¾, 19, 19) inches (45 [45, 45.5, 45.5, 46.5, 46.5, 47, 47, 47.5, 47.5, 48.5, 48.5] cm) from cast-on edge. *At the same time,* on final rnd, stop 2 (2, 3, 3, 3, 3, 3, 3, 4, 4, 4) sts short of end. Then shape sleeve cap.

Shape Sleeve Cap

Begin 2 (2, 3, 3, 3, 3, 3, 3, 4, 4, 4) sts before end of rnd.

Next row (RS) (dec): Bind (cast) off 4 (4, 6, 6, 6, 6, 6, 6, 6, 8, 8, 8), knit to end. 68 (72, 72, 78, 80, 82, 86, 88, 92, 92, 94, 100) sts.

Next row (WS): Purl across.

Next row (RS) (dec): K2, ssk, knit to 4 sts before end, k2tog, k2. 2 sts dec'd. 66 (70, 70, 76, 78, 80, 84, 86, 90, 90, 92, 98) sts.

Work a dec on the next 2 (3, 3, 3, 3, 4, 5, 5, 5, 5, 6, 6) RS rows. 62 (64, 64, 70, 72, 72, 74, 76, 80, 80, 80, 86) sts.

Bind (cast) off remaining sts.

Finishing

Block to finished measurements.

Sew shoulder seams together.

Neck

With smaller needles for working in a small round, rejoin yarn and starting at left shoulder, pick up and knit 3 sts for every 4 rows along left side of front neck, 37 (37, 37, 37, 37, 39, 39, 41, 41, 41, 43, 45) along center bound (cast) off sts, 3 sts for every 4 rows along other side of front neck, and 41 (43, 43, 45, 45, 47, 47, 49, 51, 51, 53, 55) along back neck. Be sure you have an even number of sts.

Work 8 rnds garter stitch 1/1 rib. Bind (cast) off.

Set in sleeves.

Weave in ends.

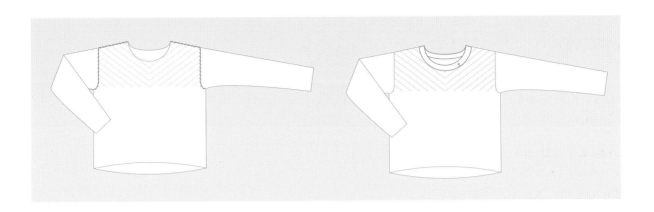

stylish sweaters

fine-knit
pullover

● ● ● ● ○

Are you drawn to classic, understated style? If so, you'll love the elegant simplicity of this fine-knit pullover. With its comfortable fit, flattering neck, and smooth silhouette, it's a sweater you'll want to knit more than once in different colors.

Instructions are given to shape the back and front armholes and neck at the same time, working with multiple balls of yarn. If you find this multitasking is too tangly, you can work the back, front neck, and shoulders separately.

Skills Needed

Knit/purl, working in the round, picking up and knitting, mattress stitch

Finished Measurements

Bust: 32 (36¼, 39¼, 43¾, 48, 52¼, 55¼, 59¾) inches (81.5 [92, 99.5, 111, 122, 132.5, 140.5, 152] cm)

Length: 23¾ (24, 24½, 24¾, 25, 25¼, 25¾, 26) inches (60.5 [61, 62, 63, 63.5, 64, 65.5, 66] cm)

Yarn

7 (8, 9, 10, 11, 12, 13, 14) skeins fingering (superfine) yarn, 50 grams/221 yards (202m) each. I used Quince & Co. Tern, 75 percent wool, 25 percent silk, in Syrah.

Gauge (Tension)

22 stitches and 29 rows = 4 inches (10cm) in stockinette (stocking) stitch

Needles

1 set circular for the body and 1 set in your preferred method of working in small round in each of the following sizes:

U.S. 5 (3.75mm/UK 9) or size needed to obtain gauge (tension)

U.S. 4 (3.5mm/UK 10) or 1 size smaller than gauge (tension) needle

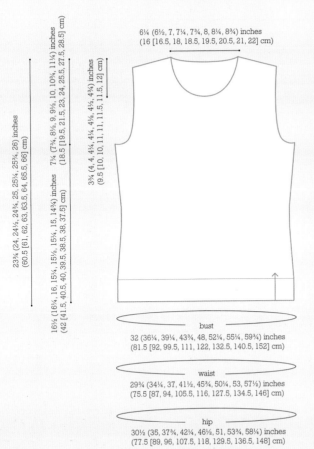

6¼ (6½, 7, 7¼, 7¾, 8, 8¼, 8¾) inches
(16 [16.5, 18, 18.5, 19.5, 20.5, 21, 22] cm)
23¾ (24, 24½, 24¾, 25, 25¼, 25¾, 26) inches
(60.5 [61, 62, 63, 63.5, 64, 65.5, 66] cm)
16½ (16¾, 16, 15¼, 15½, 15¼, 15, 14¾) inches
(42 [41.5, 40.5, 40, 39.5, 38.5, 38, 37.5] cm)
7¼ (7¾, 8½, 9, 9½, 10, 10¾, 11¼) inches
(18.5 [19.5, 21.5, 23, 24, 25.5, 27.5, 28.5] cm)
3¾ (4, 4, 4¼, 4¼, 4½, 4½, 4¾) inches
(9.5 [10, 10, 11, 11, 11.5, 11.5, 12] cm)
bust
32 (36¼, 39¼, 43¾, 48, 52¼, 55¼, 59¾) inches
(81.5 [92, 99.5, 111, 122, 132.5, 140.5, 152] cm)
waist
29¾ (34¼, 37, 41½, 45¾, 50¼, 53, 57½) inches
(75.5 [87, 94, 105.5, 116, 127.5, 134.5, 146] cm)
hip
30½ (35, 37¾, 42¼, 46½, 51, 53¾, 58¼) inches
(77.5 [89, 96, 107.5, 118, 129.5, 136.5, 148] cm)
11 (12, 12½, 14½, 16, 17, 18¼, 19¼) inches
(28 [30.5, 34.5, 37, 40.5, 43, 46.5, 49] cm)
5¼ (5¼, 5¾, 5¾, 6, 6, 6½, 6½) inches
(13.5 [13.5, 14.5, 14.5, 15, 15, 16.5, 16.5] cm)
12 (12½, 12¾, 13¾, 13½14, 14¼, 14¾) inches
(30.5 [32, 32.5, 33.5, 34.5, 35.5, 36, 37.5] cm)
9½ (9½, 10¼, 11, 11, 11¾, 12¼, 13) inches
(24 [24, 26, 28, 28, 30, 31, 33] cm)

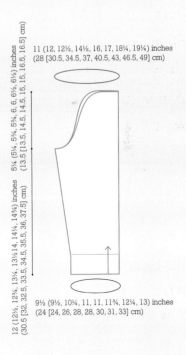

Other Supplies

4 stitch markers, blunt yarn needle, scrap yarn for holding stitches

Construction Notes

The body and sleeves are worked in the round from the bottom up to the underarms. The body and sleeves are then worked flat. The shoulders are joined, the sleeves are set in, and the neck is picked up and knit.

Tips for Modifying

- Change the sleeve or body length.
- Adapt the neck shape, or add a collar.
- Work the front in two halves to make a cardigan.
- Add texture, lace, or cables.

Stitch Patterns and Techniques

K2/P2 rib (worked in the round over a multiple of 4 sts):

All rnds: *K2, p2; rep from * to end.

Stockinette (stocking) stitch (worked in the round over any number of sts):

All rnds: Knit all sts.

Shaping Notes

Sleeve dec (RS): K1, ssk, knit to last 3 sts, k2tog, k1. 2 sts dec'd.

Armhole dec (RS): K1, ssk, knit to last 3 sts, k2tog, k1. 2 sts dec'd.

Fine-Knit Pullover

Sleeves

With smaller needles for working in a small round, cast on 52 (52, 56, 60, 60, 64, 68, 72) sts.

Join in round, being careful not to twist sts, and work 16 rnds K2/P2 rib.

Switch to larger needles.

Knit 5 (5, 5, 5, 3, 3, 3, 3) rnds.

Next rnd (inc): *K1, m1L, knit to 1 before end, m1R, k1. 2 sts inc'd. 54 (54, 58, 62, 62, 66, 70, 74) sts.

Working an inc every 18th (10th, 8th, 8th, 5th, 5th, 5th, 5th) rnd, 3 (6, 8, 9, 13, 14, 15, 16) more times, knit until sleeve measures 12 (12½, 12¾, 13¼, 13½, 14, 14¼, 14¾) inches (30.5 [32, 32.5, 33.5, 34.5, 35.5, 36, 37.5] cm) from cast-on edge. 60 (66, 74, 80, 88, 94, 100, 106) sts. Then shape sleeve cap.

Shape Sleeve Cap

Next row (RS) (dec): Bind (cast) off 3 (4, 4, 4, 4, 6, 7, 8), work to end. Turn work. (Sleeve cap is worked back and forth from here.)

Next row (WS) (dec): Bind (cast) off 3 (4, 4, 4, 4, 6, 7, 8), work to end. 54 (58, 66, 72, 80, 82, 86, 90) sts.

Next 2 rows (dec): Bind (cast) off 0 (3, 3, 3, 3, 5, 6, 7) at beg of row. 54 (52, 60, 66, 74, 72, 74, 76) sts.

Work sleeve dec (see "Shaping Notes") every other RS 3 (5, 5, 2, 2, 4, 6, 6) times. 48 (42, 50, 62, 70, 64, 62, 64) sts.

Work sleeve dec every RS 10 (6, 7, 13, 14, 10, 8, 8) times. 28 (30, 36, 36, 42, 44, 46, 48) sts.

Final 4 rows: Bind (cast) off 3 (3, 4, 4, 5, 5, 5, 5) at beg of row. 16 (18, 20, 20, 22, 24, 26, 28) sts.

Bind (cast) off remaining 16 (18, 20, 20, 22, 24, 26, 28) sts.

Body

With smaller needles, cast on 168 (192, 208, 232, 256, 280, 296, 320) sts.

Join in round, being careful not to twist sts, and work 16 rnds K2/P2 rib.

Switch to larger needles.

Marker setup rnd: *K82 (94, 102, 114, 126, 138, 146, 158), pm, k2, pm; rep from * once.

Rnd 1: *Knit to marker, sm, p2, sm; rep from * once.

Rnd 2: Knit all sts.

Rnds 1 and 2 establish the body pattern, with all sts knit except for a 2-st column of garter stitch at each side.

Work 40 more rnds as established. Then shape waist.

Shape Waist

Next rnd (dec): *K1, k2tog, knit to 3 before marker, ssk, k1, sm, work to next marker, sm; rep from * once. 4 sts dec'd. 164 (188, 204, 228, 252, 276, 292, 316) sts.

Cont until body measures 10¼ inches (26cm) from cast-on edge. Then shape bust.

Shape Bust

Next rnd (inc): *K1, m1L, knit to 1 before marker, m1R, sm, work to next marker, sm; rep from * once. 4 sts inc'd. 168 (192, 208, 232, 256, 280, 296, 320) sts.

With an inc rnd every 20th (19th, 19th, 18th, 17th, 17th, 16th, 15th) rnd, cont as established until you've worked 2 more inc rnds. 176 (200, 216, 240, 264, 288, 304, 328) sts.

Stopping 3 (4, 4, 4, 4, 6, 7, 8) sts short on final rnd, cont until body measures 16½ (16¼, 16, 15¾, 15½, 15¼, 15, 14¾) inches (42 [41.5, 40.5, 40, 39.5, 38.5, 38, 37.5] cm) from cast-on edge. Then shape armholes.

Shape Armholes

Beg 3 (4, 4, 4, 4, 6, 7, 8) sts short of end of row.

Bind (cast) off 6 (8, 8, 8, 8, 12, 14, 16), knit to 3 (4, 4, 4, 4, 6, 7, 8) before next marker. Join new ball of yarn, and bind (cast) off 6 (8, 8, 8, 8, 12, 14, 16), remove marker, knit to end. 82 (92, 100, 112, 124, 132, 138, 148) sts each front and back.

Next 2 rows (dec): Bind (cast) off 0 (3, 3, 3, 3, 5, 6, 7) at beg of each front and back. 82 (86, 94, 106, 118, 122, 126, 134) sts each front and back.

Next 2 (2, 4, 8, 12, 12, 11, 13) RS rows (dec): K2, k2tog, work to last 4 sts, ssk, k2 on both front and back. 78 (82, 86, 90, 94, 98, 104, 108) sts each front and back.

Then dec on the *2nd* RS once. 76 (80, 84, 88, 92, 96, 102, 106) sts.

Cont until front and back measure 3½ (3¾, 4½, 4¾, 5¼, 5½, 6¼, 6½) inches (9 [9.5, 11.5, 12, 13.5, 14, 16, 16.5] cm) from underarm, ending with WS row. Then shape front neck.

Shape Front Neck

For easier finishing and smooth seams, use a sloped bind (cast) off for the front neck and shoulders.

Next row (RS) (dec): On front, k32 (34, 35, 37, 38, 40, 43, 44), join new ball, bind (cast) off 12 (12, 14, 14, 16, 16, 16, 18) center sts, knit to end. Knit across back. Cont to work back in stockinette (stocking) stitch while you shape front neck.

Next row (WS) (dec): On front, purl across 1st set of sts. On next set, bind (cast) off 5 (5, 6, 6, 7, 7, 7, 8) at neck edge, purl to end.

Next row (RS) (dec): On front, knit across 1st set of sts. On next set, bind (cast) off 5 (5, 6, 6, 7, 7, 7, 8) at neck edge, knit to end. 27 (29, 29, 31, 31, 33, 36, 36) sts each side of front neck.

Over next 2 rows: Bind (cast) off 3 each neck edge. 24 (26, 26, 28, 28, 30, 33, 33) sts each side.

Over the next 2 rows: Bind (cast) off 2 each neck edge. 22 (24, 24, 26, 26, 28, 31, 31) sts each side.

Next 2 (2, 2, 2, 2, 2, 4, 4) RS rows (dec): Knit to 4 sts before neck edge (on 1st set of sts), ssk, k2. On next set, k2, k2tog, knit to end. 20 (22, 22, 24, 24, 26, 27, 27) sts each side.

Cont until front and back measure 6¼ (6¾, 7½, 8, 8½, 9, 9¾, 10¼) inches (16 [17, 19, 20.5, 21.5, 23, 25, 26] cm) from underarm, ending with a WS row. Then shape shoulders.

Shape Shoulders

Next 6 rows (dec): Bind (cast) off 5 (6, 6, 6, 6, 7, 7, 7) at armhole edges. 5 (4, 4, 6, 6, 5, 7, 7) each side of front neck, 46 (44, 48, 52, 56, 54, 60, 64) sts back.

Next 2 rows (dec): Bind (cast) off remaining 5 (4, 4, 6, 6, 5, 7, 7) of each front, and 5 (4, 4, 6, 6, 5, 7, 7) at armhole edges of back. 36 (36, 40, 40, 44, 44, 46, 50) sts remain on back. Set aside remaining sts on holder or scrap yarn.

Finishing

Block all pieces to schematic measurements.

Sew shoulder seams together.

Neck

On smaller needles for working in a small round, place 36 (36, 40, 40, 44, 44, 46, 50) back neck sts from holder.

With RS of work facing and beg at left shoulder, join yarn and pick up and knit 3 sts for every 4 rows along edge of left front neck, 12 (12, 14, 14, 16, 16, 16, 18) sts along center bound (cast) off sts, 3 sts for every 4 rows along right side of neck (matching number of sts picked up on left), knit across back neck stitches. Arrange for working in the round. Adjust as you pick up sts so you end up with a multiple of 4 sts.

Work 8 rnds K2/P2 rib.

Bind (cast) off, being careful to maintain a relaxed tension on bound (cast) off edge.

Set in sleeves and join.

Weave in ends.

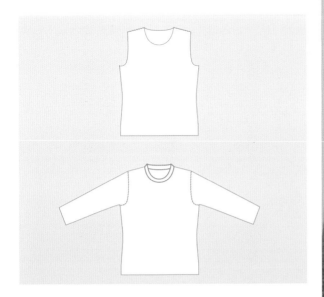

cropped
cardigan

●●●○○

A classic silhouette that flatters the waist with a cropped length, deep ribbed edges, and a deep V front, this little cardigan is wonderfully easy to make. Knitted seamlessly from the top down with a raglan yoke, this sweater will be ready to wear in no time!

Idiot's Guides: Knitting Sweaters

Skills Needed

Knit/purl, working in the round, picking up and knitting

Finished Measurements

Choose a size 1 to 3 inches (2.5 to 7.5cm) larger than the actual bust measurement

Bust: 30½ (34¾, 38, 41½, 45, 47½, 51, 55¼) inches (77.5 [88.5, 96.5, 105.5, 114.5, 120.5, 129.5, 140.5] cm)

Length: 20½ (20¾, 21, 21¼, 21½, 21¾, 22, 22¼) inches (52 [52.5, 53.5, 54, 54.5, 55, 56, 56.5] cm)

Yarn

4 (5, 6, 6, 7, 7, 8, 9) skeins sport (fine) yarn, 50 grams/175 yards (160m) each. I used Swans Island Merino Silk, 50 percent merino wool, 50 percent silk, in Slate.

Gauge (Tension)

21 stitches and 29 rows = 4 inches (10cm) in stockinette (stocking) stitch

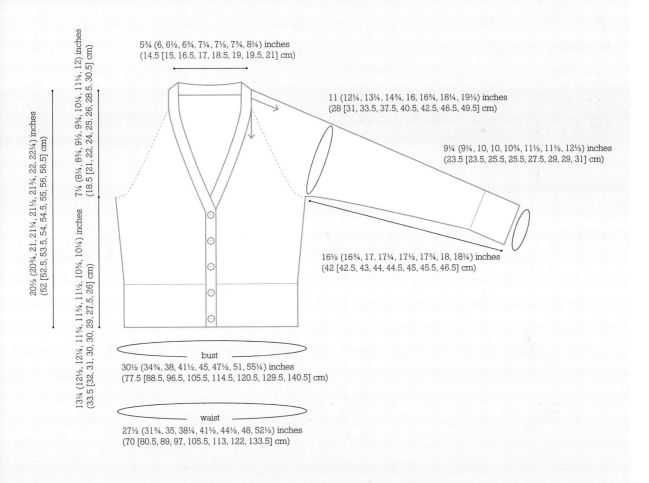

5¾ (6, 6½, 6¾, 7¼, 7½, 7¾, 8¼) inches (14.5 [15, 16.5, 17, 18.5, 19, 19.5, 21] cm)

11 (12¼, 13¼, 14¾, 16, 16¾, 18¼, 19½) inches (28 [31, 33.5, 37.5, 40.5, 42.5, 46.5, 49.5] cm)

9¼ (9¼, 10, 10, 10¾, 11½, 11½, 12½) inches (23.5 [23.5, 25.5, 25.5, 27.5, 29, 29, 31] cm)

16½ (16¾, 17, 17¼, 17½, 17¾, 18, 18¼) inches (42 [42.5, 43, 44, 44.5, 45, 45.5, 46.5] cm)

20½ (20¾, 21, 21¼, 21½, 21¾, 22, 22¼) inches (52 [52.5, 53.5, 54, 54.5, 55, 56, 56.5] cm)

7¼ (8¼, 8¾, 9¼, 9½, 9¾, 10¼, 11¼, 12) inches (18.5 [21, 22, 24, 25, 26, 28.5, 30.5] cm)

13¾ (12½, 12¼, 11¾, 11¾, 11½, 10¾, 10¼) inches (33.5 [32, 31, 30, 29, 27.5, 26] cm)

bust
30½ (34¾, 38, 41½, 45, 47½, 51, 55¼) inches (77.5 [88.5, 96.5, 105.5, 114.5, 120.5, 129.5, 140.5] cm)

waist
27½ (31¾, 35, 38¼, 41½, 44½, 48, 52½) inches (70 [80.5, 89, 97, 105.5, 113, 122, 133.5] cm)

Needles

1 set circular (long enough to accommodate a large number of stitches) and 1 for your preferred method of working in a small round in each of the following sizes:

U.S. 6 (4mm/UK 8) or size needed to obtain gauge (tension)

U.S. 4 (3.5mm/UK 10) or 2 sizes smaller than gauge (tension) needles

Other Supplies

4 stitch markers, blunt yarn needle, scrap yarn for holding stitches, 5 safety pins, 5 medium (⅝-inch [15mm]) buttons

Construction Notes

The body is worked in one piece from the neck down to the underarms. The rest of the body is worked to the bottom edge with shaping at the sides. The sleeves are knit in the round from the underarms. The bands are picked up and knit.

Tips for Modifying

- Easily change the silhouette by working fewer decreases at the sides and adding length to the body.

- For a warmer-weather version, make short sleeves.

Stitch Patterns and Techniques

K2/P2 rib (worked flat over a multiple of 4 plus 2 sts):

All RS rows: K2, *p2, k2; rep from * to end.

All WS rows: P2, *k2, p2; rep from * to end.

Rep Rows 1 and 2 for pattern.

K2/P2 rib (worked in the round over a multiple of 4 sts):

All rnds: *K2, p2; rep from * to end.

Stockinette (stocking) stitch (worked in the round over any number of sts):

All rnds: Knit all sts.

Stockinette (stocking) stitch (worked flat over any number of sts):

All RS rows: Knit all sts.

All WS rows: Purl all sts.

1-row buttonhole:

Bring yarn to front, slip 1 st, take yarn to back, wrapping st.

*Slip next st, and pass 1st slipped st over it. Rep from * 1 time.

Turn your work. Slip 1 st back to right needle.

With a cable cast on, cast on 3.

Turn. Slip 1 st purlwise. Pass 1 st over slipped st.

Shaping Notes

Neck inc: K1, m1L at beg of row, m1R, k1 when you get to last st of row. 2 inc'd (1 each front).

Full raglan inc: *Work to 1 st before marker, m1R, k1, sm, k1, m1L; rep from * 3 times, work to end. 8 inc'd (2 sts each sleeve, 1 each front, and 2 back).

Body only inc: Work to 1 st before marker, m1R, k1, sm, work to next marker, sm, m1L; rep from * once, work to end. 4 inc'd (1 st each front and 2 back).

Side dec: Work to 3 sts before side marker, ssk, k1, sm, k1, k2tog; rep from * once. 4 dec'd (1 st each front and 2 back).

Sleeve dec: K1, k2tog, work to 3 sts before end, ssk, k1. 2 dec'd.

Cropped Cardigan

Yoke

With gauge needles, cast on 58 (59, 62, 63, 70, 71, 72, 75) sts.

Raglan marker setup (WS): P2 (front), pm, p12 (12, 12, 12, 14, 14, 14, 14) (sleeve), pm, p30 (31, 34, 35, 38, 39, 40, 43) (back), pm, p12 (12, 12, 12, 14, 14, 14, 14) (sleeve), pm, p2 (front).

Please read "Shaping Notes" before working yoke.

Work yoke in stockinette (stocking) stitch over 46 (54, 58, 62, 64, 68, 74, 80) rows, as follows:

Work a neck inc (see "Shaping Notes") every other RS row throughout.

Shape body and sleeves as follows:

Batch 1: Over next 34 (34, 38, 46, 44, 44, 50, 52) rows, work a full raglan inc (see "Shaping Notes") every RS row 17 (17, 19, 23, 22, 22, 25, 26) times.

8 (8, 9, 11, 11, 11, 12, 13) neck inc worked. 27 (27, 30, 36, 35, 35, 39, 41) sts each front, 64 (65, 72, 81, 82, 83, 90, 95) sts back, 46 (46, 50, 58, 58, 58, 64, 66) sts each sleeve.

Batch 2: Over the next 4 (12, 12, 16, 20, 24, 24, 28) rows, alt body only inc and full raglan inc as follows:

*On next RS, work a body only inc (see "Shaping Notes").

On following RS, work a full raglan inc.

Rep from * 0 (2, 2, 3, 4, 5, 5, 6) times more.

1 (3, 3, 4, 5, 6, 6, 7) neck inc worked. 30 (36, 39, 48, 50, 53, 57, 62) sts each front, 68 (77, 84, 97, 102, 107, 114, 123) sts back, 48 (52, 56, 66, 68, 70, 76, 80) sts each sleeve.

Batch 3: Over next 8 (8, 8, 0, 0, 0, 0, 0) rows, alt body only inc and full raglan inc *every other* RS row as follows:

*On 2nd RS, work a body only inc.

On following 2nd RS, work a full raglan inc.

Rep from * 1 (1, 1, 0, 0, 0, 0, 0) time.

2 (2, 2, 0, 0, 0, 0, 0) neck inc worked. 34 (40, 43, 48, 50, 53, 57, 62) sts each front, 72 (81, 88, 97, 102, 107, 114, 123) sts back, 50 (54, 58, 66, 68, 70, 76, 80) sts each sleeve.

Separate Sleeves from Body

Cont to work neck inc every other RS 2 (1, 1, 0, 0, 0, 0, 0) times more as you separate sleeves and begin body, as follows:

Next row (RS): *Work to marker, remove marker. Transfer sleeve sts to scrap yarn or spare circular needle, remove next marker. Cast on 4 (5, 6, 6, 8, 9, 10, 11) (using backward loop), pm for side, cast on 4 (5, 6, 6, 8, 9, 10, 11). Rep from * once, work to end.

Shape Sides

Working a side dec (see "Shaping Notes") every 16th (14th, 14th, 14th, 14th, 14th, 12th, 10th) row 4 times, cont in stockinette (stocking) stitch until work measures 9¾ (9, 8¾, 8¼, 8¼, 8, 7¼, 6¾) inches (25 [23, 22, 21, 21, 20.5, 18.5, 17] cm) from underarm cast on, ending with a WS row. 144 (167, 184, 201, 218, 233, 252, 275) sts. 36 (42, 46, 50, 54, 58, 63, 69) each front, 72 (83, 92, 101, 110, 117, 126, 137) back.

Switch to smaller needles.

Next row (RS): K1, K2/P2 rib to last st, K1.

Next row (WS): P1, K2/P2 rib to last st, p1.

Cont as set until rib measures 3½ inches (9cm).

Bind (cast) off.

Sleeves

Transfer sleeve sts to needle. Rejoin yarn.

Pick up and knit 4 (5, 6, 6, 8, 9, 10, 11) sts from body underarm, pm, pick up and knit another 4 (5, 6, 6, 8, 9, 10, 11) sts, join in the round, being careful not to twist sts. 58 (64, 70, 78, 84, 88, 96, 102) sts.

Working a sleeve dec (see "Shaping Notes") every 18th (11th, 10th, 7th, 6th, 7th, 5th, 5th) rnd 5 (8, 9, 13, 14, 14, 18, 19) times, cont in stockinette (stocking) stitch until sleeve measures 13 (13¼, 13½, 13¾, 14, 14¼, 14½, 14¾)

inches (33 [33.5, 34.5, 35, 35.5, 36, 37, 37.5] cm) from underarm. 48 (48, 52, 52, 56, 60, 60, 64) sts.

Switch to smaller needles.

Work in K2/P2 rib 3½ inches (9cm).

Bind (cast) off.

Finishing

Block to finished measurements. Then work front bands.

Front Bands

Lay cardigan out flat and, with safety pins, mark 5 positions for buttonholes, evenly spaced, starting 1 inch (2.5cm) from bottom edge and ending at base of V on right side (as worn).

With smaller circular needles, starting at lower right front with RS facing, pick up and knit 3 sts for every 4 rows along right front edge, 1 st for every st along sleeves and back neck, and the same number from the left from edge as for the right. Adjust your pick-up rate as necessary to end up with a multiple of 4 sts plus 2.

Work 3 rows in K2/P2 rib.

Buttonhole row (RS): Work in K2/P2 rib to 1st buttonhole marker. Make a 1-row buttonhole (see "Stitch Patterns and Techniques"). [Work in K2/P2 rib to next buttonhole marker, make buttonhole] 4 more times. Work in K2/P2 rib to end of row. For neatest look, start buttonholes right after a K2.

Work 3 rows of K2/P2 rib.

Bind (cast) off.

Sew buttons onto left front button band, being careful to line buttons up with buttonholes.

Weave in ends, and block band.

draped front
cardigan

● ● ● ○ ○

Easy style and drape are the keys to this fine-knit cardigan. Fitted long sleeves, draped fronts, and a wide shaped collar all flatter your silhouette. Wear it loose and open, or wrap it closed with your favorite shawl pin. As you knit, you'll enjoy the top-down seamless construction and easy short rows on the collar. Treat yourself to a merino silk blend, like the one shown here, for something really elegant.

Skills Needed

Knit/purl, working in the round, picking up and knitting, short rows

Finished Measurements

Bust (closed, with fronts overlapping slightly): 29¾ (33, 37¾, 41, 46¼, 49, 53, 57, 61) inches (75.5 [84, 96, 104, 117.5, 124.5, 134.5, 145, 155] cm)

Length: 22¾ (23½, 24, 24¼, 24¾, 25, 25½, 25¾, 26½) inches (58 [59.5, 61, 61.5, 63, 63.5, 65, 65.5, 67.5] cm)

Yarn

3 (4, 4, 5, 5, 5, 6, 6, 7) skeins fingering (superfine) yarn, 115 grams/375 yards (343m) each. I used SweetGeorgia Silk Crush, 50 percent superwash merino wool, 50 percent silk, in Bison.

Gauge (Tension)

24 stitches and 33 rows = 4 inches (10cm) in stockinette (stocking) stitch

Needles

1 set circular (long enough to accommodate a large number of stitches) and 1 set for your preferred method of working in a small round: U.S. 5 (3.75mm/UK 9) or size needed to obtain gauge (tension)

Other Supplies

4 stitch markers, blunt yarn needle, scrap yarn for holding stitches

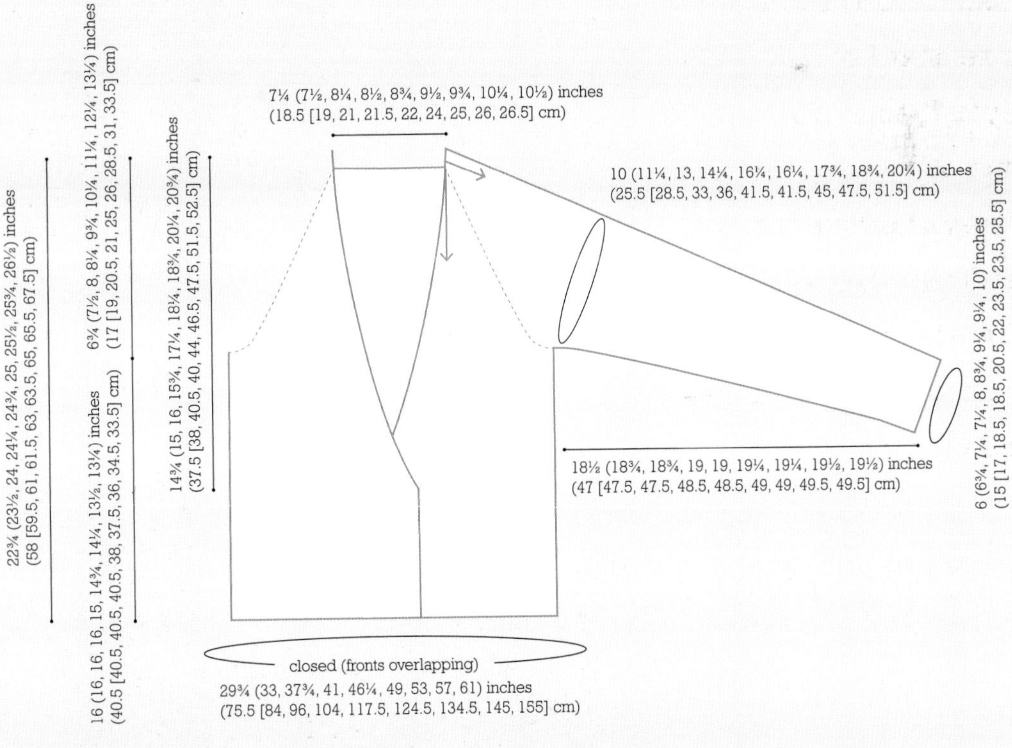

22¾ (23½, 24, 24¼, 24¾, 25, 25½, 25¾, 26½) inches
(58 [59.5, 61, 61.5, 63, 63.5, 65, 65.5, 67.5] cm)
16 (16, 16, 16, 15, 14¾, 14¼, 13½, 13¼) inches
(40.5 [40.5, 40.5, 40.5, 38, 37.5, 36, 34.5, 33.5] cm)
6¾ (7½, 8, 8¼, 9¾, 10¼, 11¼, 12¼, 13¼) inches
(17 [19, 20.5, 21, 25, 26, 28.5, 31, 33.5] cm)
14¾ (15, 16, 15¾, 17¼, 18¼, 18¾, 20¼, 20¾) inches
(37.5 [38, 40.5, 40, 44, 46.5, 47.5, 51.5, 52.5] cm)
7¼ (7½, 8¼, 8½, 8¾, 9½, 9¾, 10¼, 10½) inches
(18.5 [19, 21, 21.5, 22, 24, 25, 26, 26.5] cm)
10 (11¼, 13, 14¼, 16¼, 16¼, 17¾, 18¾, 20¼) inches
(25.5 [28.5, 33, 36, 41.5, 41.5, 45, 47.5, 51.5] cm)
18½ (18¾, 18¾, 19, 19, 19¼, 19¼, 19½, 19½) inches
(47 [47.5, 47.5, 48.5, 48.5, 49, 49, 49.5, 49.5] cm)
6 (6¾, 7¼, 7¼, 8, 8¾, 9¼, 9¼, 10) inches
(15 [17, 18.5, 18.5, 20.5, 22, 23.5, 23.5, 25.5] cm)
closed (fronts overlapping)
29¾ (33, 37¾, 41, 46¼, 49, 53, 57, 61) inches
(75.5 [84, 96, 104, 117.5, 124.5, 134.5, 145, 155] cm)

Construction Notes

The body is worked in one piece from the neck down to the underarms. The rest of the body is worked to the bottom edge with a row of decorative eyelets before the bottom ribbing. The sleeves are knit in the round from the underarms. The draped collar is picked up and knit and shaped with short rows.

Tips for Modifying

- Shorten the sleeves for a summery look.
- Knit the collar narrower and in broken rib.
- Modify the length of the body to suit your height.

Stitch Patterns and Techniques

Broken K2/P2 rib (worked flat over a multiple of 4 plus 2 sts):

All RS rows: Knit all sts.

All WS rows: P2, *k2, p2; rep from * to end.

Broken K2/P2 rib (worked in the round over a multiple of 4 sts):

All odd-numbered rnds: Knit all sts.

All even-numbered rnds: *K2, p2; rep from * to end.

Stockinette (stocking) stitch (worked flat over any number of sts):

All RS rows: Knit all sts.

All WS rows: Purl all sts.

Stockinette (stocking) stitch (worked in the round over any number of sts):

All rnds: Knit all sts.

Lifted-m1R: On back of work, knit into top of st directly below 1st st on left needle.

Lifted-m1L: On back of work, with left needle, pick up st 2 rows below 1st st on right needle and knit into it.

If you prefer, you can substitute the regular m1L and m1R, as seen in the Cropped Cardigan, for the lifted increases.

Shaping Notes

Neck inc: K1, lifted-m1L at beg of row, lifted-m1R, k1 when you get to last st of row. 2 inc'd (1 each front).

Full raglan inc: *Work to 1 st before marker, lifted-m1R, k1, sm, k1, lifted-m1L; rep from * 3 times, work to end. 8 inc'd (2 sts each sleeve, 1 each front and 2 back).

Body only inc: Work to 1 st before marker, lifted-m1R, k1, sm, work to next marker, sm, lifted-m1L; rep from * once, work to end. 4 inc'd (1 st each front and 2 back).

Sleeve dec: K1, k2tog, work to 3 sts before end, ssk, k1. 2 sts dec'd.

Short rows: Short rows are partial rows: before reaching the end of a row or round, turn your work and begin the next one. To avoid creating a gap at the turning point, *wrap* the next stitch before turning. To do this, move the yarn to the opposite side (i.e., if the yarn is at the back, bring it to the front, and vice versa), slip the next stitch pwise, move the yarn back to its original position, slip the stitch back to the left needle, and turn your work. This is called a *wrap and turn* (w&t).

The wraps are camouflaged in the reverse stockinette (stocking) stitch of the collar so they don't need any special handling on the following row.

Draped Front Cardigan

Yoke

Cast on 75 (77, 81, 83, 93, 97, 99, 101, 103) sts.

Marker setup (WS): P2 (front), pm, p14 (14, 14, 14, 18, 18, 18, 18, 18) (sleeve), pm, p43 (45, 49, 51, 53, 57, 59, 61, 63) (back), pm, p14 (14, 14, 14, 18, 18, 18, 18, 18) (sleeve), pm, p2 (front).

Please read "Shaping Notes" before shaping the yoke.

Shape yoke in stockinette (stocking) stitch over 46 (52, 56, 58, 68, 72, 80, 88, 96) rows, as follows:

Batch 1: Over 8 rows, work a full raglan inc (see "Shaping Notes") every RS row 4 times. 107 (109, 113, 115, 125, 129, 131, 133, 135) sts, 6 each front, 22 (22, 22, 22, 26, 26, 26, 26, 26) each sleeve, 51 (53, 57, 59, 61, 65, 67, 69, 71) back.

Batch 2: Over next 20 (20, 8, 0, 0, 0, 0, 0, 0) rows, work a full raglan inc and a neck inc *every other* RS row. 157 (159, 133, -, -, -, -, -, -) sts, 16 (16, 10, -, -, -, -, -, -) each front, 32 (32, 26, -, -, -, -, -, -) each sleeve, 61 (63, 61, -, -, -, -, -, -) back.

- -

When used in the stitch count, - means there's no change.

- -

Batch 3: Over next 18 (24, 40, 50, 0, 0, 0, 0, 0) rows, work a full raglan inc every RS and a neck inc *every other* RS. 237 (267, 313, 339, -, -, -, -, -) sts, 29 (34, 40, 43, -, -, -, -, -) each front, 50 (56, 66, 72, -, -, -, -, -) each sleeve, 79 (87, 101, 109, -, -, -, -, -) back.

Batch 4: Over next - (-, -, -, 60, 64, 72, 80, 88) rows, while working a neck inc *every other* RS, work a full raglan inc every RS *except* on every - (-, -, -, 8th, 6th, 6th, 5th, 5th) RS, work a body only inc instead of a full raglan inc.

Final st counts: 237 (267, 313, 339, 383, 397, 431, 461, 499) sts, 29 (34, 40, 43, 51, 54, 60, 66, 72) each front, 50 (56, 66, 72, 80, 80, 86, 90, 98) each sleeve, 79 (87, 101, 109, 121, 129, 139, 149, 159) back.

Separate Sleeves from Body

Next row (RS): *Work to marker, remove marker. Transfer sleeve sts to scrap yarn, remove next marker. Cast on 10 (12, 12, 14, 18, 18, 20, 22, 24) on right needle (using backward loop cast on); rep from * once, work to end. 157 (179, 205, 223, 259, 273, 299, 325, 351) sts for body.

Cont to work neck inc *every other* RS 14 (13, 14, 13, 13, 14, 13, 14, 13) times. 185 (205, 233, 249, 285, 301, 325, 353, 377) sts.

Then work a neck inc *every* RS 5 times. 195 (215, 243, 259, 295, 311, 335, 363, 387) sts.

Next RS row: Cast on 4 to left needle using cable cast on. K4, pm, knit to end.

Next row: Cast on 4 to left needle using cable cast on. K4, pm, purl to marker, k4. 203 (223, 251, 267, 303, 319, 343, 371, 395) sts.

Cont as set, knitting 4 at beg and end of every row, until body measures 13 (13, 13, 13, 12, 11¾, 11¼, 10½, 10¼) inches (33 [33, 33, 33, 30.5, 30, 28.5, 26.5, 26] cm) from underarm, ending with a WS row. Then work eyelets.

Eyelets

Next row (RS): K4 to marker, sm, k2 (2, 4, 4, 2, 3, 2, 4, 3), *yo, k2tog, k3; rep from * to marker, ending last rep k1 (1, 2, 3, 1, 1, 1, 2, 2) instead of k3, sm, k4.

Work 7 rows stockinette (stocking) stitch. Then work rib.

Rib

Next row (RS) (dec): K4 to marker, sm, k1, ssk, knit to end. 202 (222, 250, 266, 302, 318, 342, 370, 394) sts.

Switch to smaller needles.

Starting on WS, work 17 rows as follows:
Knit to marker, sm, broken K2/P2 rib to marker, sm, knit to end.

Bind (cast) off.

Sleeves

Transfer sleeve sts to needle. Rejoin yarn.

Pick up and knit 5 (6, 6, 7, 9, 9, 10, 11, 12) sts from body underarm, pm, pick up and knit

another 5 (6, 6, 7, 9, 9, 10, 11, 12) sts, join in the round, being careful not to twist sts. 60 (68, 78, 86, 98, 98, 106, 112, 122) sts.

Working a sleeve dec (see "Shaping Notes") every 11th (9th, 7th, 6th, 5th, 6th, 5th, 5th, 4th) rnd 12 (6, 2, 11, 14, 23, 12, 28, 15) times and then every 0 (10th, 8th, 7th, 6th, 0, 6th, 0, 5th) rnd 0 (8, 15, 10, 11, 0, 13, 0, 16) times, cont in stockinette (stocking) stitch until sleeve measures 16½ (16¾, 16¾, 17, 17, 17¼, 17¼, 17½, 17½) inches (42 [42.5, 42.5, 43, 43, 44, 44, 44.5, 44.5] cm) from underarm. 36 (40, 44, 44, 48, 52, 56, 56, 60) sts.

Switch to smaller needles.

Work 18 rnds broken K2/P2 rib.

Bind (cast) off.

Finishing

Block garment to schematic measurements.

Collar

Starting at lower right front neck edge on RS, join yarn, and pick up and knit 4 sts across garter stitch band, then 3 sts for every 4 rows along right front edge, then 1 st for every st of sleeves and back, then the same number of sts along left edge as right.

Next row (WS): K4, purl to last 4 sts, k4.

Next row (RS) (dec): K4, ssk, knit to last 6 sts, k2tog, k4. 2 dec'd.

Rep these 2 rows for 33 more rows, ending with a WS row. Then shape collar.

Shape Collar

The collar is shaped by working short rows (see "Stitch Patterns and Techniques").

Short row 1 (RS) (dec): K4, ssk, knit to 20 sts before end of row, wrap next st, and turn work.

Short row 2 (WS): Purl to 20 sts before end of row, wrap next st, and turn work.

Short rows 3 and 4: Work to 25 sts before end of row, wrap, and turn.

Cont as set, working each pair of short rows 5 sts shorter than the previous pair, for 16 more rows.

Next row (RS) (dec): Knit to last 6 sts, k2tog, k4. 2 dec'd.

Next row (WS): K4, purl to last 4 sts, k4.

Knit 8 rows.

Bind (cast) off with a stretchy bind (cast) off.

Weave in ends, stitching shut any gaps at the underarms if necessary. Block collar.

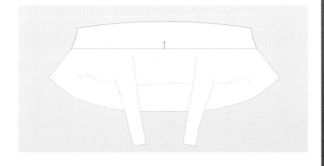

for the guys

IN THIS CHAPTER

Classic Raglan Crew Sweater

Easy Fisherman's Sweater

Rugged Layering Vest

classic raglan crew
sweater

● ● ○ ○ ○

Knitting for guys can be a challenge. They often prefer something plain, which isn't all that exciting for the knitter. The raglan shaping and pieced construction of this sweater will keep you interested, and he'll like the traditional style. Choose a heathery superwash wool like this one for a fabric that's richly colored and a sweater that's easy to wash.

Skills Needed

Knit/purl, mattress stitch, picking up and knitting

Finished Measurements

Choose a size 2 to 4 inches (5 to 10cm) larger than the actual chest measurement

Chest: 37$\frac{1}{4}$ (39, 41, 42$\frac{3}{4}$, 44$\frac{1}{2}$, 46$\frac{1}{4}$, 49$\frac{3}{4}$, 51$\frac{1}{2}$, 53$\frac{1}{4}$) inches (94.5 [99, 104, 108.5, 113, 117.5, 126.5, 131, 135.5] cm)

Length: 26 (26$\frac{3}{4}$, 26$\frac{3}{4}$, 26$\frac{3}{4}$, 27$\frac{1}{2}$, 27$\frac{3}{4}$, 27$\frac{3}{4}$, 28$\frac{1}{4}$, 28$\frac{1}{4}$) inches (66 [68, 68, 68, 70, 70.5, 70.5, 72, 72] cm)

Yarn

11 (11, 12, 12, 13, 14, 15, 16, 16) balls worsted (medium) yarn, 50 grams/110 yards (100m) each. I used Knit Picks Swish Worsted, 100 percent superwash merino, in Merlot Heather.

Gauge (Tension)

18 stitches and 28 rows = 4 inches (10cm) in stockinette (stocking) stitch

Needles

1 set straight or circular in each of the following sizes:

U.S. 8 (5mm/UK 6) or size needed to obtain gauge (tension)

U.S. 7 (4.5mm/UK 7) or 2 sizes smaller than gauge (tension) needle

Plus 1 set in the smaller size for your preferred method of working in a small round

Other Supplies

Blunt yarn needle

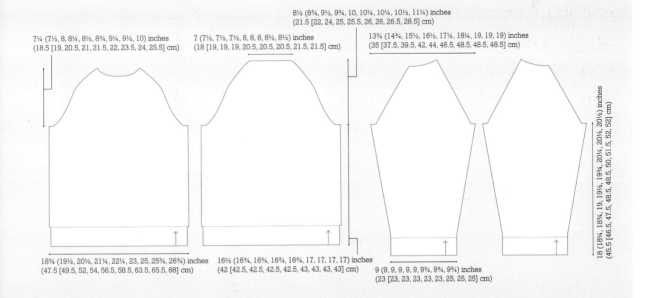

7$\frac{1}{4}$ (7$\frac{1}{2}$, 8, 8$\frac{1}{4}$, 8$\frac{1}{2}$, 8$\frac{3}{4}$, 9$\frac{1}{4}$, 9$\frac{1}{2}$, 10) inches (18.5 [19, 20.5, 21, 21.5, 22, 23.5, 24, 25.5] cm)

7 (7$\frac{1}{2}$, 7$\frac{1}{2}$, 7$\frac{1}{2}$, 8, 8, 8, 8$\frac{1}{2}$, 8$\frac{1}{2}$) inches (18 [19, 19, 19, 20.5, 20.5, 20.5, 21.5, 21.5] cm)

8$\frac{1}{2}$ (8$\frac{3}{4}$, 9$\frac{1}{2}$, 9$\frac{3}{4}$, 10, 10$\frac{1}{4}$, 10$\frac{1}{4}$, 10$\frac{1}{2}$, 11$\frac{1}{4}$) inches (21.5 [22, 24, 25, 25.5, 26, 26, 26.5, 28.5] cm)

13$\frac{3}{4}$ (14$\frac{3}{4}$, 15$\frac{1}{2}$, 16$\frac{1}{2}$, 17$\frac{1}{4}$, 18$\frac{1}{4}$, 19, 19, 19) inches (35 [37.5, 39.5, 42, 44, 46.5, 48.5, 48.5, 48.5] cm)

18$\frac{3}{4}$ (19$\frac{1}{2}$, 20$\frac{1}{2}$, 21$\frac{1}{4}$, 22$\frac{1}{4}$, 23, 25, 25$\frac{3}{4}$, 26$\frac{3}{4}$) inches (47.5 [49.5, 52, 54, 56.5, 58.5, 63.5, 65.5, 68] cm)

16$\frac{1}{2}$ (16$\frac{3}{4}$, 16$\frac{3}{4}$, 16$\frac{3}{4}$, 16$\frac{3}{4}$, 17, 17, 17, 17) inches (42 [42.5, 42.5, 42.5, 42.5, 43, 43, 43, 43] cm)

9 (9, 9, 9, 9, 9, 9$\frac{3}{4}$, 9$\frac{3}{4}$, 9$\frac{3}{4}$) inches (23 [23, 23, 23, 23, 23, 25, 25, 25] cm)

18 (18$\frac{1}{4}$, 18$\frac{3}{4}$, 19, 19$\frac{1}{2}$, 19$\frac{3}{4}$, 20$\frac{1}{4}$, 20$\frac{1}{2}$, 20$\frac{1}{2}$) inches (45.5 [46.5, 47.5, 48.5, 50, 51.5, 52, 52] cm)

Construction Notes

The front, back, and sleeves are worked flat and joined at the raglan seams and sides. The neckband is picked up and worked in the finishing.

Tips for Modifying

- Sneak in a little texture across the chest or up the sleeves.

- Change the neck to a V if he prefers.

- Classic sweaters are great for women, too! Choose the appropriate chest size, shorten the sleeves, and add a little side shaping to flatter you.

Stitch Patterns and Techniques

K2/P2 rib (worked flat over a multiple of 4 plus 2 sts):

> **All RS rows:** P2, *k2, p2; rep from * to end.
>
> **All WS rows:** K2, *p2, k2; rep from * to end.
>
> Rep Rows 1 and 2 for pattern.

K2/P2 rib (worked in the round over a multiple of 4 sts):

> **All rnds:** *P2, k2; rep from * to end.

Stockinette (stocking) stitch (worked over any number of sts):

> **All RS rows:** Knit all sts.
>
> **All WS rows:** Purl all sts.

Classic Raglan Crew Sweater

Back

With smaller needles, cast on 82 (86, 90, 94, 98, 102, 110, 114, 118) sts.

Work 18 rows K2/P2 rib.

Switch to larger needles.

Next row (RS) (inc): K2 (1, 1, 2, 1, 1, 1, 1, 2), *m1R, k26 (28, 29, 30, 32, 33, 36, 37, 38); rep from * 2 times, m1R, k2 (1, 2, 2, 1, 2, 1, 2, 2). 86 (90, 94, 98, 102, 106, 114, 118, 122) sts.

Work in stockinette (stocking) stitch until piece measures 16½ (16¾, 16¾, 16¾, 16¾, 17, 17, 17, 17) inches (42 [42.5, 42, 42.5, 42.5, 43, 42.5, 43, 43] cm) from cast-on edge, ending with a WS row. Then shape back raglan.

Shape Back Raglan

Over next 60 (62, 66, 68, 70, 72, 74, 76, 80) rows, bind (cast) off for underarm and work raglan shaping as follows:

Next 2 rows (dec): Bind (cast) off 3 (3, 3, 3, 4, 4, 4, 4, 4) at beg of row. 80 (84, 88, 92, 94, 98, 106, 110, 114) sts.

Next 4 (4, 4, 3, 4, 3, 0, 0, 0) *alt* RS rows (dec): K2, k2tog, knit to 4 sts before end, ssk, k2. 2 dec'd each time. 16 (16, 16, 12, 16, 12, 0, 0, 0) rows worked. 72 (76, 80, 86, 86, 92, 106, 110, 114) sts.

Next 21 (22, 24, 27, 26, 29, 36, 37, 39) RS rows (dec): K2, k2tog, knit to 4 sts before end, ssk, k2. 2 dec'd each time. 42 (44, 48, 54, 52, 58, 72, 74, 78) rows worked. 30 (32, 32, 32, 34, 34, 34, 36, 36) sts.

Bind (cast) off.

Front

Work the same as back to underarm. Then shape front raglan.

Shape Front Raglan

Over next 44 (46, 50, 52, 54, 56, 66, 68, 72) rows, bind (cast) off for underarm and work raglan shaping as follows:

Next 2 rows (dec): Bind (cast) off 3 (3, 3, 3, 4, 4, 4, 4, 4) at beg of row. 80 (84, 88, 92, 94, 98, 106, 110, 114) sts.

Next 21 (22, 24, 25, 26, 27, 32, 33, 35) RS rows (dec): K2, k2tog, knit to 4 sts before end, ssk, k2. 2 dec'd each time. 38 (40, 40, 42, 42, 44, 42, 44, 44) sts. Then shape front neck.

Shape Front Neck

Beginning on a RS row, over next 7 rows, cont raglan shaping and shape front neck as follows:

Divide front (RS) (dec): K2, k2tog, k10 (11, 11, 12, 12, 13, 12, 12, 12), join 2nd ball, bind (cast) off 10 (10, 10, 10, 10, 10, 10, 12, 12), k10 (11, 11, 12, 12, 13, 12, 12, 12) (including 1 st on right needle from binding [casting] off), ssk, k2. 13 (14, 14, 15, 15, 16, 15, 15, 15) sts each side of front.

Next row (WS) (dec): Purl across 1st set of sts, then on next set bind (cast) off 4 (5, 5, 6, 6, 7, 6, 6, 6).

Next row (RS) (dec): K2, k2tog, knit to end of 1st set, then on next set bind (cast) off 4 (5, 5, 6, 6, 7, 6, 6, 6), knit to last 4, ssk, k2. 8 sts each side of front.

Next 2 rows (dec): Binding (casting) off 3 instead of 4 (5, 5, 5, 5, 5, 5, 6, 6), rep previous 2 rows. 4 sts each side of front.

Next 2 rows (dec): Bind (cast) off 2 sts at neck edge. 2 sts.

Bind (cast) off remaining 2 sts.

Sleeves

With smaller needles, cast on 42 (42, 42, 42, 42, 42, 46, 46, 46) sts.

Work 18 rows K2/P2 rib.

Switch to larger needles.

Next row (inc) (RS): K2, kfb, knit to 3 sts before end, kfb, k2. 44 (44, 44, 44, 44, 44, 48, 48, 48) sts.

Work in stockinette (stocking) stitch, with an inc row every 6th (9th, 8th, 0, 7th, 6th, 0, 7th, 7th) RS row 2 (10, 12, 0, 6, 16, 0, 2, 2) times, then every 5th (8th, 7th, 7th, 6th, 5th, 6th, 6th, 6th) RS row 8 (2, 2, 16, 12, 4, 20, 18, 18) times. 64 (68, 72, 76, 80, 84, 88, 88, 88) sts.

Cont without shaping until sleeve measures 18 (18¼, 18¾, 19, 19½, 19¾, 20¼, 20½, 20½) inches (45.5 [46.5, 47.5, 48.5, 49.5, 50, 51.5, 52, 52] cm) from cast-on edge, ending with a WS row. Then shape sleeve raglan.

Shape Sleeve Raglan

Over next 52 (54, 58, 60, 62, 64, 66, 68, 72) rows, bind (cast) off for underarm and work raglan shaping as follows:

Next 2 rows (dec): Bind (cast) off 3 (3, 3, 3, 4, 4, 4, 4, 4) at beg of row. 58 (62, 66, 70, 72, 76, 80, 80, 80) sts.

*Next 1 (1, 2, 2, 2, 3, 4, 3, 2) RS row (dec): K2, k2tog, knit to 4 sts before end, ssk, k2. 2 dec'd each time. 56 (60, 62, 66, 68, 70, 72, 74, 76) sts.

Work a dec on *2nd* RS 1 time. 54 (58, 60, 64, 66, 68, 70, 72, 74) sts.

Rep from * 7 (6, 6, 5, 6, 5, 4, 5, 7) times. 26 (34, 24, 34, 30, 28, 30, 32, 32) sts.

Work a dec on the next 1 (5, 0, 5, 2, 1, 2, 3, 3) RS row. 24 (24, 24, 24, 26, 26, 26, 26, 26) sts.

Right Sleeve

Next RS row (dec): Bind (cast) off 6 (6, 6, 6, 7, 7, 7, 7, 7) at beg of row, knit to 4 sts before end, ssk, k2. 17 (17, 17, 17, 18, 18, 18, 18, 18) sts.

Next RS row (dec): Bind (cast) off 5 (5, 5, 5, 6, 6, 6, 6, 6) at beg of row, knit to 4 sts before end, ssk, k2. 11 sts.

Next RS row (dec): Bind (cast) off 4 at beg of row, knit to 4 sts before end, ssk, k2. 6 sts.

Next RS row (dec): Bind (cast) off 2 at beg of row, knit to 4 sts before end, ssk, k2. 3 sts.

Bind (cast) off remaining sts.

Left Sleeve

Next WS row (dec): Bind (cast) off 6 (6, 6, 6, 7, 7, 7, 7) at beg of row, purl to end. 18 (18, 18, 18, 19, 19, 19, 19, 19) sts.

Next row (RS) (dec): K2, k2tog, knit to end. 17 (17, 17, 17, 18, 18, 18, 18, 18) sts.

Next row (WS) (dec): Bind (cast) off 5 (5, 5, 5, 6, 6, 6, 6, 6) at beg of row, purl to end. 12 sts.

Next row (RS) (dec): K2, k2tog, knit to end. 11 sts.

Next row (WS) (dec): Bind (cast) off 4 at beg of row, purl to end. 7 sts.

Next row (RS) (dec): K2, k2tog, knit to end. 6 sts.

Next row (WS) (dec): Bind (cast) off 2 at beg of row, purl to end. 4 sts.

Next row (RS) (dec): K2, k2tog. 3 sts.

Bind (cast) off remaining sts.

Finishing

Block pieces, using schematic as guide.

Join sleeves to front and back along raglan lines. Be sure to place the *shorter* sleeve edge at the front.

Join sides and sleeves.

Neck

With smaller circular needles for working in a small round, starting at back left shoulder on RS, join yarn and pick up and knit 1 st for every bound (cast) off st around neck (not including sts used for seams). Adjust the pick-up rate as necessary for a total multiple of 4 sts. You should have about 96 (100, 100, 104, 108, 112, 108, 112, 112) sts.

Work in K2/P2 rib for 10 rnds.

Bind (cast) off.

Weave in ends. Block neck if desired.

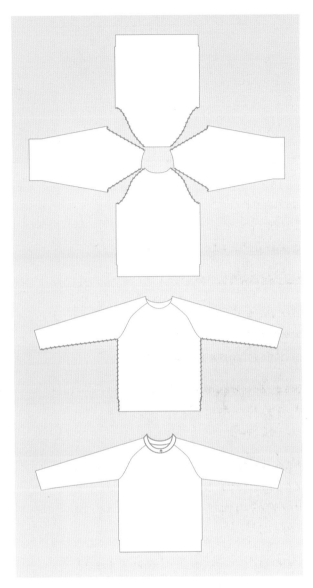

easy fisherman's
sweater

●●●●○

Who doesn't love a man in a rugged fisherman's sweater? He'll look sharp in this modern interpretation of a traditional favorite. Masculine details like the traveling cables, textured panels, set-in sleeves, and a folded turtleneck all work well in a naturally sophisticated wool like this one.

Skills Needed

Knit/purl, cables, mattress stitch, picking up and knitting

Finished Measurements

Choose a size 2 to 4 inches (5 to 10cm) larger than the actual chest measurement

Chest: 38 (42, 46, 50, 54) inches (96.5 [106.5, 117, 127, 137] cm)

Length: 26½ (27¼, 28¼, 29, 29½) inches (67.5 [69, 72, 73.5, 75] cm)

Yarn

6 (7, 8, 9, 10) skeins medium (aran) yarn, 100 grams/164 yards (150m) each. I used Cascade Yarns Eco Cloud, 70 percent merino, 30 percent baby alpaca, in Wild Dove.

Gauge (Tension)

16 stitches and 24 rows = 4 inches (10cm) in stockinette (stocking) stitch

Needles

1 set circular or straight in each of the following sizes, plus 1 set for your preferred method of working in a small round in the smaller size:

U.S. 9 (5.5 mm/UK 5) or size needed to obtain gauge (tension)

U.S. 7 (4.5 mm/UK 4) or 2 sizes smaller than gauge (tension) needle

Other Supplies

4 stitch markers, blunt yarn needle, cable needle

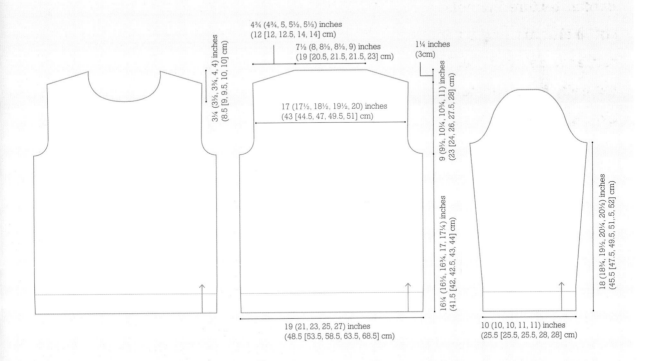

3¼ (3½, 3¾, 4, 4) inches (8.5 [9, 9.5, 10, 10] cm)

4¾ (4¾, 5, 5½, 5½) inches (12 [12, 12.5, 14, 14] cm)

7½ (8, 8½, 8½, 9) inches (19 [20.5, 21.5, 21.5, 23] cm)

1¼ inches (3cm)

9 (9½, 10¼, 10¾, 11) inches (23 [24, 26, 27.5, 28] cm)

17 (17½, 18½, 19½, 20) inches (43 [44.5, 47, 49.5, 51] cm)

16¼ (16½, 16¾, 17, 17¼) inches (41.5 [42, 42.5, 43, 44] cm)

19 (21, 23, 25, 27) inches (48.5 [53.5, 58.5, 63.5, 68.5] cm)

18 (18¾, 19½, 20¼, 20½) inches (45.5 [47.5, 49.5, 51.5, 52] cm)

10 (10, 10, 11, 11) inches (25.5 [25.5, 25.5, 28, 28] cm)

Construction Notes

The front, back, and sleeves are worked separately. The shoulders are joined, the sleeves are set in, and the sides are joined. The collar is picked up and worked.

Stitch Patterns and Techniques

Cable 3 front (C3F): Hold 2 sts to front on cable needle, p1, k2 from cable needle.

Cable 3 back (C3B): Hold 1 st to back on cable needle, k2, p1 from cable needle.

Cable 4 back (C4B): Hold 2 sts to back on cable needle, k2, k2 from cable needle.

K2/P2 rib (worked flat over a multiple of 4 plus 2 sts):

All RS rows: P2, *k2, p2; rep from * to end.

All WS rows: K2, *p2, k2; rep from * to end.

Rep Rows 1 and 2 for pattern.

K2/P2 rib (worked in the round over a multiple of 4 sts):

All rows: *K2, p2; rep from * to end.

Stockinette (stocking) stitch (worked flat over any number of sts):

All RS rows: Knit all sts.

All WS rows: Purl all sts.

Cable panel (multiple of 20 plus 10, worked over 70 sts):

Row 1 (RS): P10, [k2, p6, p2, p10] 3 times.

Row 2 (WS): K2, [p6, k2, p2, k6, p2, k2] 3 times, p6, k2.

Row 3: P10, [C3F, p4, C3B, p10] 3 times.

Row 4: K2, [p6, k3, p2, k4, p2, k3] 3 times, p6, k2.

Row 5: P2, [k6, p3, C3F, p2, C3B, p3] 3 times, k6, p2.

Row 6: K2, [p6, k4, p2, k2, p2, k4] 3 times, p6, k2.

Row 7: P2, [k6, p4, C3F, C3B, p4] 3 times, k6, p2.

Row 8: K2, [p6, k5, p4, k5] 3 times, p6, k2.

Row 9: P13, [C4B, p16] 3 times, ending p13 instead of p16.

Row 10: Rep Row 8.

Row 11: P12, [C3B, C3F, p14] 3 times, ending p12 instead of p14.

Row 12: Rep Row 6.

Row 13: P2, [k6, p3, C3B, p2, C3F, p3] 3 times, k6, p2.

Row 14: Rep Row 4.

Row 15: P2, [k6, p2, C3B, p4, C3F, p2] 3 times, k6, p2.

Row 16: Rep Row 2.

Rep Rows 1 to 16 for pattern.

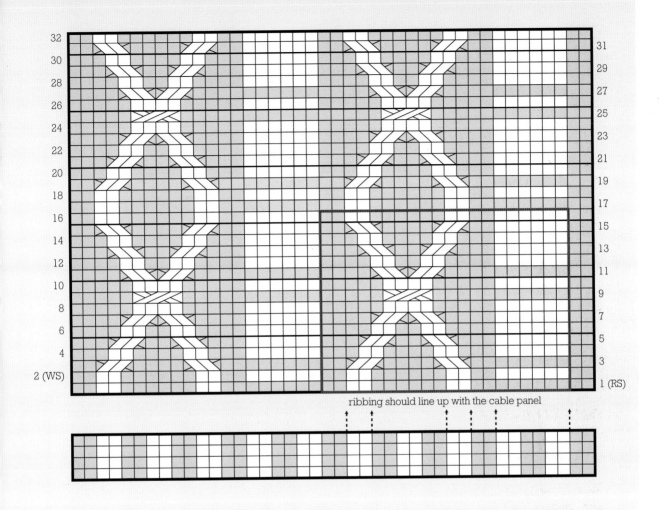

ribbing should line up with the cable panel

	Knit on RS, purl on WS
	Purl on RS, knit on WS
	Cable 3 Back (C3B): Hold 1 st to back on cable needle, knit 2, purl 1 from cable needle
	Cable 3 Front (C3F): Hold 2 sts to front on cable needle, purl 1, knit 2 from cable needle
	Cable 4 Back (C4B): Hold 2 sts to back on cable needle, knit 2, knit 2 from cable needle

Easy Fisherman's Sweater

Back

With smaller needles, cast on 78 (86, 94, 102, 110) sts.

Work 16 rows K2/P2 rib.

Switch to larger needles.

Work in stockinette (stocking) stitch until back measures 16¼ (16½, 16¾, 17, 17¼) inches (41.5 [42, 42.5, 43, 44] cm) from cast-on edge, ending with a WS row. Then shape underarms.

Shape Back Underarms

For easier finishing and smooth seams, use a sloped bind (cast) off for underarms, shoulders, front neck, and sleeve caps.

Next 2 rows: Bind (cast) off 2 (3, 3, 4, 4) sts at beg of row. 74 (80, 88, 94, 102) sts.

Next 2 rows: Bind (cast) off 1 (2, 3, 3, 3) sts at beg of row. 72 (76, 82, 88, 96) sts.

Next 2 rows: Bind (cast) off 1 (1, 2, 2, 2) sts at beg of row. 70 (74, 78, 84, 92) sts.

Next row (RS) (dec): K3, k2tog, work to last 5 sts, ssk, k3. 68 (72, 76, 82, 90) sts.

Cont in stockinette (stocking) stitch with a dec every RS 0 (1, 1, 2, 5) more times. 68 (70, 74, 78, 80) sts.

Cont without shaping until armhole measures 9 (9½, 10¼, 10¾, 11) inches (23 [24, 26, 27.5, 28] cm) from underarm, ending with a WS row. Then shape shoulders.

Shape Shoulders

Next 2 rows: Bind (cast) off 7 (7, 6, 8, 8) sts at beg of row. 54 (56, 62, 62, 64) sts.

Next 4 rows: Bind (cast) off 6 (6, 7, 7, 7) sts at beg of row. 30 (32, 34, 34, 36) sts.

Bind (cast) off remaining sts for back neck.

Front

Cast on and work 16 rows same as back.

Switch to larger needles.

Next row (RS) (marker setup): K4 (8, 12, 16, 20), pm, cable panel from Row 1 for 70 sts, pm, k4 (8, 12, 16, 20).

Next row (WS): Purl to marker, sm, cable panel to marker, sm, purl to end.

Maintaining cable panel pattern throughout front, work until front measures 16¼ (16½, 16¾, 17, 17¼) inches (41.5 [42, 42.5, 43, 44] cm) from cast-on edge, ending with a WS row (matching length of back). Then shape underarms.

Shape Front Underarms

Next 2 rows: Bind (cast) off 2 (3, 3, 4, 4) sts at beg of row. 74 (80, 88, 94, 102) sts.

Next 2 rows: Bind (cast) off 1 (2, 3, 3, 3) sts at beg of row. 72 (76, 82, 88, 96) sts.

Next 2 rows: Bind (cast) off 0 (1, 2, 2, 2) sts at beg of row. 72 (74, 78, 84, 92) sts.

Next row (RS) (dec): K3, k2tog, work to last 5 sts, ssk, k3. 70 (72, 76, 82, 90) sts.

Work a dec every RS 0 (0, 0, 1, 4) more times. 70 (72, 76, 80, 82) sts.

Cont front until it measures 5¾ (6, 6½, 6¾, 7) inches (14.5 [15, 16.5, 17, 18] cm) from underarm, ending with WS row. Then shape front neck.

Shape Front Neck

Continue to maintain cable panel.

Next row (RS): Work 30 (30, 32, 34, 35), join new ball, bind (cast) off center 10 (12, 12, 12, 12), work to end.

Work left and right sides of front at the same time.

Next 2 rows: Work across 1st set of sts. On next set, bind (cast) off 4 at neck edge, work to end.

Next 2 rows: Bind (cast) off 3 sts at neck edge.

Next 2 rows: Bind (cast) off 2 sts at neck edge.

Work 1 WS row.

Next 2 (2, 3, 3, 4) RS rows (dec): On 1st set of sts, work to 4 before neck edge, ssk, k2. On next set, k2, k2tog, work to end. 19 (19, 20, 22, 22) sts each side of neck.

Cont without shaping until armhole measures 9 (9½, 10¼, 10¾, 11) inches (23 [24, 26, 27.5, 28] cm) from underarm, ending with a WS row (matching back armhole). Then shape shoulders.

Shape Shoulders

Maintaining cable panel, shape front shoulders same as back.

Sleeves

With smaller needles, cast on 42 (42, 42, 46, 46) sts.

Work 16 rows K2/P2 rib.

Switch to larger needles.

Next row (RS) (inc): K2, kfb, knit to 3 sts before end, kfb, k2. 2 sts inc'd. 44 (44, 44, 48, 48) sts.

Work in stockinette (stocking) stitch with an inc every 12th (10th, 8th, 8th, 8th) row a total of 7 (9, 13, 13, 15) more times. 58 (62, 70, 74, 78) sts.

Cont without shaping until sleeve measures 18 (18¾, 19½, 20¼, 20½) inches (45.5 [47.5, 49.5, 51.5, 52] cm) from cast-on edge, ending with a WS row.

Shape Sleeve Cap

Next 2 rows: Bind (cast) off 3 (3, 3, 4, 4) sts at beg of row. 52 (56, 64, 66, 70) sts.

Next 2 rows: Bind (cast) off 1 (2, 3, 3, 3) st at beg of row. 50 (52, 58, 60, 64) sts.

Next 2 rows: Bind (cast) off 1 (1, 1, 1, 1) st at beg of row. 48 (50, 56, 58, 62) sts.

Next row (RS) (dec): K3, k2tog, work to last 5 sts, ssk, k3. 46 (48, 54, 56, 60) sts.

Cont, working a dec *every* RS 3 (0, 1, 2, 4) more times. 40 (48, 52, 52, 52) sts.

Work a dec *every other* RS row 2 (4, 4, 4, 2) more times. 36 (40, 44, 44, 48) sts.

Then work a dec *every* RS row 6 (5, 5, 5, 7) more times. 24 (30, 34, 34, 34) sts.

Next 2 rows: Bind (cast) off 2 (4, 4, 4, 4) sts at beg of row. 20 (22, 26, 26, 26) sts.

Final 2 rows: Bind (cast) off 3 (4, 5, 4, 4) sts at beg of row. 14 (14, 16, 18, 18) sts.

Bind (cast) off remaining sts.

Finishing

Block all pieces to schematic measurements.

Join shoulders.

Neck

With smaller needles for working in the round and RS of work facing, beg at left shoulder, pick up and knit approximately 3 sts for every 4 rows along edge of left front neck, 1 st for every center bound (cast) off st, 3 sts for every 4 rows along right side of neck (matching number of sts picked up on left), 1 st for every bound (cast) off st of back neck.

Purl 1 round.

Knit 1 round, and if necessary dec evenly across to change number of sts to a multiple of 4.

Work K2/P2 rib for 4 inches (10cm). Switch to larger needles. Work rib for another 4 inches (10cm).

Bind (cast) off, being careful to maintain a relaxed tension on the bound (cast) off edge.

Set in sleeves and join.

Join sides using mattress stitch.

Weave in ends.

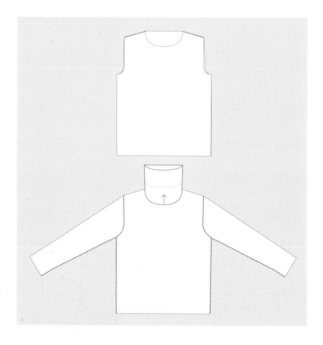

● ● ○ ○ ○

A classic garment for a classy guy, the sweater vest can be refined when knitted in cashmere or rugged in tweed; it's up to you to match the yarn to the man. Worked in a fine yarn, with tailored shoulders and traditional V neck, this sleeveless sweater looks equally good under a blazer or over a T-shirt.

Skills Needed

Knit/purl, mattress stitch, picking up and knitting

Finished Measurements

Choose a size 2 to 4 inches (5 to 10cm) larger than the actual chest measurement

Chest: 36¾ (39, 41, 43¼, 45¼, 47¼, 49½, 50¾, 52¾) inches (93.5 [99, 104, 110, 115, 120, 125.5, 129, 134] cm)

Length: 25½ (26, 26½, 26¾, 27¼, 27¾, 28, 28½, 28½) inches (65 [66, 67.5, 68, 69, 70.5, 71, 72.5, 72.5] cm)

Yarn

6 (7, 7, 7, 8, 8, 9, 9, 10) balls sport (fine) yarn, 50 grams/145 yards (133m) each. I used Berroco Ultra Alpaca Light, 50 percent alpaca, 50 percent wool, in Dark Chocolate.

Gauge (Tension)

23 stitches and 27 rows = 4 inches (10cm) in stockinette (stocking) stitch

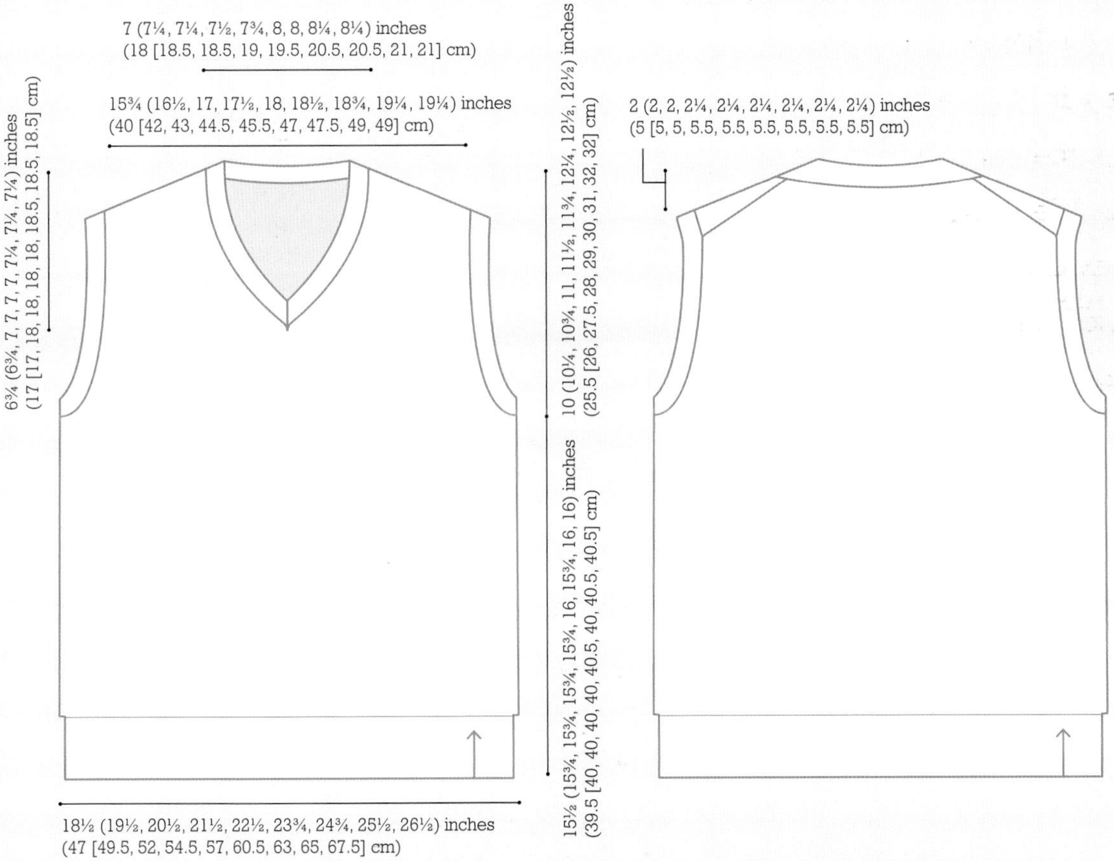

7 (7¼, 7¼, 7½, 7¾, 8, 8, 8¼, 8¼) inches
(18 [18.5, 18.5, 19, 19.5, 20.5, 20.5, 21, 21] cm)
15¾ (16½, 17, 17½, 18, 18½, 18¾, 19¼, 19¼) inches
(40 [42, 43, 44.5, 45.5, 47, 47.5, 49, 49] cm)
6¾ (6¾, 7, 7, 7, 7, 7¼, 7¼, 7¼) inches
(17 [17, 18, 18, 18, 18.5, 18.5, 18.5, 18.5] cm)
10 (10¼, 10¾, 11, 11½, 11¾, 12¼, 12½, 12½) inches
(25.5 [26, 27.5, 28, 29, 30, 31, 32, 32] cm)
15½ (15¾, 15¾, 15¾, 15¾, 16, 15¾, 16, 16) inches
(39.5 [40, 40, 40, 40, 40.5, 40, 40.5, 40.5] cm)
18½ (19½, 20½, 21½, 22½, 23¾, 24¾, 25½, 26½) inches
(47 [49.5, 52, 54.5, 57, 60.5, 63, 65, 67.5] cm)
2 (2, 2, 2¼, 2¼, 2¼, 2¼, 2¼, 2¼) inches
(5 [5, 5, 5.5, 5.5, 5.5, 5.5, 5.5, 5.5] cm)

Needles

1 set straight or circular in each of the following sizes, plus 1 set in the smaller size for your preferred method of working in the round:

U.S. 5 (3.75mm/UK 9) or size needed to obtain gauge (tension)

U.S. 2 or 3 (3.25mm/UK 11) or 2 sizes smaller than gauge (tension) needle

Other Supplies

Blunt yarn needle

Construction Notes

The front and back are worked flat and joined together at the sides and shoulders. The front shoulders are straight while the back shoulders are sloped so the shoulder seams lie slightly toward the back. The neckband and arm edges are picked up and worked in the finishing.

Stitch Patterns and Techniques

K2/P1 rib (worked over a multiple of 3 plus 2 sts):

> **All RS rows:** K2, *p1, k2; rep from * to end.

> **All WS rows:** P2, *k1, p2; rep from * to end.

> Rep Rows 1 and 2 for pattern.

K2/P2 rib (worked over a multiple of 4 plus 2 sts):

> **All RS rows:** P2, *k2, p2; rep from * to end.

> **All WS rows:** K2, *p2, k2; rep from * to end.

> Rep Rows 1 and 2 for pattern.

K2/P2 rib (worked in the round over a multiple of 4 sts):

> **All rnds:** *K2, p2; rep from * to end.

Stockinette (stocking) stitch (worked over any number of sts):

> **All RS rows:** Knit all sts.

> **All WS rows:** Purl all sts.

Double decreases:

> **Ssk-slL-psso-slR (right-leaning double decrease):** Ssk, slip st just worked back to left needle, pass next st over it and off needle, slip st (purlwise) back to right needle. 2 dec.

> **Sl-k2og-psso (left-leaning double decrease):** Slip 1 st knitwise, k2tog, pass slipped st over and off needle. 2 dec.

Layering Vest

With smaller needles, cast on 104 (110, 116, 122, 128, 134, 140, 143, 149) sts.

Work 18 rows K2/P1 rib.

Switch to larger needles.

Next row (RS) (inc): K1 (1, 1, 1, 1, 1, 1, 1, 2), *m1R, k34 (36, 38, 40, 42, 44, 46, 35, 36); rep from * 2 (2, 2, 2, 2, 2, 2, 3, 3) times, m1R, k1 (1, 1, 1, 1, 1, 1, 2, 3). 108 (114, 120, 126, 132, 138, 144, 148, 154) sts.

Work in stockinette (stocking) stitch until piece measures 15½ (15¾, 15¾, 15¾, 15¾, 16, 15¾, 16, 16) inches (39.5 [40, 40, 40, 40, 40.5, 40, 40.5, 40.5] cm) from cast-on edge, ending with a WS row. Then shape underarms.

Shape Underarms

Next 2 rows (dec): Bind (cast) off 3 (3, 4, 4, 5, 5, 6, 6, 7) at beg of row. 102 (108, 112, 118, 122, 128, 132, 136, 140) sts.

Next 2 rows (dec): Bind (cast) off 2 (2, 3, 3, 4, 4, 5, 5, 6) at beg of row. 98 (104, 106, 112, 114, 120, 122, 126, 128) sts.

Next 2 (3, 3, 4, 4, 5, 6, 6, 7) RS rows (dec): K2, k2tog, knit to 4 sts before end, ssk, k2. 2 dec'd each time. 94 (98, 100, 104, 106, 110, 110, 114, 114) sts.

Then dec on *2nd* RS 1 time. 92 (96, 98, 102, 104, 108, 108, 112, 112) sts.

Cont until piece measures 21¼ (21½, 21¾, 22, 22¼, 22¾, 23, 23¼, 23¼) inches (54 [54.5, 54.5, 56, 56.5, 58, 58.5, 59, 59] cm) from cast-on edge, ending with a WS row. Then shape back shoulders.

Shape Back Shoulders

Next 13 (14, 14, 15, 15, 15, 15, 16, 16) RS rows (dec): K2, ssk-slL-psso-slR (see "Stitch Patterns and Techniques"), knit to last 5 sts, sl-k2tog-psso (see "Stitch Patterns and Techniques"), k2. 4 dec'd each time.

Bind (cast) off remaining 40 (40, 42, 42, 44, 48, 48, 48, 48) sts.

Front

Work same as back until piece measures 18¾ (19¼, 19¼, 19¾, 20¼, 20¾, 20¾, 21¼, 21¼) inches (47.5 [49, 49, 50, 51.5, 52.5, 52.5, 54, 54] cm) from cast-on edge, ending with a WS row. Then shape front neck.

Shape Front Neck

Instructions are given to work left and right sides of neck at the same time.

K46 (48, 49, 51, 52, 54, 54, 56, 56), join new ball, and k46 (48, 49, 51, 52, 54, 54, 56, 56) to end.

Next 3 rows: Work in stockinette (stocking) stitch across both sets of sts.

Next 2 (2, 2, 2, 2, 3, 3, 3, 3) RS rows (dec):
Knit to 5 before neck edge, sl-k2tog-psso, k2.
On 2nd set of sts, k2, ssk-slL-psso-slR, knit to
end. 2 dec'd both sets of sts each time. 42 (44,
45, 47, 48, 48, 48, 50, 50) sts each set.

**Next 16 (16, 17, 17, 18, 18, 18, 18, 18) RS
rows (dec):** Knit to 4 before neck edge, ssk k2.
On 2nd set of sts, k2, k2tog, knit to end. 1 dec'd
on each. 26 (28, 28, 30, 30, 30, 30, 32, 32) sts
each set.

Work about 6 more rows without shaping, or
until fronts measure ½ inch (1.25cm) longer
than back at highest point. Bind (cast) off.

Finishing

Block pieces, using schematic as guide.

Join shoulders using mattress stitch.

Join sides using mattress stitch.

Neck

With smaller needles for working in a small
round, starting at base of front neck and working from the RS, pick up and knit 3 sts for every
4 rows along right front neck edge, 40 (40,
42, 42, 44, 48, 48, 48, 48) sts along back neck
edge, and 3 sts for every 4 rows along left front
neck edge, matching right front. Count sts and
adjust your picked-up sts as you go to end up
with a multiple of 4 plus 2 sts.

Work 8 rows, back and forth, in K2/P2 rib.

Bind (cast) off.

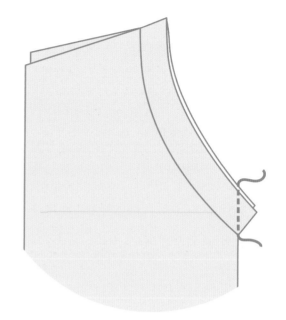

Lightly block neck band; fold front in half vertically with RS facing; and join left and right neck
bands together vertically.

Unfold front, and join ends of left and right
neck bands to neck selvedge.

Armhole Edges

With smaller needles for working in a small round, starting and ending at the underarm and working from the RS, pick up and knit 1 st for every bound (cast) off stitch, and 3 sts for every 4 rows around armhole. Count sts and adjust your picked-up sts as you go to end up with a multiple of 4 sts.

Join in the round, being careful not to twist sts.

Work 8 rounds K2/P2 rib.

Bind (cast) off.

appendix A
glossary

as established, as set To continue working after an interruption in the texture or shaping as previously established by a written pattern. For example, an established pattern might be interrupted to work a buttonhole and then continue "as set."

bar increase *See* knit front and back.

bind (cast) off (BO) To secure the final row of stitches and remove them from the needles.

blanket stitch A decorative sewing technique worked along the edge of fabric.

block A finishing technique in which the knitted piece or project is set with steam or water. Blocking smooths stitches and straightens edges.

blocking wire A specialty finishing tool, this is a long, straight wire used for anchoring the edge of knitting during blocking, most often for lace.

cable A texture that resembles knitted rope, made by crossing groups of stitches.

cable cast on A firm cast-on edge made by putting the tip of the needle between the first 2 stitches on the left needle, working a stitch knitwise, and placing it on the left needle. Although it's called "cable," it has nothing in particular to do with making cables.

cable needle (cn) A short knitting needle with a point at each end used to temporarily hold a small number of stitches while making cables. Cable needles are often curved or bent to prevent the stitches from sliding off.

cast on (CO) To put the foundation row of stitches on the needles.

circular knitting When the fabric is created in a tube by working the stitches around and around, in a spiral, unlike flat knitting, which is worked back and forth. *See also* flat knitting.

circular needle A needle with a point at each end and a flexible cable in the center. Circular needles can be used for circular or flat knitting.

decrease (Dec) To take away 1 or more stitches. The technique that takes away the stitch is also called a decrease.

double-pointed needle (dpn) A knitting needle with a point at each end, usually used in a set of 4 or 5 needles to work in the round. Double-pointed needles are available in varying lengths and diameters, but all the needles within a set are identical.

drop shoulder A sweater construction in which the armhole is vertically aligned with the side of the body and the sleeve has no cap.

dropped stitch A stitch that has fallen off the needle and is not secured; a column of dropped stitches is called a *ladder*. Sometimes, ladders are created intentionally for textural interest.

duplicate stitch A technique in which you run a strand of yarn along the same path as existing knitted stitches. Duplicate stitch can be used on the wrong side to conceal yarn ends or on the right side with a contrasting color as a decorative element.

ease In a garment, the difference between the garment's measurements and the wearer's measurements. A garment with larger measurements has positive ease; one with smaller measurements has negative ease.

eyelet   A single hole in knitted fabric, usually made with a yarn over.

Fair Isle   Refers to both the motifs and the technique derived from the particular tradition of color knitting from the Shetland Islands and Fair Isle, north of Scotland. Generally, in Fair Isle knitting, two colors of fine wool are used in each row, with the currently unused color carried across the wrong side of the work. Sometimes the term is used to refer to stranded colorwork in general.

felt   Felt is made by agitating animal fiber to lock the individual strands together.

finishing   The final phase in a knitted project when the ends are secured and hidden, pieces are joined, buttons are sewn, and the fabric is blocked.

flat knitting   When the knitted fabric is worked in a flat piece by working the stitches back and forth, unlike circular knitting, which is worked around and around to form a tube. *See also* circular knitting.

garter stitch   Reversible, ridged fabric where both sides are made of alternating knit and purl rows.

gauge (tension)   The size of a stitch, often expressed in the number of stitches and rows that fit into a 4-inch (10cm) square of the knitted fabric.

half-hitch cast on   A simple cast-on technique in which the stitches are made by twisting the yarn into a loop and placing it on the right needle.

I-cord   A narrow knitted tube made by knitting every row without turning the work on a double-pointed needle.

in pattern   When the stitch count changes and interrupts the established stitch pattern, staying "in pattern" means to continue the flow of the pattern without interruption.

increase (Inc)   To add 1 or more stitches. The technique that adds the stitch is also called an increase.

intarsia   A technique of working blocks of color. The yarn for each color is used only as required and is not carried across the back, as it is in Fair Isle or stranded colorwork.

join   Joining can mean either adding a new ball of yarn, turning a flat row into a circular round, or sewing two or more pieces of knitted fabric together.

Kitchener stitch   A stitch made by weaving a length of yarn in and out of two sets of live stitches, mimicking a knitted row, to create a join that looks like a row of stockinette (stocking) stitch. Also called *grafting*.

knit (k, K)   Specifically, the smooth side of the basic stitch. (The reverse side is the purl side.) Generally, to work any kind of knitted fabric.

knit 2 stitches together (k2tog)   To decrease by 1 stitch by putting the needle through 2 stitches and knitting them together.

knit 3 stitches together (k3tog)   To decrease by 2 stitches by putting the needle through 3 stitches and knitting them together.

knit front and back (kfb)   To increase by 1 stitch by knitting first into the front and then into the back of the same stitch. Also called a *bar increase*.

knitted cast on   A cast-on technique in which you create a stitch by working the yarn through the first stitch on the left needle knitwise and placing it on the left needle.

knitwise (kwise)   To work as if you were going to knit.

lace   A knitted fabric with a decorative arrangement of holes.

live stitch   The stitches that are not bound (cast) off.

long tail cast on   A cast-on technique that uses two strands of yarn at once, a long tail and the working yarn. The yarn from the tail is twisted into a half-hitch loop, and the working yarn is brought through the loop and placed on the right needle.

marker, stitch marker (m)   A small ring or safety pin–shape tool used to mark a location or stitch. A ring marker is placed on the knitting needle; a safety pin–shaped marker can be placed either on the needle or on a stitch.

mattress stitch   A sewing method that creates a strong, thick, barely visible seam.

multiple (mult)   Indicates the number of stitches or rows that are repeated in a stitch pattern.

needle gauge   A measuring tool that contains different-size holes used to measure the diameter of knitting needles.

place marker (pm, PM)   To put a marker on the knitting needle.

plain knitting   When working on a project that includes texture, lace, or color motifs, plain knitting is usually stockinette (stocking) stitch.

purl (p, P)   The rounded side of the basic stitch. (The reverse side is the knit side.)

purlwise (pwise)   To work as if you were going to purl.

raglan   A sleeve or yoke that's shaped with prominent diagonal lines from the underarm to the neck. A raglan sweater has no shoulder seam.

repeat (Rep)   An instruction to repeat all steps between two indicated points (often indicated by "rep from * to end"). Can also refer to a repeated section of a motif. For example, a Knit 1/Purl 1 ribbing has a repeat of 2 stitches.

reverse stockinette (stocking) stitch (rev st st)   A stitch made in the same way as stockinette (stocking) stitch, but with the purl side as the right side.

right side (RS)   The side of the knitted fabric that will be seen when the item is worn or used. A fabric that's reversible has no right or wrong side.

round (Rnd)   A horizontal line of stitches in circular knitting.

row   A horizontal line of stitches in flat knitting.

seamless   A method of knitting a sweater by joining live stitches of the different sections without seams.

selvedge, selvage   A decorative or functional edge. For example, a functional edge can be made by knitting the first and last stitch of every row, making the row edges more visible for joining.

set-in sleeve   A style of sleeve in which the cap, or the part that goes over the upper arm and shoulder, is curved to fit around the underarm and shoulder, and is sewn into the oval-shape armhole.

short row   Truncated rows of knitting made by stopping short of the end of a row and turning the work. Short rows create extra fabric in a selected area and are used for shaping.

sleeve cap   The portion of the sleeve above the underarm.

slip   To put the needle into next stitch as if to purl (unless otherwise noted) and transfer it to opposite needle without knitting or purling it.

slip, slip, knit together (ssk) The mirror of knit 2 together, to decrease 1 stitch by slipping 2 stitches, one at a time, knitwise, and then knitting them together by putting left needle through the fronts of the slipped stitches.

stitch holder A specialty tool, often shaped like a large blunt safety pin, used to hold stitches aside to be worked later.

stockinette (stocking) stitch (st st) A smooth knitted fabric in which the right side is made of knit stitches.

straight needle A knitting needle with a point at one end and a stopper at the other.

stranded A type of colorwork in which all the colors being used in a row are carried in strands across the wrong side of the work. *See also* Fair Isle.

swatch A square or rectangle of knitting used to test stitch patterns and/or measure gauge (tension).

tail A short end of yarn that's not being used (as opposed to the working yarn).

tapestry needle *See* yarn needle.

through back loop (tbl) To put the needle through the back of the stitch instead of the front.

twisted stitch A stitch that's worked through the back loop.

weave in A finishing step in which you hide and secure yarn ends on the wrong side of the work.

weight When referring to yarn, weight is the thickness of the yarn (rather than the weight of the ball).

working yarn The longer end of the yarn, leading to the ball of yarn, that's being used to work the next stitch (as opposed to the yarn tail).

wrong side (WS) The side of the work that will be totally or partially hidden when the item is worn or used.

yarn needle A blunt, thick needle with a large eye used for sewing or weaving in yarn ends. The blunt end is designed to go between the strands of yarn instead of piercing them, and the eye should be large enough to thread the yarn through. Also called a *tapestry needle*.

yarn over (yo) A strand of yarn placed over the needle to make a new stitch.

yarn tail The beginning or end of a ball of yarn not being used to work the next stitch (as opposed to the working yarn).

yoke The shaped area of a sweater around the shoulders.

appendix B
resources

Knitting has its own special language. To help you decode that language, this appendix offers a handy guide to knitting abbreviations, needle size conversions, yarn weight terminology, and a list of yarn sources.

Knitting Abbreviations

The following table gives you some commonly used knitting abbreviations and their meanings. From time to time, I abbreviate a special technique to save space in a pattern, and in those situations, the abbreviation is explained in the pattern itself.

abbreviation	meaning	abbreviation	meaning
*	repeat the instructions following the * as directed	p2tog	purl 2 stitches together
(), []	work the instructions within parentheses or brackets as directed	pat or patt	pattern
		pm, PM	place marker
		psso	pass stitch over
alt	alternate, alternating	pwise	purlwise
approx	approximately	rem	remain, remaining
beg	begin, beginning	rep	repeat, repeating
bet	between	rnd	round
BO	bind (cast) off	RS	right side
CC	contrast color	sl	slip
CO	cast on	ssk	slip, slip, knit these 2 together
cont	continue, continuing	st(s)	stitch(es)
dec, dec'd	decrease, decreased	st st	stockinette (stocking) stitch
dpn	double-pointed needle	tbl	through back loop
inc, inc'd	increase, increased	tog	together
k, K	knit	w&t	wrap and turn
k2tog	knit 2 stitches together	WS	wrong side
kwise	knitwise	wyib	with yarn in back
m1L	make 1 stitch left leaning	wyif	with yarn in front
m1R	make 1 stitch right leaning	yo	yarn over
MC	main color		
p, P	purl		

Needle Size Conversions

Note that not all sizes have an *exact* equivalent among U.S., metric, and UK systems, especially the smaller sizes.

U.S.	metric (mm)	UK
2	2.75	12
3	3.25	11
4	3.5	10
5	3.75	9
6	4	8
7	4.5	7
8	5	6
9	5.5	5
10	6	4

Yarn Weights

The following table serves as a guide to yarn weight terminology. Although suggested standards for yarn terminology do exist, each yarn manufacturer may use its own particular system. When choosing a needle size, consult the yarn label and the pattern.

weight category	possible names on label
Lace	Light fingering, fine, 2-ply
Super fine	Fine, sock, fingering, 3-ply, 4-ply
Fine	Sport, baby, 4-ply, 5-ply, 6-ply, light DK
Light	DK, light worsted, 8-ply
Medium	Worsted, afghan, aran, 10-ply
Bulky	Chunky, craft, rug, 12-ply
Super bulky	Bulky, roving, super chunky

Yarn Suppliers

Whether you shop locally, online, or both, an inspiring selection of yarn is available. Visit the following yarn websites for more information.

Americo Original

americo.ca

Berroco

berroco.com

Blue Sky Alpacas

blueskyalpacas.com

Brooklyn Tweed

brooklyntweed.com

Cascade Yarns

cascadeyarns.com

The Fibre Company

thefibreco.com

Knit Picks

knitpicks.com

Lorna's Laces

lornaslaces.net

Louet North America

louet.com

Madelinetosh

madelinetosh.com

Malabrigo

malabrigoyarn.com

The Plucky Knitter

thepluckyknitter.com

Quince & Co.

quinceandco.com

Skacel

skacelknitting.com

Swans Island Company

swansislandcompany.com

SweetGeorgia Yarns

sweetgeorgiayarns.com

index

T–U

V–W–X

Y–Z